001 W9-CHL-483

SECOND EDITION

What Is Linguistics?

SUZETTE HADEN ELGIN

San Diego State University

PRENTICE-HALL, INC., Englewood Cliffs, New Jersey 07632

Library of Congress Cataloging in Publication Data

ELGIN, SUZETTE HADEN.
    What is linguistics?

    (Prentice-Hall foundations of modern linguistics
series)
    Includes bibliographies and index.
    1. Linguistics.   2. Generative grammar.
I. Title.
P121.E58   1979   410   78-23900
ISBN 0-13-952333-2

PRENTICE-HALL FOUNDATIONS OF MODERN LINGUISTICS SERIES
SANFORD A. SCHANE, *Editor*

*Editorial/production supervision
and interior design:* Hilda Tauber
Cover design: Wanda Lubelska
Manufacturing buyer: Harry P. Baisley

© 1979, 1973 by Prentice-Hall, Inc., *Englewood Cliffs, N.J.*   07632

All rights reserved. No part of this book
may be reproduced in any form or by any means
without permission in writing from the publisher.

Printed in the United States of America

10   9   8   7   6

PRENTICE-HALL INTERNATIONAL, INC., *London*
PRENTICE-HALL OF AUSTRALIA PTY. LIMITED, *Sydney*
PRENTICE-HALL OF CANADA, LTD., *Toronto*
PRENTICE-HALL OF INDIA PRIVATE LIMITED, *New Delhi*
PRENTICE-HALL OF JAPAN, INC., *Tokyo*
PRENTICE-HALL OF SOUTHEAST ASIA PTE. LTD., *Singapore*
WHITEHALL BOOKS LIMITED, *Wellington, New Zealand*

Contents

Preface

What Is Linguistics? provides basic information about the analysis and description of languages on this earth, and about the ways in which human beings use their languages to communicate with one another. That is what linguistics is all about, and how it should be defined.

The book is intended to serve as an introduction to more advanced and more specialized material for those students who wish to continue the study of linguistics. It also provides a basic foundation in concepts and terminology for those students—particularly in education, computer science, and the various service professions—who do not plan to be linguists but who feel that the ability to read linguistic literature related to their own field of expertise would be a useful skill. Finally, the book is written for those who have no specific professional goals, but who are simply interested in the subject.

The field of linguistics has changed a great deal since the first edition of *What Is Linguistics?* was published, and many areas throughout the book have had to be revised and updated. Over the past few years, I have had discussions with teachers who were using the book in their classrooms, and

I have incorporated into the new edition some of their many helpful suggestions. Feedback from my students has also been relied on in the revision. I hope the users will enjoy and benefit by the exercises and the lists of selected readings I have provided at the end of each chapter.

Despite my efforts to include the most interesting and significant new developments, within the space and scope limitations of the book, by the time this second edition appears there will no doubt be newer developments in the field of linguistics. It is both the frustration and the joy of serving in a fast-developing discipline that no matter how quickly writers and publishers work, the researchers are always far ahead of us.

If I tried to thank everyone who has helped me in the preparation of this book the list of names would be longer than the Begats. Linguistics is the sort of field, I am happy to say, that is distinguished by a constant and lively exchange of information. The names mentioned below are but a minimal expression of my gratitude.

Thanks are due to my editor, Sanford Schane, whose patience and direction have been invaluable during the process of revision. Thanks are due to Ronald Langacker, who did his best to teach me what linguistic theory is; to Margaret Langdon, who taught me what it is *for*; and to Leonard Newmark, who taught me how to put the resulting knowledge to practical use. Thanks are due to Kathy Begaye, who taught me patience; to John Grinder, who taught me endurance; and to my husband and children, who have truly earned the sometimes loosely-awarded adjective "long-suffering." Thanks are due to Kenneth Hale, whose work and counsel have been a constant reminder to me of what linguistics is really supposed to accomplish in this world. Finally, I am grateful to my students, who have been unfailingly helpful. None of them, or anyone else mentioned, is responsible for my errors and omissions.

SUZETTE HADEN ELGIN

ONE

The Nature of Human Language

In science fiction, as in any other sort of writing, there are certain trite and overly predictable devices that once were effective but now inspire either amusement or annoyance. The all-purpose ray gun is one such device, and the "Buck Rogers Aloft" type of space opera is another. Most readers (or viewers) have ceased to be tolerant about the standard bug-eyed monster chomping and slurping and oozing its way across the countryside, destroying everything in its path. Most have begun to demand also that the *science* in science fiction be accurate, in accord with the facts (to the extent that we know them), or offered plausibly as an extension of those known facts. It is surprising, then, how indifferent these same demanding individuals remain to the antiquated information presented in much science fiction about linguistics, the science of language.

Consider, for example, how science fiction all too frequently deals with what would probably be the major problem of human encounters with intelligent alien beings—communication. The spacecraft lands, after scrupulously scientific maneuverings, and the investigating team makes an intensive analysis of the atmosphere outside to determine whether it is safe for humans.

1

Clad in spacesuits, the humans follow a rigorous exit procedure and go forth to meet their alien counterparts. The Terrans approach the Aliens, and the suspense builds. . . . Will they be friendly? Will they be creatures with whom we have enough in common to establish some mutually enjoyable relationship?

At this point all the science falls down a rhetorical rat hole. In Greek tragedy, when things got tight, the gods could be counted on to drop out of the sky and save the day. More recently we have accorded that same privilege to Tarzan, Captain Marvel, Superman, Wonder Woman, and to a variety of television supersleuths. In science fiction the big Human/Alien confrontation scene is "saved" by a device which—if named at all—is usually called something like the *universal translator* (UT, for short). Sometimes the UT is a computer; sometimes it is a gadget worn on the head like a football helmet. Its output may be described by the writer as a direct silent transmission, or as actual pronounced sounds, or as a display of words printed out on a viewing screen. Whatever the physical description, the effect is always the same: the human beings perceive the aliens' speech as their own native language, and vice versa. *Shazam!* End of communication problems.

Frank Herbert, the linguist turned science fiction writer, neatly sidestepped the problem in his novel, *Dune,* by assuming that all the languages dealt with had developed from Earth languages as Terrans moved out into space to colonize the galaxies. In that story he defines "Galach" as the official language of the interplanetary culture and describes its development from a "hybrid Inglo-Slavic" ancestor.

Television's *Star Trek* did not have time for lengthy linguistic investigations, and did not want all its aliens to be humanoid in origin. Aliens that are light-forms or crystals or similarly exotic creatures are far more likely to fascinate a viewing audience than a non-Terran who simply happens to have evolved into a human-like being with a tail or an extra eye or a few tentacles. You will therefore find, on page TO:03:02:04 of the *Starfleet Technical Manual,* a full-page illustration of the Starfleet's Universal Translator. This particular UT is very convenient, since it is hand-held; we are informed that it is 28 centimeters long, 4.8 centimeters around, and weighs 500 grams. It looks extraordinarily like a flashlight.

Unfortunately, although the UT's have a lot of charm and are useful for moving right along with the plot, from a scientific point of view they are very dubious instruments.

Some science fiction writers, perhaps burned in the past by a gadget that provoked reader rebellion, instead provide a living expert linguist. The linguist spends some time analyzing the alien language, after which he or she teaches it to the rest of the team or serves as an interpreter for them. This is a more respectable approach, since there would certainly have to be a linguist somewhere behind any UT to program it for its task. But this approach is only the smallest fraction more likely to be successful.

Now linguists on this earth do go out and analyze languages that have never been studied before. That is indisputable. They do so without being frightened at the prospect, although they ordinarily expect it to take years of their time rather than being an instantaneous process. You would therefore be justified in asking: since it can be done on earth, why not in space?

The answer is that, like the development of a method for traveling faster than the speed of light, *maybe* it is possible. If Frank Herbert's human migration framework is maintained, and no truly alien intelligence is ever encountered, the possibility increases—but we have no reason to believe that if we do encounter aliens they will of necessity all be slightly altered versions of ourselves. If they are not (and things will be more interesting if they are not), the arguments against the UT are many and compelling. To understand why that should be so, it is necessary to understand why the linguist is so calm about the prospect of analyzing a previously undescribed human language from scratch.

If you were to listen first to English being spoken, then Swahili, then Vietnamese, and finally Hopi, it would seem to you that all these streams of sound were completely different from one another. That is an obvious and reasonable first impression. But linguists know that despite their apparent differences, these four languages have a great many things in common. And it is safe to predict that any human language you might encounter would also share certain common characteristics.

In any human language we can anticipate at least the following ten basic characteristics.

1. Except for sign languages, which are rare, the language will be composed of meaningful sounds.

Thus, human language will not be made up of, say, colors, or smells, or variations in temperature, or combinations of chemicals. We may find minor systems of signals, such as the red for *stop*, green for *go*, and yellow for *caution* used in American traffic lights, but no actual language will develop in this way.

2. The language will have from about 10 to 70 meaningful sounds; furthermore, all languages will choose from the same potential set of sounds.

Human beings are capable of making thousands of noises. It is possible to make quite a distinctive noise by slapping your cheek with your open hand or cracking your knuckles. But there is no language in which a word begins with either of these sounds or contains them in any other position.

Many languages have words containing sounds produced by touching the lower lip to the upper teeth (as for English *f* and *v*), but no language uses the sound that would result from touching the upper lip to the lower teeth. There is no particularly logical reason for this, since we could certainly make such a sound and distinguish it, but it does not happen. No matter how many human languages are examined, we find the same sounds occurring again and again, so that it is possible to say that the upper limit of seventy meaningful sounds constitutes a universal set from which all languages will choose.

> 3. The language will have both consonant and vowel sounds, and the number of vowels will be at least two.

The terms *consonant* and *vowel*, as associated with our writing systems, are misleading; later in this book we will try to clarify them. For the moment, think of a consonant as being a sound that cannot be used as a syllable by itself. English *p* is a consonant in every sense of the word. Our English *n*, however, although we call it a consonant, *can* be pronounced as an independent syllable, as in the word *button*. No language could ever have words composed entirely of real consonants like *p* and *k* (though some languages have writing systems that give that impression), because they could not be pronounced.

> 4. The language will have a way to make statements, questions, commands, and exclamations.

You will recognize this four-way classification as the traditional division of sentences into declaratives, interrogatives, imperatives, and exclamations. These are called *speech acts*, because in pronouncing or writing the sentence you are at the same time performing an action—stating, asking, ordering, or exclaiming. There are of course more subtle divisions than these. There are threats, promises, pleas, laments, boasts, and many more. However, while languages do not usually have special forms for these other speech acts, all known languages have a particular way of indicating the basic four.

English relies primarily on word order and intonation (the tone of voice and its "melody") to distinguish one speech act from another. Lakota Sioux has a set of separate words which must be placed at the end of a sentence to indicate a command, with one for female speakers and another for males.

A *morpheme* is a meaningful sequence in a language which cannot be divided into any smaller meaningful units; it may or may not be a word. Thus, *elephant* is both a word and a morpheme; *books* contains the morpheme (and word) *book* and an additional morpheme, the *s* that marks the plural, which is not an independent word. In Kumeyaay, an American Indian language of California, commands are indicated by a morpheme attached to the verb. The Kumeyaay word *menak* has two morphemes—*me-* ('you') and *-nak* ('sit down')—and is a statement. *Kenak* is made up of *ke-*, the imperative marker, and the same *-nak*, and is a command meaning 'Sit down!'

5. The language will have a way of making sentences negative.

From the earliest stages of speech in the child, human beings need some way to assert the contrary of statements, to negate them. The variety of negative forms used by different languages (including English) is astonishing. Two-part negatives are very common in human languages; for example:

NAVAJO
Jáan doo naalnish da.
John NEG he-is-working NEG   John isn't working.

FRENCH
Jean ne travaille pas.
John NEG is-working NEG   John isn't working.

French differs from Navajo in having various possible morphemes for the second half of the negative—for example, *ne . . . point* is more emphatically negative than *ne . . . pas*—whereas the Navajo form is always *da*.

6. The language will have both noun-like and verb-like elements.

The basic noun/verb distinction is universally found in human languages, but is expressed more differently from one language to another than might be anticipated. An element may be a noun in one language and a verb in another, and vice versa. Furthermore many languages have verbs that would be considered adjectives in English.

In Kumeyaay the negative element itself (*maaw* 'not') is used as a verb, and has the following set of forms in the singular:

emaaw	*e* (I) + *maaw* (not)
memaaw	*me* (you) + *maaw*
umaaw	*u* (he, she, it) + *maaw*

The negative command in Kumeyaay is always composed of two verbs, one of which is *kemaaw*.

7. The language will have a way of indicating the case relationships between nouns and verbs.

In every human language, once you have located the verb in a sentence, a number of questions may arise about that verb. Who is doing it? Who or what is it being done to? Where and when is it being done? What is being used to do it? And many others, depending on the particular verb. The relationship that a noun has to a verb in a sentence, based upon this sort of information, is called its *case*; and case is crucial to keeping straight what is going on in sentences.

The methods used by languages to indicate case include one or more of the following: word order, special morphemes added to the nouns, prepositions, and postpositions. (Postpositions are like prepositions, except that they follow instead of precede the noun. English and Samoan have prepositions; Navajo has postpositions.)

Latin has a full set of case morphemes in the form of endings on its nouns. Such a set is called a *declension*, and an example in the singular is given below:

port*a*	the gate, a gate	Nom.	(subject)
port*ae*	of the gate	Gen.	(possessive)
port*ae*	to/for the gate	Dat.	(indirect object)
port*am*	the gate, a gate	Acc.	(direct object)
port*ā*	by/with/from the gate	Abl.	(other relationships)
port*a*	O gate!	Voc.	(thing addressed)

Another set of case endings is used for the plural, giving *portae, portārum, portīs, portās, portis,* and *portae* to complete the declension.

English like Latin once had declensions, but our case endings have almost completely disappeared. All that remains in nouns is the 's of the possessive, and in pronouns we find a remnant of the old case system in a set like the following:

who	*who* + no ending	(subject)
whose	*who* + *s* (and "silent" *e*)	(possessive)
whom	*who* + *m*	(direct object, indirect object, and a number of other relationships)

Having lost our subject and object case endings for full nouns, we have to rely on some other mechanism to keep track of things, and word order is the chosen method. "John bit the dog" and "The dog bit John" mean very different things in English. In Latin, since both *John* and *the dog* would have endings marking them clearly as subject or object, the order of the words is not very important.

    8. The language will have a way to indicate the tense and aspect of the verb.

Tense and aspect are complicated concepts (examined more fully in Chapter Nine). Roughly speaking, tense has to do with the time of a state or an event, while aspect expresses its frequency, its duration, and whether or not it has been completed. Some languages place more emphasis on one than on the other, and the ways chosen to indicate the two in speech or writing will reflect this preference. Some languages demand a great deal of detail and precision in these matters. In Navajo, for example, it is not sufficient to state simply that someone has gone somewhere. The form of the verb must specify whether that person has gone and returned, gone and arrived and gone no farther, gone and arrived and continued on past the original destination, gone and is still on the way to the destination, and so on. The degree of specificity demanded has as one result the fact that there are more than three thousand separate forms for the Navajo verb *go*.

The perception of time and duration may also vary from one language to another. For instance in Navajo the verb *sidá*, which is translated into English as 'he, she, it is sitting' or 'the two of them are sitting', is a Navajo past tense form. From the Navajo point of view, to be sitting is a completed action by one who has stopped moving, and hence is an event in the past.

Many languages add morphemes to the verb (forming a set called a *conjugation*) to indicate tense and/or aspect. An example from Spanish is the following conjugation of *hablar* ('to speak') in the future tense.

hablaré	I will speak
hablarás	you (singular) will speak
hablará	he, she, it will speak
hablaremos	we will speak
hablaréis	you (plural) will speak
hablarán	they will speak

Although English has a past tense verb ending (usually *-ed*), it has no future conjugation and conveys the same information either by placing the auxiliary verb *will* before the main verb, or—to the frequent astonishment of people learning English—by using the present tense and a time word, as in "We leave tomorrow."

    9. The language will have grammar rules that allow the deletion of parts of sentences, and rules that allow them to be moved about.

English forms most imperatives by deleting the *you* in commands, as does French. Similarly, the English speaker may say either "I know that Maria is here" or "I know Maria is here"; in the second sentence, the word *that* has been deleted. Samoan allows the deletion of the preposition which marks a noun as a direct object; since this is the only one of the case-marking prepositions that may be deleted, no confusion is caused by the rule.

Both Spanish and Navajo allow the deletion of subject pronouns, since they are marked on the verb. However, the morpheme *-o* on the word *trabajo* ('I am working') has combined tense and aspect and the information that the subject is singular and first person (*I*) into one indivisible chunk. The Navajo word for 'I am working', *naashnish*, contains the information about the subject in the morpheme *-sh-* which appears before *-nish*; for tense and aspect one must look elsewhere.

No human language has absolutely fixed word order for its sentences, although some languages are much stricter about movement rules than others. French, English, and Spanish all use movement rules in the formation of questions; all languages appear to have movement rules that are used to emphasize one element over another. Languages such as Russian and Hungarian, which have full sets of case endings, will tend to allow far more freedom of word order than languages like English and Chinese, which lack such markers of noun function.

10. The language will have at least two ways of combining small sentences into larger ones.

One way to combine sentences is *conjunction* (also called *coordination*). It consists of simply hooking sentences together, as English does in "I saw Bill come into the room and I left at once." The other way is called *embedding*, and consists of putting one sentence *inside* another sentence. We can do this many times, as shown by the example below:

Carlos said that Mary had forgotten that Bill would not remember that Elizabeth had promised that Aaron would bring the can opener.

That example, which is well on its way to becoming something like "The House That Jack Built," has put four sentences inside one bigger sentence; notice that each one of the embedded sentences is marked by the word *that* at the beginning. Navajo does this by adding *-ígíí* to the last word in the embedded sentence; Hopi has the same process, but the marker is *-q*.

There is no human language that does not have both conjoining and embedding, which means that it would never be possible to write down all of the sentences of any human language or to state how many sentences the language could contain. It is not even possible to state how *long* a "longest" sentence of a human language would be, since no matter how long it was a speaker could always embed another sentence in it or add another sentence to it by conjunction.

Without conjoining and embedding, human communication would undoubtedly be a tedious matter, since we would all be restricted to a language style like the average pre-primer.

This list could be made much longer, but it is sufficient for purposes of illustration. People often react to items on the list by commenting on how "obvious" they are, and by asking "How could there possibly be a language that didn't have _____?," with the blank filled by one or more of the ten characteristics listed.

Which is precisely the point. All human languages ever encountered have had those ten characteristics. They are part of what a human being means by the very word *language*. We have every reason to believe that no human language will ever be encountered that does *not* possess those ten characteristics.

On the other hand, we have no particular reason to suppose that a truly alien language would possess any of them. What a human language is like is tied to what the human brain and vocal apparatus are like. There is no more reason to expect that an intelligent gas-cloud would use consonants and vowels than that it would have a human heart or a pair of human kidneys. What, then, would an alien language be like? And how could a linguist—or a translating or interpreting device programmed by a linguist—begin to work with such a language?

Nobody knows. It is part of being human that we are unable to imagine clearly any other sort of language than a human language.

EXERCISES AND PROBLEMS

1. In his book *Is Anyone There?*, Isaac Asimov suggests that the formal system of mathematics might serve as one way to approach the problem of communication between human beings and aliens in space. Do you agree or disagree? Why?

2. Assume that a planet once settled by an English-speaking group of Terrans has seen its civilization rise, develop, and die. All that remain are a few ruined buildings, inscriptions, and artifacts. Assume that the inscription below was found in two columns on the side of a pillar. Can you decipher it?

COLUMN I	COLUMN II
WOMAN	THREETEEN
WOMANID	TOO-TENTY-SEFFAN
MOMAN	FORETEEN
MOMANID	THREE-TEN
INFAN	ELEFFAN
FOREPED	TOO
FOREPEDID	SEFFAN
THREEPED	TOO-TEN
THREEPEDID	TOO
BERD	FIFE
BERDID	MULTY

3. Remember that a morpheme is a unit of meaning that cannot be divided into any smaller meaningful units. Divide the words in Exercise 2 into their morphemes and explain what each of the morphemes means.

4. The words listed below are all from English. As in Exercise 3, divide them into morphemes and state the meanings of each.

   (a) house, trees, walking, water, waiter, friendly
   (b) unpacking, indisputable, abandonment, emphasis, misunderstanding, unkindness, friendship
   (c) philodendron, telegraph, telephone, anthropology, theology, locomotive, automobile

   Is there any problem with the morpheme division for group (c)? Can you explain the source of the difficulty?

5. The following sentences are from Esperanto, an artificial language. English translations are given. Make a list of the Esperanto words, with their translations, and then divide them into morphemes. Specify the meaning of each morpheme.

(a)	Mi kuŝas sur la liton.	I sleep on the bed.
(b)	Mi kuŝas sur la plankon.	I sleep on the floor.
(c)	La infano kuŝas sur la liton.	The child sleeps on the bed.
(d)	Mi kuŝis sur la liton.	I slept on the bed.
(e)	La infanoj kuŝis sur la liton.	The children slept on the bed.
(f)	La infanoj kuŝis sur la litojn.	The children slept on the beds.
(g)	Mi vidas la infanon.	I see the child.
(h)	Mi vidas la infanojn.	I see the children.

(i)   Mi vidis la liton.   I saw the bed.
(j)   La knabo timas la bovon.   The boy fears the bull.
(k)   La knabino timas la bovon.   The girl fears the bull.
(l)   Mi vidas la bovinon.   I see the cow.
(m)   Mi vidos la knabon.   I will see the boy.
(n)   La bovo vidos la knabon.   The bull will see the boy.

Note: The *ŝ* is pronounced like *sh* in *ship*. The *j* is pronounced like English *y*. All other sounds are approximately as in English.

6. Using the information from Exercise 5, write translations into Esperanto for the English sentences below.

(a) The cow sees the child.
(b) The cows see the children.
(c) The boy will fear the bull.
(d) I will see the beds.
(e) The boys slept on the floor.

7. Look at the following Esperanto sentences and their translations:

(a) Mi vidas la knabon.   I see the boy.
(b) Min vidas la knabo.   The boy sees me.
(c) La knabo vidas min.   The boy sees me.
(d) La knabo min vidas.   The boy sees me.
(e) Mi la knabon vidas.   I see the boy.
(f) Vidas mi la knabon.   I see the boy.
(g) La knabon vidas mi.   I see the boy.
(h) La knabon mi vidas.   I see the boy.

The system for marking subject/object case relationships in Esperanto is clearly very different from that of English. State how Esperanto distinguishes subjects and objects and explain the effect this has on sentence structure.

8. A proposal that comes up from time to time in science fiction is that there might be an interstellar or intergalactic Sign Language. Does this seem plausible to you? Comment on the difficulties that might arise with such a system in the following two situations:

(a) communication between Terrans and alien beings who are of Terran ancestry but migrated from Earth three thousand years ago;

(b) communication between Terrans and alien beings who have no shared ancestry but have evolved completely independently on another world.

9. The following examples are from an entirely hypothetical language which we will call Fáda. Look at the examples (usually called the *data* in linguistics); then answer the questions underneath them.

Vocabulary

hóna	planet	ganéy	discover
kaamíyo	spaceship	poróy	be-safe
elába	captain	anamóy	be-beautiful
biníssa	passenger	binéy	die
sarelfáda	food	kiféy	land (*verb*)
farelfáda	water	haróy	be-tragic
		poréy	settle

Sentences

(a) Kiféye kaamíyo dep hóna dep kol.   The spaceship landed on the planet.

(b) Poréye biníssaba dep hóna dep.   The passengers settled the planet.

(c) Poróyo fass anamóyo hóna.   The planet was safe and beautiful.

(d) Poróyo sarelfáda dep fass farelfáda dep.   The food and water were safe.

(e) Binéye elába dep-sa haróyo.   That the captain died was tragic.

(f) Po binéye po biníssaba dep.   The passengers did not die.

(g) Po haróyo po baf.   That was not tragic.

Questions

(a) Does Fáda lack any of the ten characteristics of a human language described in this chapter?

(b) How does Fáda show that a noun is plural?

(c) How does Fáda show that a verb is past tense?

(d) How does Fáda embed one sentence in another? *Hint:* Look at sentence (e).

(e) How would you write in Fáda: "The water was not safe and the passengers died."

(f) How does Fáda indicate subjects and objects?

SUGGESTED READINGS

Note: Nontechnical readings are indicated throughout by an asterisk.

ARTICLES AND EXCERPTS

*ASIMOV, I. 1967. *Is Anyone There?* pp. 189–211. Ace Publications, New York. Originally published as "A Science in Search of a Subject," *New York Times Magazine*, May 23, 1965.

*BOHANNAN, L. 1966. "Shakespeare in the Bush." *Natural History*, Aug.–Sept. 1966.

*CHAFE, W. 1965. "The Nature of Language." *The National Elementary Principle* 45:10–15.

*CHASE, S. 1954. "How Language Shapes Our Thoughts." *Harpers*, April 1954.

*CLARKE, A. 1968. *The Promise of Space*, Chap. 27. Pyramid Books, New York.

DOUGHERTY, R. 1970. "Recent Studies on Language Universals." *Foundations of Language* 6:505–61.

*DYKEMA, K. 1961. "Where Our Grammar Came From." *College English* 22:455–65.

*FERRIS, T. 1975. "The Universe as an Ocean of Thought." *Harpers*, July 1975.

*HERBERT, F. 1965. *Dune*, pp. 523–41 ("Terminology of the Imperium"). Ace Publications, New York.

HOCKETT, C. 1960. "The Origins of Speech." *Scientific American* 203:89–96.

*KANFER, S. 1974. "Is There Intelligent Life on Commercials?" *Time*, April 16, 1974.

KRUEGER, J. 1968. "Language and Techniques of Communication as Theme or Tool in Science Fiction." *Linguistics* 39:68–86.

MCNEILL, D. 1966. "Speaking of Space." *Science* 152:875–80.

*SAGAN, D. 1973. *The Cosmic Connection*, Chaps. 3, 4, and 30. Dell Publishing, New York.

SECHREST, L. et al. 1972. "Problems of Translation in Cross-Cultural Communication." *Journal of Cross-Cultural Psychology* 3:41–56.

*SHENKER, I. 1971. "Chomsky is difficult to please. Chomsky is easy to please. Chomsky is certain to please." *Horizon*, Spring 1971.

*SULLIVAN, W. 1966. *We Are Not Alone*, pp. 261–70 ("Celestial Syntax"). Signet Books, New York.

*WANG, W. 1973. "The Chinese Language." *Scientific American* 228:50–63.

*WOOLFSON, P. 1970. "Sapir's Theory of Language." *Language Sciences* 11:8–10.

BOOKS

GREENBERG, J. (ed.). 1966. *Universals of Language, 2nd ed.* M.I.T. Press, Cambridge, Mass.

WHORF, B. 1964. *Language, Thought and Reality*. J. CARROLL (ed.). John Wiley and Sons, New York.

TWO

Semantics

For the native speaker of English, the following sentence will not be acceptable:

(1)   Even Einstein could have solved that equation.

There is nothing grammatically wrong with that sentence. It has all its words in the right places, and its spelling and punctuation are everything they ought to be. Why, then, doesn't it make sense?

The difficulty with sentence (1) is that if *it* is true, a number of other things must also be true, including both of the following:

(2)   a. The equation was fairly easy.
      b. Einstein wasn't very good at solving equations.

The two propositions of (2) must be true if (1) is, but we know that in reality Einstein was a mathematical genius and that no equation that would have been a challenge for him could have been simple. To make this more clear, let's rewrite sentence (1) as in (3).

(3)   Even Billy could have solved that equation.

Since the mathematical skills of the unidentified Billy are unknown, the sentence is now perfectly all right.

What matters here is not the respective abilities of Albert Einstein and the hypothetical Billy with regard to the solving of equations. Notice that neither of the sentences of (2) appears anywhere in the series of words that make up sentence (1). How then, just by looking at (1), did you *know* that the sentences of (2) were involved?

The science that attempts to answer such questions is semantics, the study of meaning. Its goal is to explain how sequences of language are matched with their proper meanings by the speakers of that language.

Like many other scientific goals, this one has yet to be achieved. Every question answered turns out to have more questions lurking behind it; that is the nature of scientific investigation, and what makes it fun to do. This chapter will present some of the basic concepts and methods used by semanticists in their work toward that ultimate goal.

PROPERTIES OF LANGUAGE

In Chapter One we stated that all human languages have certain shared characteristics. Linguists call these characteristics universal properties of language, and consider them to be parts of the definition of a human language. An understanding of those properties which are most directly concerned with meaning is essential to the study of semantics. Those we will examine here are *synonymy*, *ambiguity*, and *presupposition*.

Synonymy

To say that two differing sequences of language have the same meaning is to claim that they are *synonymous*.[1] The term is often used carelessly. The sentences in (4) can be considered synonymous in the strictest and most precise sense of the word.

(4)   a. Marian set down the football.
　　　b. Marian set the football down.

---

[1] It is also common to say that such sequences are *paraphrases* of one another, especially for longer units of language.

We can claim that these two sentences really "mean the same thing," because it is impossible to imagine any situation in which one of them could be used and the other could not, and because native speakers of English have no feeling that there is any subtle difference of meaning between them. But good examples like (4) are not easy to find. Consider the following pair of sentences, for instance.

(5)   a. Sam is a vegetarian.
       b. Sam doesn't eat meat.

Are these two sentences also synonymous, in the way that the sentences of (4) are? We can only answer "it depends," which is an immediate indication of semantic trouble. The difficulty is in the word *vegetarian*. For most of us, being a vegetarian implies a philosophical or religious or perhaps ecological objection to the eating of meat. If Sam doesn't eat meat simply because he dislikes the taste, or because he can't afford it, or because his doctor has told him not to, that is not exactly the same thing as vegetarianism. Similar subtle differences can be seen in the following pairs.

(6)   a. Evelyn is a spinster.
       b. Evelyn is not married.

(7)   a. Christopher is a bachelor.
       b. Christopher is not married.

In examples (5) to (7) a major reason for the impossibility of deciding whether the sentence pairs are synonymous or not is the problem of specifying the exact meaning for a single word. A different kind of problem is shown in the sentences of (8).

(8)   a. John ate the spaghetti.
       b. The spaghetti was eaten by John.
       c. What John ate was the spaghetti.
       d. It was John who ate the spaghetti.
       e. It was the spaghetti that John ate.
       f. The spaghetti was what John ate.
       g. What John did was eat the spaghetti.
       h. It was the spaghetti which was eaten by John.
       i. What was eaten by John was the spaghetti.

Here the meanings of individual words are not the source of the difficulty. The words are almost the same from sentence to sentence. But are these sentences synonymous? Do they mean exactly the same thing? Let's repeat the strictly synonymous pair of (4):

(9)   a. Marian set down the football.
      b. Marian set the football down.

In (9) it is Marian who does something, and the football that something (being set down) happens to. Changing the order of the words does not change these facts. Similarly, in all the sentences of (8), it is John who acts, it is the spaghetti which undergoes the action, and the act—eating—remains constant throughout the examples. Both (8) and (9) are very different in this respect from (10), where rearrangement of the pieces creates a drastic rearrangement of events as well.

(10) a. The lion killed the water buffalo.
      b. The water buffalo killed the lion.

Example (10) shows clearly that synonymy cannot be the result of just having a pair of sentences whose *words* are identical, although that is a characteristic of the synonymous sentences of (9). Nor, as example (8) shows, is synonymy as simple a matter as maintaining a shared set of facts about who is doing what and what is being done. Native speakers of English agree that although the sentences of (8) are very *close* in meaning, and although the differences among them are not easy to explain, they don't mean exactly the same thing.

One way to characterize roughly the meaning differences in (8) is to say that some of the sentences seem to be about John, while others are about the spaghetti. No analogous difference can be found between (9a) and (9b).

Another aspect of the difference becomes apparent when you consider how the sentences of (8) could be used. You will find that there are some situations in which one member of the set would be acceptable, while another would seem very odd, as shown by (11).

(11) a. Q: What did John do?
          A: John ate the spaghetti.
      b. Q: What did John do?
          A: *The spaghetti was what John ate.[2]

---

[2] An asterisk before a sentence is used in linguistics to indicate that this is not an acceptable sequence of English.

No native speaker of English would accept a question/answer sequence like (11b). Contrast this with:

(12) a. Q: What did Marian do?
          A: Marian set down the football.
      b. Q: What did Marian do?
          A: Marian set the football down.

If discussion of synonymy had to be restricted absolutely to such flawless example pairs as (9), it would be brief, because such examples are rare. On the other hand, we cannot let the conditions for synonymy become too casual. Semantics is a scientific endeavor, and a statement such as "Two sentences are synonymous if they are only a *little* bit different in meaning" is not very scientific. How different is "only a little bit different"? And how is that degree of difference to be measured? One speaker's "only a little bit" might be another speaker's "not the same thing at all," and the two individuals would then be said (accurately) to be quarreling over "just semantics."

The solution most linguists accept involves the concept of semantic *focus*. Focus can be informally defined as "what the sentence is about," and is the part of the sentence having greatest semantic importance for the speaker or writer. Certainly this does not mean that the other parts of the sentence are irrelevant, or are of no importance at all to the speaker. If this were true, presumably they would just be left out of the sentence altogether. And it is true that in a sentence such as "John saw Mary" it is somewhat arbitrary to say that the sentence is any more "about John" than it is "about Mary." Consider, however, the sentences in (8), and compare (g) with (i).

g. What John did was eat the spaghetti.
i. What was eaten by John was the spaghetti.

Although both these sentences, and all the sentences of (8), are in a sense "about" both John and the spaghetti, in (g) the element that is most clearly foregrounded or brought to the reader's attention is neither one. It is instead John's action, his eating of the spaghetti. In (i) this is no longer true. Here the primary focus is on the spaghetti in its role of something being eaten. Similarly, in the sentence "It was John who ate the spaghetti" (8d), the speaker has made a point of indicating the particular importance of John. In "It was the spaghetti that John ate" (8e), the same point has been made on behalf of the spaghetti, at John's expense. The differences are subtle, but the basic concept should be clear.

Linguists agree that perfect synonymy is rare, but point out that all speakers of English recognize that the sentences of (8) constitute a set with a common core of meaning, differing only in regard to focus. No sentence in the set could be true unless *all* the sentences are. So long as this is true of any two sequences, so long as meaning differences are rigidly restricted to differences of this kind and no others, they can be said to be synonymous. This solution will allow us to include the sentences of (8) and (9), but will exclude those of (5) to (7) and (10), where the differences clearly go beyond the limit specified.

No language exists which does not have sequences demonstrating the property of synonymy. Similarly, no language exists which does not have grammatical resources available for producing sets of sentences differing only in the element which the speaker chooses to indicate as the focus of his or her interest and expression. This is a stylistic resource, and a valuable one; without it we would be severely limited in our ability to communicate nuances of meaning.

Ambiguity

When two sequences are synonymous, they have a different form but share a single meaning. Ambiguity is the opposite of synonymy—an ambiguous sequence is one with a single form which represents *more than one* meaning. For example:

(13) Fighting elephants can be dangerous.

There is no way to tell, by looking at sentence (13) in isolation, which of the meanings represented in (14) is intended by the speaker.

(14) a. For someone to fight elephants can be dangerous.
      b. Elephants which are fighting can be dangerous.

The important phrase here is "in isolation." Ambiguity in real life—either in conversation or in reading—is not likely to be met with frequently. The context of the potentially ambiguous sequence (the other sentences around it, or the real world situation in which it is used, or both) will ordinarily serve to make clear which meaning is intended. You will not usually be aware that a sentence you have heard or read in context is ambiguous, unless that fact is pointed out to you.

The ambiguity of a sequence like (13) is due to a lack of clarity as to the functions of the various pieces of the sentence (usually referred to as its constituents). We cannot tell whether those elephants are doing the fighting themselves or are being attacked. Ambiguity can also be caused—again, in isolation—by the multiple possible meanings of a single word, as in:

(15) George gave Benjamin a plane for Christmas.

© THE WIZARD OF ID by permission of
Johnny Hart and Field Enterprises, Inc.

Although *a plane* could be either a carpentry tool or an airplane, in real life you probably would know whether George could afford to buy something so expensive as an airplane, whether Benjamin was old enough for such a gift to be suitable, and so on. Thus the context would be sufficient to specify the meaning in the vast majority of cases.

Like synonymy, ambiguity is found in every human language, both for single words and for longer sequences.

The two properties of language just discussed, ambiguity and synonymy, are not major problems in daily conversation between native speakers of the same language. Translations, however, can be utterly destroyed by them. The point of a translation (whether spoken or written) is to produce a sequence in one language which will be equivalent to a sequence in the other, and the resulting sequence must not be ambiguous. When two languages are very closely related, there is a fairly good chance for success in translation, although it is by no means a simple matter. With languages which share no common ancestor in their history, success becomes much more difficult to achieve.

Every English-speaking linguist who has ever worked with the Navajo language, for example, has come upon the interesting fact that the most common Navajo equivalent for the English sentence "There is a road from the house to the cornfield" must be literally translated as "It is roading from the house to the cornfield." *Road* is always a noun in English; this is not true for Navajo. We can say that the Navajo sentence and the English sentence are *equivalent* to one another in that they would be used in the same situation to convey the same perceived facts, but by no means can we claim that they are synonymous.

The following pair of sentences, one English and one Navajo, is also equivalent.

(16) a. Rebecca was riding a horse.
      b. Łį́į' Rebecca bił naaldloosh ńt'éé'.

The Navajo sentence, however, if translated literally rather than freely, says "The horse was going about with Rebecca." Notice that the English sentence has Rebecca doing something *to* a horse, while the Navajo sentence has the horse doing something *together with* Rebecca. The case relationships expressed are not the same at all.

It is not necessary to go as far from the English language as Navajo to encounter difficulties in translation, nor are they confined entirely to idioms, or to the famous "false friends" of the foreign language classroom—pairs of words which appear almost identical but turn out to have quite different meanings.[3] Compare the two very brief sentences below:

(17) a. Be good. ENGLISH
b. Sois sage. FRENCH

The two sentences are equivalent, in the sense that a French-speaking parent would use (17b) in the same situation in which an English-speaking parent would use (17a) in speaking to a child. However, the French sentence, literally translated, instructs the child to be wise (*sage*), which is not precisely the same thing as an instruction to be good.

Computer translations must be very carefully set up to avoid any sequences where either ambiguity or synonymy is involved, unless it is so trivial that a clarification can be built in. Programming a computer to translate Navajo into English, or vice versa, would be very tricky. The literal translation of (16b), for example, is ambiguous in English, since we cannot tell whether Rebecca is sitting on the horse as the two of them "go about" or not. This ambiguity is not present in the original Navajo sentence, because the Navajo motion verb is one which cannot be used to speak of a human being. It would require an exceedingly skillful programmer to provide a computer with all the information needed to produce unambiguous, and sufficiently synonymous, sequences under circumstances like these.

Presupposition

The word presupposition is used in a number of different ways in the literature of philosophy, logic, and linguistics. In this text the term is used somewhat loosely to refer to all those things which a native speaker of a language knows are meant by a sequence of that language, but which are not actually stated in that sequence. (You may have encountered this concept before in connection with the term *logical entailment*.) The first example sentence in this chapter—"Even Einstein could have solved that equation"—illustrates this property very well. It presupposes at least the following propositions:

a. there was once an individual named Einstein;
b. there exists some mathematical equation, referred to in the sentence;
c. the equation is not very difficult;
d. the individual named Einstein was not very good at solving equations.

---

[3] A common example of "false friends" is the English/French pair *sympathetic/sympathique*. The French word appears almost the same as the English one, but to say that Marie is *sympathique* means that she is pleasant to be with, that her company is enjoyable. The English word *sympathetic* is used to describe someone who is inclined to show an attitude of interest and concern towards other people's problems.

As used in this text, presupposition also includes the concept of the *connotation* of a sequence of language as understood by native speakers. The strict definition of a word is its *denotation*, which is usually fairly easy to provide; the connotation(s) are something else again.

To make this clearer, let's consider again two sentences we looked at earlier:

(18) a. Evelyn is a spinster.
     b. Christopher is a bachelor.

In terms of their denotations, we would say that *spinster* and *bachelor* are different in meaning only in that one refers to females and the other to males. In a strict denotational sense this is true; *bachelor* denotes an unmarried man, while *spinster* denotes an unmarried woman. When we consider the connotations, however—that is, the things that a native speaker of English is likely to know about these two words in addition to their precise definitions—it is clear that they are not so close in meaning as they seem. Sentence (18a) presupposes that there is someone named Evelyn, that this Evelyn is female, and that she is not married; (18b) presupposes that Christopher is male, and that, like Evelyn, he is not married. In addition, for most speakers of English in contemporary America, (18a) has the following presuppositions:

(19) a. Evelyn is not a young girl.
     b. Evelyn is unmarried because she has not had the *opportunity* to marry.
     c. People should feel sorry for Evelyn.

Example 18b, on the other hand, has no presuppositions regarding Christopher's age, but does have the following presupposition:

(20) Christopher is unmarried because he has not *chosen* to marry.

Needless to say, there is no presupposition that Christopher deserves our sympathy. The connotations of *bachelor* today involve the image of a man enjoying himself in unwedded bliss; *spinster* is quite different.

Some scholars will object to this use of the term presupposition because of the presence of variability here. That is, although every native speaker of English without exception will agree that the term spinster entails the two terms 'female' and 'unmarried', it would be possible to find speakers for whom the propositions listed in (19) would not hold. However, it is precisely because of this variability that this writer finds the term so useful as a semantic concept.

People have a strong tendency to assume that if they are talking to another individual fluent in their language, and if the words being used by both are "in" the same language, they are sharing the same presuppositions and adequate communication is taking place. In real-life terms, this is often an assumption with no foundation in fact. If *spinster* for you presupposes the propositions of (19), but presupposes none of them for your grandmother, then when you and your grandmother use the word *spinster* you are not using the "same" word. For you, it has firmly attached presuppositions that may never have occurred to your grandmother, and your communication is curtailed by this difference.

The farther apart two speakers are in real-world terms—that is, in terms of native language, age, sex, race, nationality, socioeconomic background, geographic background, profession, religion, and similar factors—the more likely it is that even when they speak "the same language" they do not share the same presuppositions. The presuppositions of a language are rarely part of the content of foreign language textbooks, and native speakers usually are not consciously aware of their own presuppositions. The thickest and most prestigious dictionaries are often of little help; for example, although the word *even* is responsible for the two presuppositions of sentence (1) listed in (2), no dictionary definition of *even* will provide a non-native speaker of English with that information. We will take up this matter again in the Sociolinguistics chapter of this text, since it is a significant cause of communication difficulties in a multi-ethnic nation such as the United States.

Two additional terms should be discussed under the heading of presupposition: *anomaly* and *meaningfulness*. These terms are closely related and can profitably be discussed together. Look at these sentences:

(21)   a. I met a pregnant bachelor on the subway.
      b. Phillip was attacked by his electric typewriter.
      c. There is an exceptionally exquisite unicorn in my desk drawer.
      d. Timothy drew a square circle on the blackboard with his largest mump.

We can characterize all these sentences as weird, and some as weirder than others. Technically speaking, the sentences are semantically *anomalous*; that is, they have something semantically wrong with them. The anomaly of (21a) comes from the fact that *bachelor* presupposes maleness, while the word *pregnant* presupposes that the individual so described is female. Sentence (21b) presupposes that a typewriter is capable of attacking someone, while

(21c) presupposes that unicorns exist. All four sentences could in the narrowest sense of the word be classified as meaningless.[4]

However, the term *meaningless* does not mean the same thing for all the examples. We can all understand (21a) and (21c) if we are willing to assume a universe in which pregnancy in the male human is possible and unicorns are among the inventory of existing animals. This requires a suspension on our part of concepts based upon the actual universe in which we live, but we have no difficulty deriving meaning from the sentences. Example (21b) can be understood in two ways; either we imagine a universe in which there are animate electric typewriters, or we understand the sentence as not being meant literally. It's not especially unusual to ask someone how he or she acquired a bruise and to be told that it is the result of having been "attacked" by one machine or another. The speaker does not mean to imply that the machine really is alive, but rather that it "behaves" as if it were. Anyone who has ever had to deal with a jammed garbage disposal unit or a broken bicycle chain or any similar mechanical device will find the sentence fully meaningful.

But then there is (21d). It would take much ingenuity to make this anomalous example meaningful. Like sentence (1), it has all its parts in their proper places, it contains no errors of spelling or punctuation, and there are no missing or superfluous pieces. Well and good—but what could it mean?

No damage will be done if, as is likely, we are unable to find a suitable interpretation for (21d). What matters is to understand that anomaly and meaningfulness, like many other characteristics of human language, are not either/or matters. Rather, they exist in varying degrees, and particular sequences fall at different points on the scale. Example (21d) is definitely more anomalous, and far less meaningful, than the other three examples of (21).

When we consider all of the problems discussed above for the interpretation of meaning even within a single human language, not to mention those that arise when we attempt to achieve roughly adequate translations between two or more human languages, the dubious nature of the universal translator of science fiction becomes exceedingly clear. The problem of specifying meaning to the degree necessary for satisfactory communication, whether through a human being or by means of a computer programmed by a human being, is still one of the major difficulties we must face on this planet. To attempt to face an extension of the quandary *beyond* human civilization requires a leap of faith; first, we must be convinced that it is at least possible.

---

[4] This sort of rigidity has many advantages in formal academic situations. It also leads to practical absurdities. For instance, if all the sentences of (21) are meaningless, they are exactly equivalent in meaning, and therefore synonymous. No native speaker of English is likely to accept this formal result.

SEMANTIC FEATURES AND
SELECTIONAL RESTRICTIONS

From previous examples, it will be clear that even when the discussion of meaning is restricted to the meaning of a single word, we cannot talk of a single *unit* of meaning at that level. To say that the meaning of "bleb" is "blister" is to say nothing useful; it merely gives us two words to define instead of one. The meaning of a word is composed of parts, each of which must be specified to determine the full meaning accurately, and it may be that the concept of the "full meaning" of a word is never going to be more than an ideal. When we think of "bachelor," for example, we know that part of its meaning is humanness, another part animacy, another maleness, and still another the state of being unmarried—but how much more must be included?

In many instances, what a semanticist needs to know does not involve a search for the hypothetical full meaning. Instead, what is needed is the answer to a question something like the following: Given a group of words which share enough meaning in common to be considered a semantic set, what characteristics of each member of that set does a native speaker have to recognize in order to identify it? For instance, for the set of words denoting "footwear," how does a native speaker of English recognize one pair of footwear as bedroom slippers, another as sneakers, another as sandals, and so on?

We see this process of making distinctions developing in small children as they learn their language, with finer and finer distinctions indicating greater linguistic sophistication. A child may begin by calling all animals "doggy," for example, and then move to a stage where—on the basis of size—all animals are either a "doggy" or a "horse." This will suffice for cats, dogs, and guinea pigs, and for cows, bears, deer, and horses. But a semantic crisis will arise the first time the child comes in contact with an animal such as a large sheep. Is it a dog or is it a horse?

Similarly, anyone who has eaten many meals with a child is familiar with the following conversational sequences:

(a) CHILD: Can I have another roll?
    ADULT: Sure, honey, but that's not a roll. It's a biscuit.
    CHILD: Oh.

(*and the following evening*)

(b) CHILD: Can I have another biscuit?
    ADULT: Sure, honey, but that's not a biscuit. It's a roll.
    CHILD: Oh.

To deal with the system by which native speakers identify members of semantic sets such as kinship terms, footwear, foods, musical instruments, etc., many linguists use a device called the *semantic feature*. There are a number of other ways to write down the information for definitions, beginning with the standard dictionary definition and proceeding through various kinds of formal diagrams. However, the semantic feature allows the linguist to prepare a chart called a feature *matrix*, which does not attempt to present a full definition for the items that appear on it, but rather to list those characteristics of the listed items that are *distinctive*—that is, those that enable a native speaker to identify members of the set and assign them to categories.

English has a set of kinship terms which includes the words *mother, father, daughter, son, aunt, uncle, grandfather, grandmother, cousin, nephew, niece, mother-in-law*, etc. The use of kinship terms varies from culture to culture, so that what is viewed as an uncle/nephew relationship in English may be considered a father/son or older brother/younger brother relationship in another language. If you select just four basic terms from the English list, looked at from your own point of reference, a semantic matrix can be set up for them as in Table I. If the feature (customarily written in capital letters) is present, we write a plus, if absent, a minus.

Table I

	Mother	Father	Sister	Brother
[MALE]	−	+	−	+
[SAME GENERATION]	−	−	+	+

If you added the terms *aunt* and *uncle* to this matrix, the features given would no longer be sufficient to separate all the items. You would still need the feature [MALE] to indicate the sex, but [SAME GENERATION] would become problematical. It isn't the fact that a female relative is of a different generation that makes her your aunt; it is the fact that she is the sister of your mother or father. There are families in which the aunt or uncle is many years younger than the niece or nephew. In such a situation the concept of same or different generation may be formally the same but becomes very different in practical terms. The addition of *first cousin* would introduce new complications, and the feature [MALE] would not even be relevant. English, unlike many languages, does not have separate terms to distinguish a male cousin from a female one.

Throughout all human languages, there is a system which is usually referred to as *agreement* (or *concord*). We are all accustomed to reading grammar rules that tell us that one thing must "agree" with something else.

This system is interwoven with semantic feature analysis, because the grammar of any language will require that the features associated with various elements in a sequence be compatible with one another. The name for such requirements is *selectional restrictions*, and violation of these restrictions will produce a semantically anomalous sentence. For example:

(22)   *The boy injured herself.

Since *the boy* and *herself* in a sentence like this are assumed to refer to identical individuals, traditional grammar says that the pronoun *herself* does not "agree" with its antecedent, *the boy*. In terms of semantic features, *the boy* would be marked with the feature [+ MALE], while *herself* would be marked [− MALE]. This violates the rules of agreement for English, and results in an unacceptable sentence.

A more extreme example is given in (23).

(23)   I ate a tennis racket for lunch.

One way of expressing what is wrong with (23) is to say that the verb *eat* must always have as its direct object a word which could be marked with the semantic feature [+ EDIBLE]. Since this cannot apply to a tennis racket, (23) is semantically impossible.

The two concepts of the *semantic feature* and the *selectional restriction* are extremely useful tools for the semanticist. Many features (sometimes called semantic *primes*) are part of the universal characteristics of language. Thus, all human languages have at least the following features, along with many others:

[HUMAN]
[ANIMATE]
[ROUND]
[FLAT]
[RIGID]
[MALE]
[LIQUID]
[MOVABLE]

However, most universal features can be viewed as representing a range rather than a fixed point, and languages differ in the limits they set for any given feature. One language may extend the limits of the feature [LIQUID] to include the kind of mud that squishes up between the toes when walked through barefoot, while another may set the limit a bit short of that point and consider that kind of mud a solid. Such differences are generally found only at the extreme ends of the scale, however; we would not expect to find a language that classifies water itself as [−LIQUID].

It should be pointed out that individual languages sometimes make arbitrary feature assignments as a result of historical tradition, religious convention, or similar factors. Many male English speakers, for instance, assign the feature [−MALE] to a boat, a car, a rifle, etc., and therefore refer to them as "she" rather than "it." The gender systems of languages like French, in which a table is [−MALE], while a bed is [+MALE], clearly cannot be explained in terms of real world facts. There are languages in which the feature [+ANIMATE] is assigned to such natural phenomena as the wind, lightning, thunder, and the like.

For the vast majority of the semantic features which are universal, however, since all human beings perceive the same universe with the same set of perceptual organs and interpret the information from those organs with the same human brain, there will be basic agreement from language to language.

A major concern in linguistics is the question of how a semantic *theory* is to be constructed, so that linguists can talk about all these matters with clarity, and can use the theory as a framework for their teaching and research. The term customarily used to describe the semantic part of the grammar—whatever it may be like—is the *semantic component*.

THE TASK OF THE SEMANTIC COMPONENT

We have been examining some of the things which a semantic component must be able to do. The fundamental task of the semantic component is to match the sequences of a language with their proper meanings. In doing so it must account for the fact that native speakers recognize sequences as synonymous, ambiguous, and/or meaningful. It must account for the way in which people make judgments about the degree to which any of those characteristics is true of a particular sequence. The semantic component must also be able to account for the native speaker's ability to understand the presuppositions of a sequence as part of its meaning.

When we say that the semantic component must "account for" a particular activity of a human being, relative to his or her language, we do not mean that the theory is expected to state what is going on "inside the speaker's head." The mental operations that take place in the course of matching sequences with their meanings are not available for our observation. A semantic theory is instead a systematic way of discussing and describing semantic activities of human speakers, and is a symbolic model of those activities. It is not intended to represent psychological reality.

Keeping this in mind, we can return to the question of how a semantic component would operate. One obvious possibility has already been eliminated; it is clear that determining the meaning of a sentence is *not* a matter of determining the meaning of each word and then adding those meanings up like a set of numbers. The pair of sentences below, like the pair in (10), demonstrates that beyond question.

(24)   a.   Billy stuck out his tongue at Wesley.
      b.   Wesley stuck out his tongue at Billy.

The semantic component will have to have access to many other kinds of information besides simple word meanings. The difference in meaning between the two sentences of (24) requires knowledge about the grammatical functions represented by particular word orders in the English sentence, for example. Real world knowledge (such as that Einstein was a great mathematician) obviously must enter into the process. Even variations in the pattern of sound in sentences with identical words in identical orders must be taken into account, as shown by (25).

(25)   a.   Patricia called John an intellectual, and then he insulted her.
      b.   Patricia called John an intellectual, and then *he* insulted *her*.

In the case of (25b), the semantic component must be able to tell, from the strong stress on *he* and *her*, that the speaker considers it an insult to call someone an intellectual. In (25a), however, there is no such meaning attached to the sentence. This particular pattern of sound can be used to produce sentences which English speakers will find very strange, much as they would the sentence about Einstein. For instance:

(26)   a.   Mary called Michael a wonderful man, and then *he* insulted *her*.
      b.   Mary called Michael a great writer, and then *he* insulted *her*.

Both of these sentences presuppose that *whatever* Mary called Michael is an insult, but neither of the phrases, "a wonderful man" or "a great writer" ordinarily qualifies as insulting. (Notice that if the two sentences are pronounced with neutral stress there is nothing odd about them at all.)

A semantic component must also be able to account for the fact that native speakers of a language know not only what a sentence means in itself, but also what *speech act* (question, command, statement, etc.) it is intended to represent. For example, if someone says to you "Bring that dog into the house before it gets soaking wet!" you understand the sequence as two things: a sentence, with its associated meaning, and an action called a command. The understanding you have that the sequence is a command is part of the total meaning of the sentence.

Linguists find it interesting that speakers are able to determine the speech act category of a sentence even when it isn't what it appears to be.[5] Consider the following sentence.

(27) Why don't you hand me that wrench?

This sentence ought to be a question, from all apparent surface clues. And there are of course situations where it *is* a question. If someone has been asked three times to hand you a certain wrench, and just stands there holding the wrench and looking at you, you are likely to ask why and really want to *know* why. Under most circumstances, however, example (27)—although it is clearly marked by both words and pattern of sound as a question—is not a question at all, but a polite command. The semantic theory must account for the fact that native speakers of English know this and respond appropriately, and that they can tell the difference between these two uses of the sentence.

Finally, a semantic component must explain the ability of speakers to understand sequences of language which, strictly speaking, ought to mean one thing but clearly mean another, in a broader sense than just that of the speech act represented. The sentences which George Lakoff (and others) have called "hedges" are examples of this type of semantic problem. Example (28) shows a number of typical hedges.

(28) a. You know I would never tell you what to do, dear, but you shouldn't buy that car.
      b. You must do exactly what you please, of course, but the blue one is really ugly.
      c. I don't believe in interfering in other people's business, Bob, but there's no excuse for the way you yell at that hound.
      d. I can't stand people who go around giving advice when they haven't been asked for any, but if you'd go see my accountant you wouldn't have to pay taxes like that.
      e. I know this is a stupid question, but what's a lambda?

It isn't enough for the semanticist to say that the semantic component must be "that part of the grammar which accounts for all these features of language." A complete theory of semantics would have to accomplish all of the tasks we have mentioned above, in a very specific and systematic way. A moment's thought about just one such task will help to underscore the difficulty of constructing such a theory. Assume that we want to write a rule

---

[5] The investigation of language phenomena of this kind is often called *pragmatics*, which can be defined as the interaction between a sequence of language and the real world situation in which it is used.

to account for sentence (27), "Why don't you hand me that wrench?" We might begin like this:

(29) *A sentence which is marked grammatically as a question is to be inter-*
     preted as a command if and only if . . .

What should one put after "if and only if"? Obviously, we know, or we would not be able to interpret such sentences properly in daily life. But a formal explanation of what we are doing, even when we realize that it is not intended to describe actual mental processes, is not automatically available to us just because we know it must exist.

This chapter has not gone deeply into the problems of formalization; the upcoming chapters on syntax and phonology will provide a more appropriate environment for such material. The most important thing to understand at this point is the reason formalization is necessary. You can see that chemistry would not be very useful if its theory consisted of statements like (30).

(30) Whan a little bit of Element X is mixed with quite a lot of Element Y,
     the result will usually be pretty close to Compound Z.

Semantics can't rely on statements like that either, and the fact that the phenomena with which semanticists must work cannot be measured out into test tubes and checked for variables like weight and temperature doesn't help matters.

In spite of the formidable difficulties, linguists have made attempts to set down the beginnings of a coherent semantic theory. The suggested readings at the end of this chapter will direct you to some of these attempts.

EXERCISES AND PROBLEMS

1. An idiom is a phrase or construction whose meaning differs from the literal sense of its constituents, and which functions as a single unit, such as "kick the bucket" for "die," or "hit the sack" for "go to bed." Look at the following examples, which illustrate a particular kind of English idiom:

(a) Mary never lifted a finger to help us.
(b) Phyllis didn't turn a hair when the gun went off.
(c) *Bill lifted a finger to help us.
(d) I didn't blink an eye in spite of the expense.

(e) *I blinked an eye in spite of the expense.
(f) Marta just doesn't give a hoot.
(g) *Phyllis turned a hair when the gun went off.
(h) *Marta just gives a hoot.
(i) It was so windy that we didn't move a muscle.
(j) *It was so windy that we moved a muscle.

Can you determine what is responsible for the unacceptability of the starred sequences? What do the two additional examples below tell you about this phenomenon?

(k) Mary refused to lift a finger.
(l) *Mary agreed to lift a finger.

2. A 30-ft. tree standing upright in a forest is described as either "thirty feet *tall*" or "thirty feet *high*." If that tree were lying full length on the ground, it would have to be described as "thirty feet *long*." Explain what semantic distinction the English speaker relies on to determine the choice of the proper adjective.

3. Explain what is causing the communication breakdown between Dennis and his mother in the cartoon on p. 34.

4. The English verbs listed below all have to do with the same basic activity, but they vary in the intensity of that activity. Rank them in order of relative intensity, and write sentences to demonstrate the correctness of your judgment. An example has been given to start you off.

Example: I reprimanded Liz for running over my dog.

(a) reprimand   (b) chastise
(c) denounce   (d) berate
(e) scold   (f) censure
(g) criticize   (h) condemn

5. All of the following sentences are semantically odd. State the characteristic they have in common which accounts for their oddness.

(a) Harry went to the drugstore for ice cream, and no pentangle has more than five sides.
(b) I like Mary very much, but thunder is rare in this part of the country.
(c) The United States is larger than Denmark, and "cat" has only three letters.
(d) I want to leave at once, and any beaver can build a dam.

"ARE YOU LOOKING FOR A SPANKING, YOUNG MAN?" "GOSH, NO! WHERE DID YOU GET A NUTTY IDEA LIKE *THAT*?"

DENNIS THE MENACE by Hank Ketcham,
© Field Newspaper Syndicate.

6. In English some creatures go about in a *herd*, others in a *flock*, and still others in a *crowd*. Prepare a semantic feature matrix that will make it clear upon what features English speakers rely to make these classifications.

7. In this chapter a number of semantic difficulties were discussed. The cartoon on the next page illustrates one such difficulty. Is it one already discussed, something new, or a combination of both? Explain your answer.

8. The terms *freedom*, *liberty*, *independence*, *justice*, and *equality* form a semantic set. Do you think it would be possible to prepare a semantic feature matrix to make clear the distinctions among the members of the set? If so, how? If not, why not?

Pass It On!

INTERLANDI
© 1976, Los Angeles Times.

9. Consider the following group of sentences:

    (a) John killed Bill.
    (b) John caused Bill to die.
    (c) John caused Bill to become dead.
    (d) John caused Bill to become not alive.

Are these sentences synonymous, as the term was defined in this chapter? Can you think of contexts in which one of them would be true and another false, or in which one could be used while another could not?

10. All of the following sentences are ambiguous. Demonstrate their ambiguity by writing paraphrases of each that are *not* ambiguous.

    (a) Will you take the chair?

(b) They are sailing boats.

(c) We bought her dog biscuits.

(d) Did you remember the burglar in the bedroom?

(e) Helen promised to stand by Claudius.

(f) Nina wrote her thesis by herself.

(g) I have never seen Martin so low before.

(h) The police were ordered to stop smoking.

(i) He saw her drawing pencils.

(j) Fifty soldiers shot three wild foxes.

11. Here are a few sequences taken from signs commonly posted in public buildings. What, exactly, do you think they mean?

(a) When not in use, turn out the lights.

(b) When locked, use the restroom on the ground floor.

(c) Passengers can be momentarily met at the front of the terminal.

Is there any disagreement in the class over the meanings of these sequences?

12. Charles Fillmore has pointed out that something unusual seems to be going on with the English verbs *come* and *go*. Look at the following sentences and try to determine what factor the speaker uses in making a choice of the proper verb.

(a) I just called you to see if you will be coming to my office tomorrow.

(b) I just called you to see if you will be going to my office tomorrow.

(c) She asked me to go to her party, but I didn't go.

(d) She asked me to come to her party, but I didn't go.

(e) *She asked me to come to her party, but I didn't come.

(f) Please come in.

(g) Please go in.

13. Describe, for your own speech, the meaning differences in the following pairs of words:

(a) scarf/muffler   (b) dress/gown

(c) curls/ringlets   (d) dinner/supper

(e) barrel/keg   (f) woman/lady

(g) porch/veranda   (h) slice (meat)/carve (meat)

(i) boots/galoshes   (j) murder/assassinate

(k) apron/pinafore   (l) bucket/pail

(m) kerchief/scarf   (n) woman/girl

(o) speech/lecture

14. All of the following sentences are semantically strange in English. Consider them carefully and state what element or elements are responsible for your reaction. Then rewrite the sentences so that they would be acceptable.

(a) He's an Eagle Scout, and he can't tie a knot, either.
(b) He's a millionaire, and he can't afford to buy our dinner, either.
(c) She's an expert cook, and she can't boil water, either.
(d) My friend is a concert pianist, and he can't swim, either.
(e) Bill is a college professor, and he can't tie a knot, either.
(f) She's good at tennis, and she can't boil water, either.

Do you see any difference between the semantic difficulty in the first three sentences and that shown by the last three?

SUGGESTED READINGS

ARTICLES AND EXCERPTS[6]

ADAMS, K. and N. CONKLIN. 1973. "Toward a Theory of Natural Classification." *CLS-9*, CORUM et al. (eds.).

ANDERSON, S. 1972. "How to Get *Even*." *Language* 48:893–906.

BIERWISCH, M. 1970. "Semantics." J. LYONS (ed.), *New Horizons in Linguistics*. Penguin Books, Harmondsworth, England.

———. 1971. "On Classifying Semantic Features." In STEINBERG and JOKOBOVITS (eds.).

BLACK, M. 1959. "Linguistic Relativity: The Views of Benjamin Lee Whorf." *Philosophical Review* 68:228–38.

BOLINGER, D. 1965. "The Atomization of Meaning." *Language* 41:555–73.

BOYD, J. and J. THORNE. 1969. "The Semantics of Modal Verbs." *Journal of Linguistics* 5:57–74.

FILLMORE, C. 1971. "Verbs of Judging." In FILLMORE and LANGENDOEN (eds.).

——— 1973. "May We Come In?" *Semiotica* 9:97–116.

FRASER, B. 1970. "Idioms Within a Transformational Grammar." *Foundations of Language* 6:22–42.

——— 1971. "An Analysis of 'even' in English." In FILLMORE and LANGENDOEN (eds.).

——— 1973. "Hedged Performatives." In MORGAN and COLE (eds.).

GORDON, D. and G. LAKOFF. 1975. "Conversational Postulates." In MORGAN and COLE (eds.).

GRICE, H. 1975. "Logic and Conversation." In MORGAN and COLE (eds.).

HORN, L. 1969. "A Presuppositional Analysis of 'only' and 'even'." *CLS-5*, BINNICK et al. (eds.).

[6] CLS entries refer to annual papers of the regional meetings of the Chicago Linguistic Society; volume number indicates the year of the meeting.

JACKENDOFF, R. 1975. "Morphological and Semantic Regularities in the Lexicon." *Language* 51:639–71.

*JACOBS, R. 1969. "Focus and Presupposition: Transformations and Meaning." *College Composition and Communication* 20:187–90.

KATZ, J. and J. FODOR. 1963. "The Structure of a Semantic Theory." *Language* 39:170–210.

KEENAN, E. 1971. "Two Kinds of Presupposition in Natural Language." In FILLMORE and LANGENDOEN (eds.).

——— 1972. "On Semantically Based Grammar." *Linguistic Inquiry* 3:413–62.

MORGAN, J. 1969. "On the Treatment of Presuppositions in Transformational Grammar." *CLS-5*, BINNICK, et al. (eds.).

McCAWLEY, J. 1968. "The Role of Semantics in a Grammar." In BACH and HARMS (eds.).

PARTEE, B. 1971. "On the Requirement that Transformations Preserve Meaning." In FILLMORE and LANGENDOEN (eds.).

WIERCZBICKA, A. 1975. "Why 'Kill' Does Not Mean 'Cause to Die': The Semantics of Action Sentences." *Foundations of Language* 13:491–528.

BOOKS

ADAMS, V. 1973. *An Introduction to Modern English Word-Formation.* Longman, London.

AUSTIN, J. 1962. *How to Do Things with Words.* Oxford University Press, Oxford, England.

BACH, E. and R. HARMS (eds.). 1968. *Universals in Linguistic Theory.* Holt, Rinehart and Winston, New York.

DILLON, G. 1977. *Introduction to Contemporary Linguistic Semantics.* Prentice-Hall, Englewood Cliffs, N.J.

FILLMORE, C., and D. LANGENDOEN (eds.). 1971. *Studies in Linguistic Semantics.* Holt, Rinehart and Winston, New York.

GLEITMAN, L. and H. GLEITMAN. 1970. *Phrase and Paraphrase.* W. W. Norton, New York.

GREEN, G. 1974. *Semantics and Syntactic Regularity.* Indiana University Press, Bloomington.

JACKENDOFF, R. 1972. *Semantic Interpretation in Generative Grammar.* M.I.T. Press, Cambridge, Mass.

LEECH, G. 1974. *Semantics.* Penguin Books, Harmondsworth, England.

MORGAN, J., and P. COLE (eds.). 1975. *Syntax and Semantics, Vol. III: Speech Acts.* Academic Press, New York.

NIDA, E. 1975. *Componential Analysis of Meaning.* Mouton, The Hague.

SADOCK, J. 1974. *Toward a Linguistic Theory of Speech Acts.* Academic Press, New York.

SEARLE, J. 1969. *Speech Acts.* Cambridge University Press, Cambridge, England.

STEINBERG, D., and L. JOKOBOVITS (eds.). 1971. *Semantics: an Interdisciplinary Reader.* Cambridge University Press, Cambridge, England.

THREE

Syntax

The following set of sentences presents an interesting problem for analysis:

(1) a. Every afternoon I go study at the library.
     b. *Every afternoon he goes study at the library.
     c. Every afternoon you go study at the library.
     d. Every afternoon we go study at the library.
     e. *Every afternoon she goes study at the library.
     f. *Every afternoon John goes study at the library.
     g. Every afternoon they go study at the library.
     h. Every afternoon John and Bill go study at the library.

Notice that these eight sentences, except for the individual carrying out the action, are almost identical; and yet native speakers of English flatly reject (1b), (1e), and (1f), while accepting all the others. The specialist in syntax (syntactician), whose major interest is the system by which smaller meaningful sequences of language are combined into larger ones, attempts to explain what is going on in (1).

The first step to take in solving the problem is to group the starred sentences together as in (2), and determine what they have in common that makes them different from the acceptable sentences.

(2)   a. *Every afternoon he goes study at the library.
       b. *Every afternoon she goes study at the library.
       c. *Every afternoon John goes study at the library.

When these sentences are compared with the others, we can see one difference immediately. The words *he, she,* and *John,* unlike the subjects of all the other sentences of (1), are third person singular forms. If this is the reason for the unacceptable sentences, we should be able to write a rule forbidding the use of third person singular subjects in sentences containing "go + study" as a sequence. (And a moment's thought will make it clear that the rule should include "go + verb" rather than just "study," since substituting other verbs for "study" would not affect the distribution of the sentences into acceptable and unacceptable examples.)

We can test this idea by constructing a sentence or sentences using the other third personal singular form, *it*. We will have to change the verb, of course, because of the selectional restrictions on *study*. Example (3) will serve the purpose.

(3)   a. Every afternoon the polar bears go swim in the icy pool.
       b. *Every afternoon the polar bear goes swim in the icy pool.
       c. *Every afternoon it goes swim in the icy pool.

We have now tested our solution, and have evidence to support it; we can therefore write down a hypothesis as follows:

(4)   *In English no sequence of the verb* go *followed immediately by another verb is allowed if the subject of the verb is a third person singular form.*

A hypothesis like this, while obviously not a matter of major scientific significance, must nonetheless be submitted to close and careful scrutiny before it can be accepted as a fact about English grammar. Notice that all the sentences so far have been declarative statements; this provides us with a way to look for a weakness in the hypothesis. What if the sentences are formulated as questions, as in (5)?

(5)   a. Do I go study at the library every afternoon?
       b. Does he go study at the library every afternoon?
       c. Do you go study at the library every afternoon?
       d. Do we go study at the library every afternoon?
       e. Does she go study at the library every afternoon?

    f. Does John go study at the library every afternoon?

    g. Do they go study at the library every afternoon?

    h. Do John and Bill go study at the library every afternoon?

And the polar bears—

(6)   a. Do the polar bears go swim in the icy pool every afternoon?

      b. Does the polar bear go swim in the icy pool every afternoon?

      c. Does it go swim in the icy pool every afternoon?

Clearly, the hypothesis in (4) cannot be correct, because we now have many acceptable sentences (called counterexamples) which contain the sequence "go + verb" and have third person singular subjects.

In such a situation, we must look again at the sentences that were starred. Although it is true that they all have third person singular subjects, that cannot be the characteristic which makes them unacceptable to native speakers of English. We have to look for something else to account for this fact.

By this time we can be reasonably certain that the verbs and their subjects are the crux of our problem. We can therefore shorten the set of starred examples and look at them again for some shared characteristic which sets them off from the others.

(7)   a. *He goes study.

      b. *She goes study.

      c. *John goes study.

      d. *The polar bear goes swim.

      e. *It goes swim.

Like Archimedes in his bathtub watching the water rise about him, we may feel a temptation to shout Eureka, since it now looks as if the problem may be in the -es ending on the verb go, which appears in every starred sentence but in none of the others. If our hypothesis is reframed to reflect this idea, it will look like this:

(8)   *In English no sequence of the verb* go *followed immediately by another verb is allowed if there is an* -es *ending on* go.

This seems to hold up, and is supported if we test it by constructing a few imperative sentences, as in (9).

(9)   a. Go study at the library every afternoon.

      b. Go swim in the icy pool.

      c. Go clean your room.

No -es, no unacceptable sentence. On the other hand, isn't there something fishy here? Does English have rules of grammar that are so idiosyncratic?

Certainly.[1] It would be satisfying, however, if we could make the rule apply more widely.

The crucial thing to notice is that what seems to trigger our rejection is an ending, a *suffix*. We can then ask ourselves this question: Are there any other suffixes that we could put between *go* and the following verb, to see if we get unacceptable sentences?

The *-ed* ending, which would ordinarily be our next testing device, won't work here, since the past tense of *go* is not *goed* but *went*. We do, however, have the verb suffix *-ing*, which can be added to *go*. Now we can rewrite the sentences in (1) to try this out.

(10) a. *I am going study at the library every afternoon.
      b. *He is going study . . .
      c. *You are going study . . .
      d. *We are going study . . .

And although we can't add *-ed* to *go*, it's reassuring to note that we would *not* accept sentences like "I went study" either, since there is a sense in which the word *went* is our way of spelling out the combination of "go + *-ed.*"[2]

The correct solution, then, is stated in (11).

(11) *No sequence of the verb* go *followed immediately by another verb is allowed in English if there is a suffix on* go.

What we have just done was to solve a problem in English syntax. Syntax is what most of us mean by "grammar," although you will be aware that the term has a somewhat different technical meaning in linguistics.

We could tell from the beginning that the problem was not a semantic one. There was nothing semantically anomalous about the starred sentences we were working with, nor did the change of subject change the meaning in any other respect. We knew that the difficulty could not be a matter of unacceptable combinations of English sounds, either, both because it makes no difference what verb is second in the two-verb sequence, and because there are many examples of the same sound combinations which are perfectly all right. For instance:

(12) a. He goes swiftly down the road toward the barn.
      b. She goes sweetly smiling into the courtroom.

---

[1] The rule of English that allows "Don't budge from that spot" but forbids "Budge from that spot" is a good example. *Budge* is the only verb in the whole English language that cannot occur in a sentence unless a negative element is also present.

[2] Notice, also, that we would not accept sentences such as "Every afternoon this week I have gone study at the library."

Notice that you have had no difficulty deciding whether to accept or reject a sequence, just as you would have no difficulty constructing completely new sentences to illustrate the points made in the discussion of this problem. This ability that native speakers have to make acceptability judgments, as well as the ability to create new sequences fitting syntactic patterns, is part of what linguists refer to as your linguistic *competence*. It demonstrates that although you probably had no conscious knowledge of the rule set down in (11)—it's not one commonly found in English grammar books—you do know the rule!

This is a very important point, particularly if you feel insecure in any way about your knowledge of grammar. The number of "grammar rules" that you are able to recite or write down is a result of whatever you may have been taught in English classes in the past, and is a separate thing from the inventory of rules that you really know.

For example, if you were asked to state the rule for forming English questions that can be answered by "yes" or "no," you would probably find it difficult. Your inability to state the rule does not interfere in any way with your ability to produce such questions; therefore you know the rule, even though you are not consciously aware of that knowledge. You know a great deal about the grammar of your native language, and you use that knowledge constantly. Your *performance* in language (also a technical term in linguistics) can be affected by many things, such as fatigue, nervousness, illness, novocaine, etc. But your competence is, formally speaking, perfect.

In addition to making judgments about acceptability, another thing that native speakers can do is divide up sentences into their *constituent* parts. For example, look at the following sentence:

(13) That man chopped down a tree.

If you were provided with a list of proposed constituents for sentence (13) and asked to indicate which were acceptable to you and which could never be, you would sort the list as shown in (14).

(14) a. that man   d. a tree
      b. *that man chopped down   e. chopped down a tree
      c. *man chopped down   f. *chopped down a

(You would also accept the individual words of the sentence as constituents, of course.)

One of the ways that a native speaker knows whether or not a sequence is a constituent is by the criterion of *substitutability*. Look at (15).

(15) a. That man chopped down a tree.

      b.   He   chopped down a tree.

The fact that there is a separate element to substitute for *that man* shows that it is a constituent of English. No element exists that can be substituted for *man chopped* or *chopped down a*, which are not constituents.

You also know the order in which constituents of sentences in your language must be arranged; while you would accept the sequences in (16), you would flatly reject those of (17).

(16) a. That man chopped down a tree.
      b. An elephant came lumbering along the road.
      c. A small kitten was sleeping under the bed.

(17) a. *Chopped down a that man tree.
      b. *Lumbering came road along the elephant an.
      c. *Bed the under a kitten was small sleeping.

Transformational grammarians call the rules which specify precisely these two things about a language—what constituents may consist of and what their basic ordering must be—Phrase Structure Grammar (PSG) rules. A complete set of such rules for English, or for any language, would be very complex; we will look only at a simplified set, in Table I, which would be adequate to account for sentences like (13).

Table I SIMPLIFIED PHRASE STRUCTURE GRAMMAR RULES FOR ENGLISH

1. S → NP VP
2. NP → Det N
3. VP → V NP
4. V → V (Part)

SYMBOL	EXPLANATION
S	Sentence
NP	Noun Phrase
VP	Verb Phrase
Det	Determiner (*a, the, this, that*, etc.)
N	Noun
V	Verb
Part	Particle (*up, down, over*, etc., in two-part verbs)
→	'is composed of' or 'is rewritten as'
( )	optional element

Note: Rule 1 is read: "A sentence is composed of a noun phrase and a verb phrase."

The four rules in Table I will account for all the sentences of (18) and many thousands like them.

(18) a. The boy kicked a rock.
     b. That man called up a friend.
     c. A woman bought the car.
     d. This child swallowed a fishbone.

They will also account for your rejection of the proposed constituents (14c, 14e, 14f) and the constituent orderings in (17). That is, no rule in Table I allows a constituent composed of a noun followed by a determiner (such as *man that*) or a sentence with the constituent order Verb + Particle + Determiner + Determiner + Noun + Noun, as in (17a).

The information shown in Table I can be converted into diagrams known as *tree* diagrams. In these diagrams the labels S, NP, VP, etc., which mark structural division points, are called *nodes*. Example (19) is a tree diagram for sentence (13), drawn by using the rules in Table I.

(19)

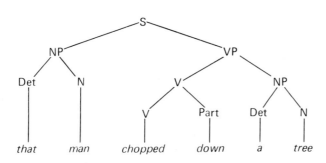

You would not accept, however, any of the trees that are proposed in (20) for the same sentence.

(20) a.

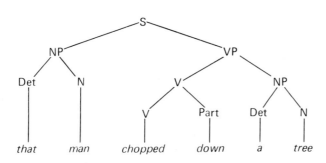

b.

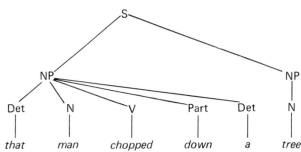

c.

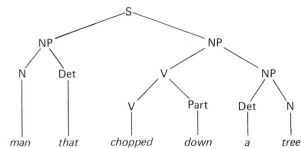

All the trees in (20) make claims about the phrase structure grammar of English that are simply false, and none of them can be constructed from the rules in Table I. The last tree in (20), for instance, makes the claim that some English NP's are composed of a noun followed by a determiner, while others have the determiner before the noun. Since no English speaker will accept a constituent like *cat a* or *boy the*, this cannot be a PSG rule of English.

In addition to these rules, transformationalists propose that a grammar must also contain a different kind of rule—the transformational rule. Unlike PSG rules, transformational rules do not simply rewrite one sequence of symbols as another sequence. Instead, they take a single sequence and make changes in its structure. We will look at an example of such a rule, and then return to the discussion of two basic questions:

a. What is the difference between a phrase structure grammar rule and a transformational rule?

b. Why do we need both types of rules?

TRANSFORMATIONAL RULES

The rule we will discuss by way of example is called Particle Movement. As you look at (21), remember that some verbs of English consist of only one element, while others consist of a verb followed by a particle (*up, down, over,* etc.).

(21) a. Mary ran down the road.
    b. Mary ran down the skunk.

The tree structures corresponding to these two sentences are shown below.[3]

a.

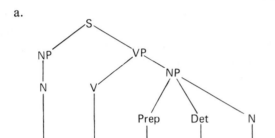

b.

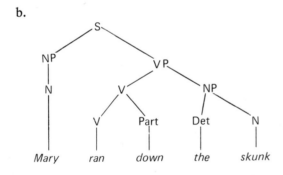

Notice that although the actual words in the two sentences are almost the same, you would have no difficulty backing up your feeling that their structures are quite different. For example:

(22) a. It was down the road that Mary ran.
    b. *It was down the skunk that Mary ran.

---

[3] The node Prep in diagram (a) refers to Preposition. A complete PSG for English would include prepositions as possible constituents in noun phrases.

c.   Down the road Mary ran.
d.   *Down the skunk Mary ran.

(23)   Q: Where did Mary run?
     A: Down the road.
     A: *Down the skunk.

Now consider the pair of sentences in (24), repeated from the semantics chapter.

(24)   a.   Marian set down the football.
     b.   Marian set the football down.

Sentence (24b) is said to be *derived from* (24a) by the application of the rule of Particle Movement, which takes the particle *down* from its original position after *set* and moves it into a position immediately after the object NP. We would then have the two trees shown in (25), in which the second is called a *derived* tree structure.

(25)   a.

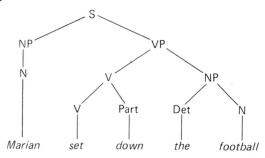

b.

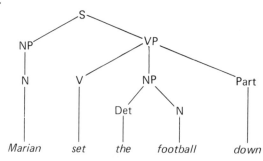

Although the sentence in (25b) is synonymous with that in (25a), it is clearly derived, because it cannot be the result of any phrase structure rule of

English. Example (25a), on the other hand, follows from the rules in Table I.

The question to be asked here is why we need a transformational rule to account for the second sentence. Why can't we simply modify our phrase structure rules by adding a rule like that shown in (26)?

(26) $\text{VP} \rightarrow \begin{Bmatrix} \text{V (Part) (NP)} \\ \text{V (NP) (Part)} \end{Bmatrix}$ [4]

If we had such a rule, it would account for our pair of sentences by giving us the two trees shown in (27).

(27) a.

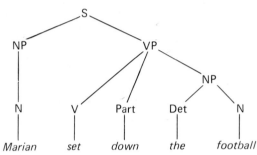

b.

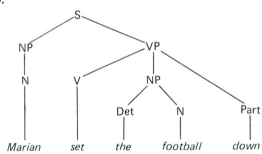

We would run into a few complications here, however. For example, look at the next pair of sentences.

(28) a. *Marian set down it.
    b. Marian set it down.

---

[4] The braces indicate that you must choose one and only one member of the enclosed set.

This pair shows that although the change in structure in (24) is a matter of free choice, since there is no situation in which a speaker could use one sentence of the pair but not the other, this does not hold true in a sentence where the object of the verb is a pronoun. Since a pronoun is one of the things that *can* serve as the object of a verb, the rule in (26) is not going to be adequate for our needs. It simply says that when there is a particle in a verb phrase it may be placed either before or after the object; the rule doesn't indicate that it makes any difference whether the object is a pronoun.

There is another problem with rule (26). Notice that this rule, which we would have to have if we were to account for both sentences of (24) in the phrase structure grammar, does not recognize as a constituent of English a multiple-part verb composed of a verb and following particle. It says instead that a particle is just another part of the verb phrase, with no more direct relationship to the verb itself than the NP's have. This does not agree with the intuitions native speakers have about such sequences. For example, many verb + particle sequences can be replaced with a single-part verb which is synonymous, or nearly so, as in (29).

(29) a. The clerk went over the figures.
      b. The clerk examined the figures.
      c. Maxine looked up the number in the phone book.
      d. Maxine   located   the number in the phone book.

Unless the particles are actually smaller constituents of a multiple-part verb, it is hard to explain why we feel that *examine* is just a more formal way of saying *go over*.

The sentences in (30) offer more evidence that verb and particle are a single constituent.

(30) a. What did you set down?   The football.
      b. What did you go over?   The figures.
      c. What did you look up?   The number.

These problems, and others which have not been mentioned here, can be avoided if we proceed as follows: Instead of attempting to write a PSG rule which will account for all possible orders of verbs and particles in verb phrases, including those with pronoun objects, we take the theoretical position that (24a) represents the basic order of the sentence. We can then write one transformational rule to move the particle, specifying that it is obligatory if the object of the verb is a pronoun.

Transformational rules are usually written in two parts. The first specifies exactly what structure a sequence must have if the rule is to apply.

The second shows the structure *after* the application of the rule. Thus, one tells you when to use the rule and the other tells you what it does. If there is a condition on the rule it is written beneath it. The various parts of the structure are given identifying numbers so that they can be easily referred to. Example (31) shows the rule of Particle Movement.

(31) NP V Part NP
    1   2   3   4   ⟹ 1, 2, ∅, 4, 3
    Obligatory if 4 is a pronoun.

The symbol ∅ (called the *null* symbol) is used to mark the position from which an element has been moved or deleted. The double-barred arrow is the transformational arrow, and can be read as 'changes to' or 'becomes'.

Transformational rules are often very formidable in appearance; the one just discussed has been somewhat simplified. In reading transformational literature you should not be surprised to find rules written in much more complex ways, nor should you be surprised to find considerable variation in rule format from one writer to another. In particular, you will find rules which contain the symbol # used to indicate the beginning and ending of sentences, as well as the letters *X* and *Y*, which are called *variables* and indicate that it makes no difference what appears in that spot in the description.

There is, for example, the rule called Imperative Deletion. This rule states that the word *you* may be deleted from a command. It obviously makes no difference what follows *you*, as shown in (32).

(32) a. You leave this room!   Leave this room!
    { b. You pick up your books and take them upstairs!
      c. Pick up your books and take them upstairs!
    { d. You carry your little brother out into the yard and put him in his playpen so that he won't get stepped on when the painters get here!
      e. Carry your little brother out into the yard and put him in his playpen so that he won't get stepped on when the painters get here!

Since this is the situation, Imperative Deletion can be written like this:

(33) # *IMP* you *X* #
    1   2   3   4 5 ⟹ 1, 2, ∅, 4, 5

The variable symbol, *X*, is used to indicate that the grammar need not take into consideration what follows the word *you*.

Notice that the second element of (33) is *IMP* (for *imperative*). This element, like the element *Q* which appears at the beginning of questions, is present to indicate formally that a part of the meaning of a sentence is the speech act which it is intended to convey. This is necessary if we are to preserve the constraint which states that transformational rules are not allowed to change meaning except with respect to focus. *IMP* is not a meaningless element here, since it is a kind of shorthand notation for a whole complex of meaning that might be written out in full as "I the speaker hereby order you the listener to . . ." followed by the action specified. It is also important to have *IMP* present in the rule in order to keep it from deleting *you* every time it appears in an English sentence. We would not want this rule to achieve results like those shown in (34).

(34) a. #you are growing older# $\Longrightarrow$ #are growing older#
　　 b. #I see you standing there# $\Longrightarrow$ #I see standing there#

There is no actual word or morpheme of English which spells out *IMP* in the surface structure. However, all speakers of English recognize the tone of voice and melodic pattern of a sentence which is intended as a command.

Students are justified in asking whether all this formal apparatus of arrows, numbers, braces, etc. is necessary. James McCawley (1974) answers the question by saying: "The biggest advantage to formalization is that it forces one to be *explicit*, to make up his mind about details."

Of course it must be added that rules written in formal notation can also be stated explicitly in ordinary English prose. Instead of setting out the rule of Particle Movement as in (31), we could do it like this:

(40) *Whenever a sentence contains a verb phrase which is composed of a verb followed immediately by a particle, which is in turn followed immediately by a pronominal object of that verb, the particle must be moved to a position directly following the object; if the object is not a pronoun, however, the rule is optional.*

You can see at once the advantage in using symbol notation. The Particle Movement rule, although relatively simple, takes a great deal of space to write out in words and is very hard to follow. More complex transformational rules are likely to require several paragraphs of prose space. Symbol notation can provide all that information in just a few lines, and in a form that is easier to analyse and work with. In doing arithmetic it makes little difference whether you write "2 + 2 = 4" or "two plus two equal four," but having to write out a column of fifteen six-digit numbers and their sum in words would be both a nuisance to do and extremely cumbersome to read. The formal notation used by linguists is a great saver of time and energy.

The major problem with formalization, however, is not the symbols themselves, but the fact that not all linguists use the *same* formalizations. Not only do the forms of rules vary from writer to writer, so do the forms of tree diagrams. At the current stage of the discipline this is unavoidable, because the notation a linguist uses expresses his or her personal conviction about the way rules and trees should be symbolized, and there is a variety of such personal convictions. An introductory text is not the place to enter into arguments about the relative degrees of superiority of any system (usually referred to as the *model* associated with a particular linguist). But it is well for the novice in linguistics to be aware of these notational differences when reading other texts. The suggested readings at the end of this chapter include source materials on this controversy.

THE FOUR TYPES
OF TRANSFORMATIONAL RULES

Only four kinds of grammatical operations exist in all human languages. There are therefore only four possible kinds of transformational rules: *deletion, insertion, substitution,* and *movement.* We have already looked at one deletion rule (Imperative Deletion) and have discussed a movement rule (Particle Movement). In this section we will take up each of the four categories in greater detail and consider examples of each.

Deletion Rules

In early work on transformational grammar (for example, Noam Chomsky 1957), it was proposed that a basic structure such as "John is sick" could be transformed into "John is not sick" by the application of an optional Negative rule. But, as linguists began to work with transformational grammar, they ran headlong into the problem discussed in the semantics chapter—that of formally specifying "a little bit" of meaning change. If a rule could be allowed to change "John is sick" into something so very different in meaning as "John is not sick," there would seem to be no way to prevent rules that would change "John is sick" into "John is tall" or "John is busy" or "Mary is sick." There had to be a way that differences in meaning could be formally specified to allow just enough change and no more. A limitation (usually called a *constraint*) was therefore proposed for the entire grammar, as follows:

(32)   *No transformational rule is allowed to change meaning.*[5]

In order to maintain this constraint, deletion rules have to be set up in such a way that the deletion is always *recoverable*—that is, so that one can always tell what has been deleted. This restriction is strongly supported by the fact that no human language has ever been encountered which had deletion rules like these:

    a. Delete every other word in the sentence.
    b. Delete every word in the sentence that comes before a three-syllable word.
    c. Delete every word in a sentence that has more than three syllables.

Human beings, given a pencil and paper, could certainly perform such operations. But once the rules had applied there would be no way to determine what had been eliminated from the sequence, and communication would become difficult, if not impossible.

All known deletion rules in human languages are of two types: rules of *constant* deletion and rules of *identity* deletion. In a constant deletion rule the element deleted is specifically named in the rule itself and will always be the same element no matter in what sentence the rule applies. The rule of Imperative Deletion is such a rule; it can delete only the word *you* and nothing else, and only from sentences identified as imperatives. All native speakers of English understand the sequence "Go pick up your coat" to mean the same thing as "You go pick up your coat," as shown by the long tradition in grammar classes about the "understood *you.*"

In an identity deletion rule, however, there is no way to know in advance what words will be deleted. To insure that the deletion is recoverable, then, the following condition must be met:

(33)   *The deleted word(s) must have an identical counterpart which is not deleted.*

Murphy's Law as stated in (34) provides an excellent example of this process.

(34) a. If anything can go wrong, it will go wrong.
      b. If anything can go wrong, it will.

---

[5] This is why sets of sentences like those discussed in Chapter Two, example (8), have been the source of controversy in linguistics. The question has been whether the constraint forbidding meaning change could be maintained in the face of such sets.

No native speaker of English has any question in his or her mind as to what has been deleted from (34b). The two sentences are among the class of perfectly synonymous pairs. The deleted portion of (34b) can only be *go wrong*, which is still present in the first clause of the sentence in the same structural position from which it has been removed in the second—that is, immediately after the auxiliary *will*. It makes no difference at all what follows the auxiliary, so long as it has an identical counterpart remaining. Example (35) will make this clear.

(35)   If Helen says she will eat chocolate ants out of her slipper at the annual festivities for the Twenty-Seventh Street Marching Band, she will.

Any native speaker of English knows what follows that final *will*, and will instantly reject the suggestion that it is anything other than "eat chocolate ants out of her slipper, etc." The rule is usually called Verb Phrase Deletion.

In the model of transformational grammar known as the Standard Theory (associated most closely with Noam Chomsky), it is customary to say that (34b) is the *surface structure* of the sentence; (34a), from which it is derived, is part of the *deep structure*. The steps that a given sequence goes through on its way to the surface structure—which may involve the application of a number of rules—constitute the *derivation* of that sequence. There is much argument among contemporary linguists about the existence of a separate deep structure level and its characteristics; like the controversy over various systems of formalizations, the arguments would be out of place in an introductory text. McCawley (1974) has a useful summary comment:

> A grammar . . . would be transformational if it involves the notion of a *derivation*, consisting of some kind of underlying structure and steps leading from it to a surface structure, where all steps of the derivation are represented as trees, and it involves a system of rules that specify how the different stages of a derivation are related to each other.

We will use the terms *deep* and *surface structure* in this sense, to refer to the various stages of a derivation.

Additional examples of deletion rules in English are given in the following pairs of sequences:

(36)   a. I know that Mario is late.
       b. I know Mario is late.

(37)   a. Everyone should eat something before we leave.
       b. Everyone should eat before we leave.

(38) a. Bill plays checkers, and Angela plays chess.
     b. Bill plays checkers, and Angela chess.

Insertion Rules

You will remember that, in order to prevent deletion rules from altering meaning, all human languages carefully restrict them to either constant or identity deletion. The corollary of this for insertion rules is that any element inserted must be meaningless. Otherwise, the inserted item would add new semantic content.

The idea of adding something meaningless to a sentence seems odd, at first glance. But look at the next example.

(39) It is raining.

Ask yourself what, precisely, is raining? What is this *it*? If you look at a sentence such as "I picked up a snake and it bit me," there is no question in your mind; *it* and the snake are one and the same. The *it* in (39) is very different, because there is no *it* that *rains*.

Many languages express this fact clearly in the surface form of their equivalent sentences, which would be translated literally as "Is-raining." English, however, has a strict rule that except in imperatives every sentence must have a surface subject. It makes no difference whether this surface subject has any logical reason for existence or not, it still has to be present.

The deep structure of (39) contains a tree like this:

(40)

This cannot be a surface structure of English. Therefore, the rule of *It*-Insertion puts a meaningless *it* in to fill the empty subject slot. The same rule is required to derive the sentences of (41).

(41) a. It snowed last night.
     b. It was thundering over the mountains.
     c. It is hot in this room.
     d. It is very pleasant in the garden.

Another insertion rule of English is the rule called *There*-Insertion, which is needed in the derivation of sentences like (42).

(42) There is a big lizard on your front porch.

The word *there* in (42) is not the same one that we find in sentences such as those of (43), where *there* has a meaning of its own.

(43) a. I don't know how that book got in your briefcase, but I certainly didn't put it there.
b. The salt is over there on the table.

The application of *There*-Insertion also involves movement, as shown in the derivation for (42) below:

(44) a. #a big lizard is on your front porch#
b. #is a big lizard on your front porch#
c. There is a big lizard on your front porch.

(Notice that there is no element Q at the beginning of (44a), therefore (44b) cannot be misinterpreted as a question.)
    There is a major difference between these two insertion rules—one is obligatory and the other optional. An obligatory rule is one that *must* apply if the resulting surface structure is to be grammatical. *It*-Insertion is obligatory, as shown by the fact that no grammatical sentence such as "Is raining" exists in English. An optional rule is one about which a speaker has some choice; thus, there is nothing wrong with simply saying "A big lizard is on your front porch" and leaving it at that. Since this is so, we know that *There*-Insertion is an optional rule. Most people agree that they tend to use *There*-Insertion as a way of introducing new information without being too abrupt, which is of course a matter of pragmatics and will vary from one individual to another.

Substitution Rules

    This class of rules substitutes one constituent—usually a member of the set of English pronouns—for another constituent with which it is identical. Look at the tree diagram in (45), where the small *i* by each NP means 'identical':

(45)

There is no acceptable surface structure "John behaved John." Therefore, the Reflexive rule must apply, to substitute the pronoun *himself* for the second instance of *John.*

Two important points about this rule should be mentioned here. First, notice that the rule always applies to the *second* identical NP, as shown by (46).

(46) a. *Himself behaved John.
      b. *Herself behaved Elizabeth.

Secondly, the Reflexive rule has to take into account various characteristics of all the NP's involved, to prevent sentences like those in (47).

(47) a. *John behaved herself.
      b. *John behaved themselves.

One way to indicate how this information is present in the deep structure is by the use of features like those discussed in the semantics chapter. The tree diagram in (48) shows how this would be done.

(48)

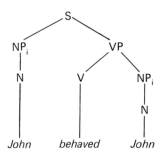

$$\begin{bmatrix} +\text{HUMAN} \\ +\text{SINGULAR} \\ +\text{MALE} \\ +\text{THIRD PERSON} \end{bmatrix} \qquad \begin{bmatrix} +\text{HUMAN} \\ +\text{SINGULAR} \\ +\text{MALE} \\ +\text{THIRD PERSON} \end{bmatrix}$$

The pronoun that is substituted by the rule must agree in features with the NP (its "antecedent") which it replaces. The only member of the set of reflexive pronouns that bears the feature specification [+HUMAN], [+SINGULAR], [+MALE], [+THIRD PERSON] is *himself,* which is therefore selected by the grammar.

The Reflexive rule would not apply to a structure like (49), because it is restricted to sequences containing a verb whose subject and object are identical.

(49)

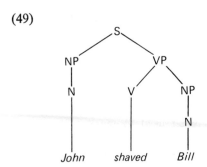

If any substitution rule applied to a sequence like (49) it would have to be simple Pronominalization. This would give us "John shaved him" if the identity of *him* were made clear by some earlier sequence such as "The assistant seated Bill and then . . ." or by the real world situation in which the sentence was used. Alternatively, if the context referred to John rather than Bill, the result of Pronominalization would be "He shaved Bill."

The ordering of rules is one of the most intricate parts of transformational theory, and will not be discussed in detail in this text. Briefly, we know that certain rules must apply before others if we are to avoid a grammar that generates unacceptable surface structures. For example, we can demonstrate that an ordered relationship must exist for the Reflexive rule and the rule of Imperative Deletion. Look at these sentences:

(50) a. You behave yourself.
  b. Behave yourself.
  c. *Behave you.

To account for this pattern, we can try two different orderings for the application of Reflexive and Imperative Deletion. First, example (51).

(51) Deep Structure: #*IMP* you$_i$ behave you$_i$#
  Apply *Imperative Deletion*: #*IMP* ∅ behave you$_i$#

Now we can go no farther. The Reflexive rule can't apply, because we don't *have* a verb whose subject and object are identical; the subject has been deleted. The resulting surface structure could only be (50c), "Behave you," which would not be accepted by native speakers of English. We therefore try the opposite ordering, shown in (52).

(52) Deep Structure: *#IMP* you*ᵢ* behave you*ᵢ#*
  Apply *Reflexive*:   *#IMP* you behave yourself*#*
  Apply *Imperative Deletion*: *#IMP* ∅ behave yourself*#*

This is the correct result, and we can be certain that the ordering must be first Reflexive, then Imperative Deletion.

Movement Rules

We will begin with a very simple movement rule, called Topicalization. Topicalization is one of the rules of English used to mark a particular constituent of a sentence as the focus of that sentence.

When there is no information present to the contrary, the subject of the sentence is usually assumed to be its focus. For example:

(53) I hate squid.

We would say that this sentence is about "I," and that "I" is the element with the greatest semantic prominence for the speaker. If, however, it is the squid which should play the major role, it can be moved to the left of the subject to indicate that fact, as in (54).

(54) Squid, I hate.[6]

This movement rule draws attention to the squid, and does so to such a degree that people will often claim that they have no such rule in *their* grammar. A typical objection is (55).

(55) That, I would never say.

Notice that (55) is the result of applying Topicalization to the sequence "I would never say that." However, the speaker's reaction to (54) is justified in many ways. A sentence like "Squid, I hate" sounds peculiar all by itself. It will seem less bizarre if it is not so isolated, as in the sentences of (56).

(56) a. I'm really fond of lobsters; but squid, I hate.
   b. Squid, I hate; lobster, on the other hand, is one of my favourite
    foods.

---

[6] The comma which appears after a topicalized NP is not inserted by the transformational rule; it is a part of the sound system of English, which is the subject of the next chapter. Not all varieties of English require the pause symbolized by this comma.

Topicalization is also common with the demonstratives (*this*, *that*, *these*, *those*, *there*), as in (55), especially when the sentence has a strong negative content. Example (57) is typical.

(57)   That stupid class, I wish I'd never taken.

Topicalization is of course an optional rule. The movement rule called Question Formation, however, is obligatory. This rule states that in a question the first auxiliary must be moved into a position immediately to the left of the subject NP. The two most common ways of indicating in deep structure that a sequence is a question are (a) to have the symbol *Q* as the first element in the sentence, or (b) to indicate that the sequence begins with "I ask you." Whether (a) or (b) is the better choice, both express a single fact: the information that a sequence is a question is part of its meaning and it must therefore be represented in the deep structure. We will use the symbol *Q* here (as we used *IMP* to indicate a command, rather than "I order you") because it is less complex. Example (58) shows the application of the rule.

(58)   Deep Structure:
       #*Q* Charles will bring the steaks#
       Apply *Question Formation*:
       #*Q* will Charles bring the steaks#

We then have the proper surface structure, "Will Charles bring the steaks?"
       It may seem trivial to point out that a rule which operates by moving an auxiliary cannot apply if no auxiliary is present. The consequences of this fact, however, are not trivial, and have led to the writing of many a lengthy article. The question is, where does the auxiliary come from?
       The modal auxiliaries (*can*, *shall*, *will*, *should*, etc.) will be present in the deep structure, since they have meanings of their own. They function in English to allow the speaker either to make a comment about the rest of the sentence, as in (59), or to indicate a speech act, as in (60).

(59)   Carlos must catch the 7:30 flight.
       (I, the speaker, say that *it is necessary* for Carlos to catch the 7:30 flight.)

(60)   Anne may take piano lessons.
       (I, the speaker, *give my permission* for Anne to take piano lessons.)

But what about a situation in which the speech act is a statement, and the speaker has no comment to make about the balance of the sentence? Then what?

There was an earlier stage of English when this was not a problem. You simply moved the first verb to the left of the subject NP. This produced sentences like those from *King Lear* in (61), which we are now familiar with only in written contexts such as Shakespeare's plays and the King James version of the Bible.

(61) a. Spake you with him?
      b. Parted you in good terms?

Any speaker of English knows that the contemporary forms of these questions are "Did you speak with him?" and "Did you part on good terms?" The needed element is then a form of *do*. The controversy is over whether we are to say that there is a rule of *Do*-Insertion which would insert *do* in questions that have no auxiliary present, or that there is a rule of *Do*-Deletion to take out a deep structure *do* not needed on the surface.

This problem must be considered again in the formation of negative sentences, as shown in (62).

(62) a. Claudine will not speak French with us.
      b. Claudine does not speak French with us.
      c. *Claudine speaks not French with us.

Just as with the questions in (61), the grammar of English at one time allowed sentences like (62c) which are not acceptable today.

We will not take up here the complicated arguments relative to *Do*-Deletion versus *Do*-Insertion. But it should be clear that *some* auxiliary verb must be present before Question Formation (as well as the rule that derives negative sentences) can be applied. If no other auxiliary is present, a form of *do* must be.

Another movement rule of English is the rule of Extraposition. One of the possible choices to serve as a subject of a sentence is another sentence; when this choice is made, the sentential subject will have a marker with it to show that it is embedded, as in (63).

(63) That you are tired upsets me.

Here *you are tired* is the embedded sentential subject.

Extraposition takes the subject and moves it all the way to the end of the sentence, leaving an empty subject slot behind. As you would expect, the rule of *It*-Insertion must then apply to fill that slot. The derivation in (64) shows this process.

(64) a. #that you are tired upsets me#

 b. #⠀⠀⠀⠀∅⠀⠀⠀⠀upsets me that you are tired#
 c. It upsets me that you are tired.

RULE INTERACTION

A major resource of human languages (called *recursion*) is their ability to combine a number of sentences into a single sentence. One such mechanism is conjunction, as in "John left and Mary stayed." Another is the use of a sentence as the subject of another sentence, which was mentioned in the description of Extraposition above.[7] A third process is *relativization*, which involves the interaction of a number of different transformational rules. We will conclude this chapter with a discussion of this embedding process.

A sentence embedded as a relative clause has no separate relationship to the verb in the higher sentence in which it is embedded. Instead, it serves as an adjective does, providing information about some noun phrase in the higher sentence and answering the question "Which one?" about that noun phrase. The requirement for relativization in English is that the two sentences to be combined have a shared NP—one that appears in both deep structures and is coreferential. For example:

(65) a. The table$_i$ is in the hall.
 b. The table$_i$ is an antique.

One of the possible choices for NP in a complete phrase structure grammar of English is a noun phrase followed by a relative clause—symbolized as NP − S. This choice will allow us to combine the two sentences of (65) as shown in (66), where we will use brackets to mark off the embedded sentence.

(66) #the table$_i$ [the table$_i$ is in the hall] is an antique#

The corresponding tree diagram is shown in (67).

[7] It should be mentioned that sentences can also be embedded as the direct objects of verbs, as in "I know that you are tired," where *you are tired* is the embedded object. Extraposition, however, applies only to sentences embedded as subjects.

(67)

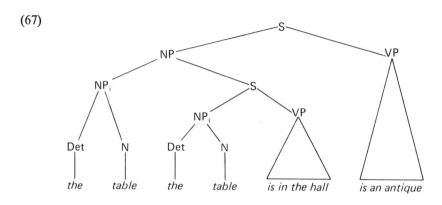

Since English will not allow a sentence such as "The table the table is in the hall is an antique," the rule of Relativization now requires a relative pronoun to be substituted for the second coreferential NP, as in (68).

(68)   #the table$_i$ [which$_i$ is in the hall] is an antique#

This rule is obligatory, since without applying it you cannot obtain an acceptable surface structure. Once it has applied, you may stop, or you may go on to use a rule known as Relative Reduction. This optional rule allows you to delete a relative pronoun, together with any form of *be* that may follow it in the relative clause, as in (68).

(68)   a. The table which is in the hall is an antique.
       b. The table in the hall is an antique.

You again have an acceptable surface structure. However, two more rules may still be involved in the relativization process. The first is a movement rule, Relative Fronting, which specifies that any relative pronoun which is not first in its clause must be moved to that position. Because the table in (65b) was a subject NP, it was already in initial position and Relative Fronting was not required. Consider the following partial derivation, in which the coreferential NP in the relative clause is an object rather than a subject.

(69)   a. #the table$_i$ [I bought the table$_i$] is an antique#
       b. #the table$_i$ [I bought   which$_i$] is an antique#

Example (69b) is not a possible surface structure of English, and Relative Fronting must now apply, as in (70).

(70) a. #the table$_i$ [I bought which$_i$] is an antique#
      b. The table which I bought is an antique.

Finally, there is a movement rule called Adjective Fronting. Just in case (after Relative Reduction has applied) there is nothing left behind but an adjective, Adjective Fronting moves the adjective to the left of the first coreferential NP. For example:

(71) a. #the table$_i$ [the table$_i$ is old] is an antique#
      b. #the table$_i$ [which$_i$ is old] is an antique#
      c. #the table$_i$ [∅   ∅ old] is an antique#
      d. The old table is an antique.

Adjective Fronting, like Relative Fronting, is an obligatory rule.

Navajo is like English in allowing sentences to be embedded either as sentential subjects or objects, or as relative clauses. However, both types of embedding are marked by the same suffix -*ígíí* which was mentioned in the first chapter. As a result, a sentence such as (72) is ambiguous and may have either one of the meanings in (73).

(72) *Ashkii léi   naalnishigíí   yish'į.*
      Boy   the   he-is-working   +   I-see
           EMBEDDED SUBJECT

(73) a. I see the boy who is working.
      b. I see that the boy is working.

The ambiguity is increased by the fact that the *yi*- morpheme of *yish'į*, which is the direct object pronoun prefix, has two possible translations in this sentence: 'he' or 'it'. If the sentence is translated as (73a), then *yi*- means 'he'. If it is translated as (72b), *yi*- means 'it'. In isolation there is no way to distinguish between the two possible meanings.

Since Navajo has no separate relative pronoun, and no separate form of *be* following it, Relative Reduction cannot be one of the inventory of transformational rules in that language. The elements called "adjectives" in English are verbs in Navajo, which eliminates Adjective Fronting as a possible Navajo rule. With no relative pronoun to be moved, Relative Fronting is also out of the question.

The *process* of relativization appears to be a part of all human languages. No language has ever been discovered that did not have it. However, the precise rules which are used to carry out that process will differ from one language to another. Navajo and English differ radically in this respect.

1. The following sentences illustrate a fact about the syntactic behavior of English idioms. Look at them carefully and determine what that fact is.

   (a) All the Scouts hit the hay.
   (b) The hay was hit by all the Scouts.
   (c) It was the hay that all the Scouts hit.
   (d) She cut off her nose to spite her face.
   (e) It was her nose that she cut off to spite her face.
   (f) What she cut off to spite her face was her nose.
   (g) I think the manager is slightly under the weather.
   (h) The weather is what I think the manager is slightly under.
   (i) Phillip had to bite the bullet.
   (j) The bullet, Phillip had to bite.
   (k) What Phillip had to bite was the bullet.
   (l) The bullet had to be bitten by Phillip.

2. From the rules in this chapter, and from your own knowledge of English, make a list of all the English constituents that can serve as noun phrases. Then rewrite the PSG rule below to show this information. (Remember that parentheses around an element are used to indicate that it is optional.)

   $$NP \rightarrow \left\{ \qquad \right\}$$

3. In this chapter a distinction was made between obligatory rules and optional ones. Do you consider the rule of Imperative Deletion obligatory or optional? Why?

4. The rule of Particle Movement in this chapter was written as if the rule could move any particle in any multiple-part verb. Write down a list of sentences with the same structure as "Mary set down the football" and determine whether the rule is accurate. A few verb + particle combinations are given below to get you started.

   pick up, look over, find out, tie up, count on

   Are there any verbs that are followed by more than one particle? If so, does the Particle Movement rule apply to them? How?

5. The following sentence was used in a television report about a bomb scare:

   They roped off a four-block area and then removed it.

   Can you explain what has gone wrong in this sentence?

6. Each of the following sentences has undergone a deletion rule of English. For each one, indicate what has been deleted and state whether the rule is an example of constant deletion or identity deletion. (It isn't necessary to state the name of the rule; not all these rules are discussed in the text.)

(a) Move down three places.
(b) Mary asked for money and Bill for a gold watch.
(c) I tried to swim the creek, and then Sue tried.
(d) She asked him to leave and he did.
(e) Mary and Ellen went to the Greyhound Station.
(f) Richard is taller than Noel.
(g) I'll ski if you ask me to.

7. In English the direct object of a verb is usually defined as the object of a transitive verb. The verb *hit* is transitive because the action of hitting carries over to that which is hit. Thus, in example (a) *the nail* is the direct object, receiving the action of the transitive verb *hit*.

(a) Edward hit the nail with a hammer.

In the examples below, the italicized noun phrase is traditionally defined as the direct object, and the verb as transitive. Ask yourself whether anything actually happens to these direct objects as a result of the action of the verb; then comment on the definition of a transitive verb. List these verbs and discuss each one briefly.

(b) Helene saw *a broken glass* in the sink.
(c) The children admired *the soccer player* very much.
(d) I like *ice cream.*
(e) We all know *that the earth is approximately round.*
(f) Eli slammed *the kitchen door.*
(g) Our parents expected *only three guests.*
(h) Can you smell *the roses* out there in the garden?
(i) Let's cut *the pie* into two pieces.

8. In English sentences some constituent must always come from one of the classes of elements that can be marked for tense (as with *-ed*) or aspect (as with *-ing*). Therefore, although Russian, Kumeyaay, and many other languages allow surface structures that would translate literally as "James a professor," English forbids this. Similarly, "James in the kitchen," "James tall," and "The party at six" are all unacceptable. The missing constituent in all these sentences is a form of the verb *be*. There are three possible ways that "be" could appear in the surface structure of such sentences; list them. Can you think of any reason(s) for a linguist to insist that one of the three was the correct choice and the other two wrong? Explain your answer.

9. For a pair of sentences to be related to one another by a transformation, they must be synonymous (as defined in the semantics chapter of this text). Decide which of the pairs below fit this description.

(a) The fact that Joseph lies is astonishing.
(b) That Joseph lies is astonishing.
(c) The window was broken by something.
(d) The window was broken.
(e) Even Elizabeth can answer that question.
(f) Elizabeth can even answer that question.
(g) Harriet stepped carefully over the broken wire.
(h) Harriet carefully stepped over the broken wire.
(i) For someone to ski on gravel would be difficult.
(j) To ski on gravel would be difficult.
(k) In the corner a little girl sat crying.
(l) A little girl sat crying in the corner.
(m) Reyes is still here.
(n) Reyes is still not here.
(o) Many students read all of the articles.
(p) All of the articles were read by many students.
(q) It is fortunate that you are here.
(r) Fortunately, you are here.

10. Pronominalization rules in English are said to apply when a sequence contains identical pairs of noun phrases; identity deletion rules are not restricted to noun phrases, but have the same requirement for a pair of identical elements. The following sentences illustrate a phenomenon called (among other things) "sloppy identity." Explain why the term *sloppy* is used.

(a) After the cat bit the lizard's tail off, it grew back.
(b) The dress Mary is wearing is the same one Helen is wearing.
(c) If you will hold your breath, I will.

11. Jesse James had been living under the alias "Mr. Howard" when he was shot to death. The folksong about this shooting ends like this:

> *And that dirty little coward*
> *that shot Mr. Howard*
> *laid Jesse James in his grave.*

Because Jesse James was using an alias, Jesse James and the "Mr. Howard" of the song were the same individual. Does this mean that you could substitute *him* for *Jesse James* in the song without changing the meaning of the line? A similar example to help you decide is the following:

> When George Washington looked in the mirror, he was looking at the father of his country.

Could Reflexive apply here?

12. The set of sentences below shows the operation of two rules of English syntax. Consider the examples carefully and answer these questions for each rule: (i) Is it a rule of deletion, insertion, substitution, or movement? (ii) What does it do?

    (a) I gave the canoe to Marie.
    (b) I gave Marie the canoe.
    (c) Sam showed his negatives to Althea.
    (d) Sam showed Althea his negatives.
    (e) Norman loaned five dollars to Sarah.
    (f) Norman loaned Sarah five dollars.
    (g) Norman borrowed five dollars from Sarah.
    (h) *Norman borrowed Sarah five dollars.
    (i) I caught a cold from Mr. Sanchez.
    (j) *I caught Mr. Sanchez a cold.
    (k) He sent the letter to his cousin.
    (l) He sent his cousin the letter.

    What further information about this rule can you learn from the following sentences?

    (m) I explained the problem to Bertrand.
    (n) *I explained Bertrand the problem.
    (o) June demonstrated the use of the machine to Mr. Higgins.
    (p) *June demonstrated Mr. Higgins the use of the machine.

13. Grammar texts of English can be found which state that the word *would* is the past tense form of *will*, the word *could* the past tense form of *can*, and the word *should* the past tense of *shall*. At one stage of the history of English this rule was accurate. Look at the sentences below and state whether you think the rule should still be in grammar books today.

    (a) Mr. Jones can leave for Houston tomorrow.
    (b) Mr. Jones could leave for Houston tomorrow.
    (c) I will leave tomorrow if I can finish my work today.

(d) I would leave tomorrow if I could finish my work today.
(e) Shall we leave tomorrow?
(f) Should we leave tomorrow?

14. One constituent which was omitted in the phrase structure grammar rules in this chapter is the *adverb*. The following sentences all contain elements that are classified as adverbs in traditional grammar; they are in italics. Do you think it would be possible to write PSG rules that would account for the constituent structure and order required for these elements? If so, write the necessary rule or rules. If not, explain why not.

(a) Stefan is *very* annoyed with me.
(b) The plumber left *quickly* with his tools.
(c) *Unfortunately*, we have *only* three sandwiches.
(d) The nurse smiled *hopefully* at his patient.
(e) There is a *rather* bedraggled swan on the lake.
(f) *Clearly*, this is an intricate problem.
(g) I can't see *clearly* in this fog.
(h) They can't *even* swim, poor things.
(i) *Probably* the road is flooded.
(j) Try to eat your peas *properly*.
(k) I will never go *there* again.
(l) He tried, *patiently*, to convince us to move.

15. Look at (14g) again. Compare it with (14c) and (14d). Does this give you any clue as to why sentences like the following are now a matter for argument in English grammar classes?

Hopefully, John will remember to bring the salt.

16. The set of rules for the relativization process in English discussed in this chapter applied only to one kind of relative clause—the *restrictive* relative clause. Restrictive relative clauses are not set off by commas and they function to restrict the meaning of the NP they refer to very strictly, almost as if they were a kind of name. The sentences below include *non-restrictive* relative clauses, which are not the same thing. Look at the data carefully and explain the difference between the two types of relative clauses. It will help you solve this problem if you decide first why "My left arm which I broke yesterday hurts badly" is not an acceptable sentence.

(a) My left arm, which I broke yesterday, hurts badly.
(b) My twin brother, who is a pilot, just left.

(c) My head, which you bumped with your elbow, is fragile.

(d) Her father, who lives in Pittsburgh, is coming to visit.

17. Here is a Reflexive derivation for French. Explain how it differs from the same syntactic process in English.

(a) $\#Paul_i$ *rase* $Paul_i\#$
              is-shaving

(b) $\#Paul_i$ *rase* $se_i\#$
                     himself

(c) *Paul se rase.*

(d) **Paul rase se.*

SUGGESTED READINGS

ARTICLES AND EXCERPTS

AKMAJIAN, A. 1970. "On Deriving Cleft Sentences from Pseudo-cleft Sentences." *Linguistic Inquiry* 1:149–68.

ANDERSON, S. 1974. "On Dis-Agreement Rules." *Linguistic Inquiry* 4:445–51.

BACH, E. 1971. "Questions." *Linguistic Inquiry* 2:153–66.

BAKER, C. 1970. "Double Negatives." *Linguistic Inquiry* 1:169–86.

———— 1970a. "Notes on the Description of English Questions: The Role of an Abstract Question Morpheme." *Foundations of Language* 6:197–219.

BEDELL, G. 1974. "The Arguments about Deep Structure." *Language* 50:423–45. (This article is an excellent historical survey of the arguments presented by the various syntactic theories on this question. Highly recommended.)

BERMAN, A. 1974. "On the VSO Hypothesis." *Linguistic Inquiry* 5:1–37.

BRESNAN, J. 1970. "On Complements: Towards a Syntactic Theory of Complement Types." *Foundations of Language* 6:297–321.

BRONCKART, J. and H. SINCLAIR. 1973. "Time, Tense and Aspect." *Cognition* 2:107–30.

CARDEN, G. 1970. "A Note on Conflicting Idiolects." *Linguistic Inquiry* 1:281–90.

CHAPIN, P. 1970. "Samoan Pronominalization." *Language* 46:366–78.

CHOMSKY, N. 1964. "A Transformational Approach to Syntax." In FODOR and KATZ (eds.), *The Structure of Language.* Prentice-Hall, Englewood Cliffs, N.J.

DOUGHERTY, R. 1969. "An Interpretive Theory of Pronominal Reference." *Foundations of Language* 5:488–519.

*DYKEMA, K. 1961. "Where Our Grammar Came From." *College English* 22:455–65.

ELLIOTT, D. 1974. "Toward a Grammar of Exclamations." *Foundations of Language* 11:231–45.

FILLMORE, C. 1963. "The Position of Embedding Transformations in a Grammar." *Word* 19:208–31.

GREEN, G. 1968. "On *too* and *either*, and not just *too* and *either*, either." *CLS-4*, DARDEN et al. (eds.).

GRINDER, J. 1970. "Super Equi-NP Deletion." *CLS-6*, CAMPBELL et al. (eds.).

——— 1971. "Chains of Coreference." *Linguistic Inquiry* 2:183–202.

——— and P. POSTAL. 1971. "Missing Antecedents." *Linguistic Inquiry* 2:269–312.

HANKAMER, J. 1973. "Unacceptable Ambiguity." *Linguistic Inquiry* 4:17–68.

HARMAN, G. 1963. "Generative Grammars without Transformational Rules: A Defense of Phrase Structure." *Language* 39:597–616.

HARRIS, Z. 1946. "From Morpheme to Utterance." *Language* 22:161–83.

——— 1957. "Co-occurrence and Transformation in Linguistic Structure." *Language* 33:283–340.

HOARD, J., and C. SLOAT. 1973. "English Irregular Verbs." *Language* 49:107–20.

HODGE, C. 1970. "The Linguistic Cycle." *Language Sciences* 13:1–7.

HOOPER, J. and S. THOMPSON. 1973. "On the Applicability of Root Transformations." *Linguistic Inquiry* 4:465–97.

JACKENDOFF, R. and P. CULICOVER. 1971. "A Reconsideration of Dative Movement." *Foundations of Language* 7:397–412.

KING, H. 1970. "On Blocking the Rule for Contraction in English." *Linguistic Inquiry* 1:134.

KIPARSKY, P. and C. KIPARSKY. 1971. "Fact." In BIERWISCH and HEIDOLPH (eds.).

KLIMA, E. 1964. "Relatedness between Grammatical Systems." *Language* 40:1–20.

KOUTSOUDAS, A. 1972. "The Strict Order Fallacy." *Language* 48:88–96.

LANGACKER, R. 1969. "On Pronominalization and the Chain of Command." In REIBEL and SCHANE (eds.).

LEHMANN, T. 1972. "Some Arguments Against Ordered Rules." *Language* 48:541–50.

McCAWLEY, J. 1970. "English as a VSO Language." *Language* 46:286–99.

———. 1974. "Dialogue." In H. PARRET, *Discussing Language*. Mouton, The Hague.

POSTAL, P. 1969. "Underlying and Superficial Linguistic Structure." In REIBEL and SCHANE (eds.).

——— 1970. "On Coreferential Complement Subject Deletion." *Linguistic Inquiry* 1:439–500.

RINGEN, C. 1972. "On Arguments for Rule Ordering." *Foundations of Language* 8:266–73.

ROSENBAUM, P. 1970. "A Principle Governing Deletion in English Sentential Complementation." In JACOBS and ROSENBAUM.

ROSS, J. 1969. "Auxiliaries as Main Verbs." In REIBEL and SCHANE (eds.).

———. 1969a. "Guess Who?" *CLS-5*, BINNICK et al. (eds.).

SANDERS, G. and H.-Y. TAI. 1972. "Immediate Dominance and Identity Deletion." *Foundations of Language* 8:161–98.

SCHACHTER, P. 1973. "Focus and Relativization." *Language* 49:19–46.

——— 1976. "A Nontransformational Account of Gerundive Nominals in English." *Linguistic Inquiry* 7:205–41.

SMITH, C. 1964. "Determiners and Relative Clauses in a Generative Grammar of English." *Language* 40:37–52.

SZAMOSI, M. 1973. "On the Unity of Subject Raising." *CLS-9*, CORUM et al. (eds.).

THOMPSON, S. 1973. "On Subjectless Gerunds in English." *Foundations of Language* 9:374–83.

——— 1971. "The Deep Structure of Relative Clauses." In FILLMORE and LANGENDOEN (eds.), *Studies in Linguistic Semantics*.

THORNE, J. 1966. "English Imperative Sentences." *Journal of Linguistics* 2:69–78.

WELLS, R. 1947. "Immediate Constituents." *Language* 23:81–117.

ZWICKY, A. 1970. "Auxiliary Reduction in English." *Linguistic Inquiry* 1:323–36.

BOOKS AND MONOGRAPHS

BIERWISCH, M. and K. HEIDOLPH (eds.). 1971. *Progress in Linguistics*. Mouton, The Hague.

BULL, W. 1960. *Time, Tense, and the Verb*. University of California Press, Berkeley and Los Angeles.

CHOMSKY, N. 1957. *Syntactic Structures*. Mouton, The Hague.

——— 1965. *Aspects of the Theory of Syntax*. M.I.T. Press, Cambridge, Mass.

——— 1967. *Language and Mind*. Harcourt Brace Jovanovich, New York.

*ELGIN, S. 1975. *A Primer of Transformational Grammar for Rank Beginners*. National Council of Teachers of English, Urbana, Ill.

EMONDS, J. 1975. *Root and Structure-Preserving Transformations*. Academic Press, New York.

FODOR, J. and J. KATZ (eds.). 1964. *The Structure of Language*. Prentice-Hall, Englewood Cliffs, N.J.

GRINDER, J. and S. ELGIN. 1973. *Guide to Transformational Grammar*. Holt, Rinehart and Winston, New York.

JACOBS, R. and P. ROSENBAUM. 1968. *English Transformational Grammar*. Ginn, Waltham, Mass.

——— (eds.). 1970. *Readings in English Transformational Grammar*. Ginn, Waltham, Mass.

KATZ, J. and P. POSTAL. 1964. *An Integrated Theory of Linguistic Descriptions*. M.I.T. Press, Cambridge, Mass.

LEES, R. 1960. *The Grammar of English Nominalizations*. Mouton, The Hague.

PALMATIER, R. 1972. *A Glossary for English Transformational Grammar*. Appleton-Century-Crofts, New York. (This indispensable and highly recommended reference work is out of print, but may be found in your library.)

PERLMUTTER, D. 1970. *Deep and Surface Structure Constraints in Syntax*. Holt, Rinehart and Winston, New York.

POSTAL, P. 1974. *On Raising*. M.I.T. Press, Cambridge, Mass.

REIBEL, D. and S. SCHANE (eds.). 1969. *Modern Studies in English*. Prentice-Hall, Englewood Cliffs, N.J.

STOCKWELL, R. et al. 1973. *The Major Syntactic Structures of English*. Holt, Rinehart and Winston, New York.

——— 1977. *Workbook in Syntactic Theory and Analysis*. Prentice-Hall, Englewood Cliffs, N.J.

STOCKWELL, R. 1977. *Foundations of Syntactic Theory*. Prentice-Hall, Englewood Cliffs, N.J.

TRAUGOTT, E. 1972. *A History of English Syntax*. Holt, Rinehart and Winston, New York.

FOUR

Phonology

All known human societies communicate by the method of meaningful sounds.[1] Human beings make many other, nonmeaningful sounds as well, however. For example, it is unlikely that a sneeze could ever be understood as having a meaning (other than the extralinguistic one that indicates physical discomfort). Sounds like coughing, crying, hand-clapping, throat-clearing, and so on, may have meaning in specific contexts, but they are very different from the sounds that actually make up human languages. Phonology concerns itself with the analysis and description of the *meaningful* sounds that human beings make, and how those sounds function in different languages. Here, as in semantics and syntax, linguists look for the systematic patterning that is characteristic of all human language.

---

[1] The sign language of the deaf is of course an exception; it is a system of meaningful gestures rather than sounds.

Look at the following lists of words:

(1)   a   b
       impossible   indecent
       improbable   indefinite
       impersonal   indescribable
       imbalanced   intolerable
       impermanent   indecipherable
       impassable   indefatigable
       imperceptible   intolerant
       impregnable   indestructible
       improper   intemperate
       immaterial   innumerable

Each of the words in (1) begins with a prefix which is a morpheme meaning 'not'; thus, *intolerant* means 'not tolerant', and so on. Now consider the data in (2) below and ask yourself, as a speaker of English, whether you would consider these forms acceptable. (Pronouncing them aloud will help in this decision.)

(2)   a   b
       inpossible   imdecent
       inproper   imtolerable
       inmaterial   imnumerable

You are correct in rejecting the data in (2). If you test it more extensively by changing the prefixes on all the words in (1), putting *im-* on the forms in Column (b) and *in-* on those in Column (a), you will find that your judgment holds for the entire sets.

Even more interesting is the fact that if you were shown a set of non-existent English words and asked to decide whether they would take *im-* or *in-* as a negative prefix, you would still have no difficulty making your decisions. For example:

(3)   a. basticulate   having eleven lumpy protrusions
      b. prednissable   possible to predniss
      c. modupulary   elected by only four voters
      d. dorifinary   having striped feathers
      e. tacatic   nervous before a test
      f. narlate   soaked with catsup

You would know at once that the proper forms must be those shown in (4).

(4) a. imbasticulate
     b. imprednissable
     c. immodupulary
     d. indorifinary
     e. intacatic
     f. innarlate

There are far too many different items involved in these decisions for the emerging pattern of choice to be accounted for by any random process; therefore, you must be deciding on the basis of a rule of some kind. A first and obvious possibility is the statement in (5).

(5) This negative prefix is *im-* before *p*, *b*, and *m*, and it is *in-* before *t*, *d*, and *n*.

This will describe the data adequately. That is, it accounts for all the sequences of the language presented above, and would account for all other sequences (even hypothetical ones) of the same kind. It accurately states the facts, both present and potential. Since the prefix has meaning, it is a *morpheme*; and the two possible forms that it might take as stated in (5) are traditionally referred to as its *allomorphs*.

It is certainly possible that nothing more is going on than what is expressed in (5). There *are* idiosyncratic rules in human languages. English, for example, will not allow any word to begin with the sound represented by the letter *s* in *measure*. There's nothing unusual about the sound, and it appears elsewhere in English words, but it is forbidden to begin one. However, before settling for this solution, it would be worth asking the following question: Is there some reason why you prefer *im-* before *p*, *b*, *m* but *in-* before *t*, *d*, *n*? If you can find a reason, you will have a solution that provides an explanation rather than just a description.

Pronounce the six hypothetical sequences in (6) aloud, paying very close attention to what is happening to the various parts of your mouth as you do so. (Pronounce the *a* in the word *father*.)

(6) ma, pa, ba; na, ta, da

You will notice that for *m*, *p*, *b* you must press both lips together, while for *n*, *t*, *d* you have to touch the front portion of your tongue to the gum ridge just behind your upper teeth. In other words, when you choose the final sound of the prefix, you choose the sound formed in the same place in the mouth as the first sound of the word to which the prefix is added. This process is more reasonable than the proposal in (5), and should remind you of the feature-matching operations discussed in semantics and syntax. It is an example of the process known as *assimilation,* in which sounds that are next to one another become very like one another, and is extremely common in human languages.

For some speakers of English the assimilation of this negative prefix is carried even farther. These speakers pronounce the prefix in words such as *ingratitude* and *incompetent* as they pronounce the suffix *-ing* in *working.* Both *gratitude* and *competence* begin with sounds formed at the back of the mouth rather than at the lips or teeth, and this is also true of the consonantal portion of *-ing.*

Phonologists and phoneticians are specialists in the investigation of such matters as these. They want to know upon what basis native speakers of languages make decisions about which combinations of sounds are allowed and which are forbidden, which are meaningful and which meaningless. They want to know how the meaningful sounds pattern within a language, how they differ from one language to another, and what implications such information has for all human languages.

In this chapter we will discuss some of the terminology, concepts, and methods needed for this sort of investigation.

ARTICULATORY PHONETICS

Articulatory phonetics describes how speech sounds are made and provides a framework for their classification. In order to understand the terminology used, you will need to have some familiarity with the vocal tract. This can most easily be accomplished by examining the accompanying diagram.

The vocal organs include the lungs, the trachea, the larynx, the pharynx, the nose, and the mouth. The term *vocal tract* is used for the throat, nose, and mouth together.

When you speak, the air exhaled from your lungs flows into the larynx, where the vocal cords are stretched across the air passage, and on out through the vocal tract. This airstream is modified by the vocal organs in a variety of ways. Some of the modifications—such as pressing the lips together or rounding them—are actions that you can readily note for yourself. Others, such as the vibration of the vocal cords or the movements of the back of the tongue, are far less accessible to conscious observation.

CONSONANTS

For consonants, the two main articulators are the lips and the tongue. Consonants are classified in terms of two factors: *where* the sound is produced (for example, at the lips), and *how* it is produced (as, for example, by pressing

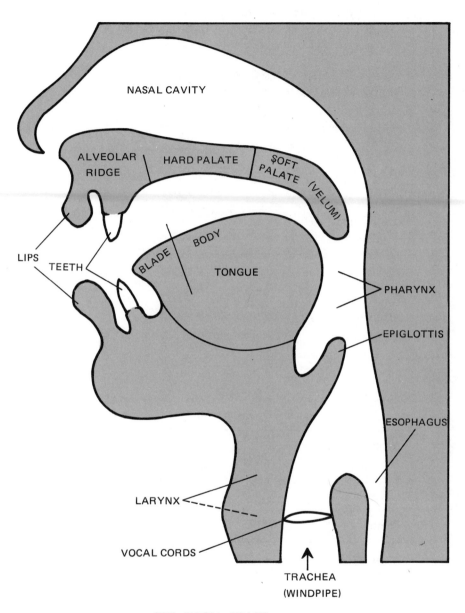

NASAL CAVITY

ALVEOLAR RIDGE

HARD PALATE

SOFT PALATE (VELUM)

LIPS

TEETH

BLADE

BODY

TONGUE

PHARYNX

EPIGLOTTIS

ESOPHAGUS

LARYNX

VOCAL CORDS

TRACHEA (WINDPIPE)

THE VOCAL TRACT

Note that the soft palate is shown lowered toward the back
of the tongue, as in the production of a nasal sound.

both lips tightly together). These two factors are called the *place and manner of articulation*. The consonant sounds of English, classified first according to their *place of articulation*, are shown in Table I.

Table I ENGLISH CONSONANT SOUNDS CLASSIFIED BY
PLACE OF ARTICULATION

	SOUND SYMBOL	AS IN:
Labial	p	*p*it
	b	*b*it
	m	*m*it
	w	*w*it
Labio-dental	f	*f*ine
	v	*v*ine
Dental	θ	*th*ick
	ð	*th*is
Alveolar	t	*t*ip
	d	*d*ip
	s	*s*ip
	z	*z*ip
	l	*l*ip
	r	*r*ip
	n	*n*ip
Alveo-palatal	č	*ch*ar
	ǰ	*j*ar
	š	*sh*ip
	ž	mea*s*ure
Palatal	y	*y*ip
Velar	k	*K*ate
	g	*g*ate
	ŋ*	si*ng*
Glottal	h	*h*ip

* This is one of the consonant sounds that is not allowed to occur at the beginning of a word in English. The other is ž.

Labial sounds have the lips as their place of articulation; if both lips are required in order to produce the sound, it is called a *bilabial. Labio-dental* sounds are made with the lower lip against the upper teeth.

Dental sounds require that the blade of the tongue touch the upper teeth. Behind the upper teeth lies the *alveolar ridge; alveolar* sounds are produced by contact between the blade of the tongue and this bony area of the gum ridge. Consonant sounds made further back in the mouth involve the body of the tongue and contact with either the *hard palate* or the *soft palate* (velum). In *alveo-palatal* sounds the blade and body of the tongue together make contact at the region from the alveolar ridge to the hard palate. *Palatal* sounds involve contact exclusively between the body of the tongue and the hard palate; for *velar* sounds the body of the tongue is in contact with the soft palate.

Still farther back in the throat, at the glottis (i.e., the opening between the vocal folds), the *glottal* sounds are formed; English has only one of these, the sound symbolized by *h* in Table I.

In Table II the consonant sounds of English are classified according to the second factor—their *manner of articulation.*

Table II ENGLISH CONSONANT SOUNDS CLASSIFIED BY MANNER OF ARTICULATION

Stops	p, b, t, d, k, g
Fricatives	f, v, θ, ð, s, z, š, ž, h
Affricates	č, ǰ
Nasals	m, n, ŋ
Liquids	l, r
Glides	w, y

Stops are sounds which require that the flow of air through the vocal tract be cut off completely. *Fricatives* allow air to escape through a narrow constriction, but with a turbulence caused by the friction as the air flows over various parts of the vocal tract. *Affricates* are a combination of the first two categories; they begin as a stop and end as a fricative. The sound represented by *č*, for example, begins like *t* and ends like *š*, but is considered a single sound just as *t* itself is.

During the production of most consonant sounds of English, the velum is raised, blocking off the flow of air through the nasal passages. For *nasals*, however, the velum is lowered, allowing air to flow out through the nose and blocking air flow through the mouth.

The *liquids* include *l* and *r*; they are grouped together primarily because they pattern similarly in sound systems. The *l* is a *lateral*, which means that it requires the lowering of one or both sides (the lateral edges) of the tongue.

This is not true of the sound *r*. For English *r* the tongue is raised toward the roof of the mouth and forms a shape that could almost be described as "cupped."

The *glides* have the least amount of vocal tract constriction of all consonant sounds. For this reason, they are sometimes called *semi-vowels*.

Finally, the information about both place and manner of articulation is combined in Table III. Here the abbreviation *Vl* (voiceless) indicates that the vocal cords are not vibrating during the production of a particular sound, and *Vd* (voiced) indicates that vocal cord vibration is required.

Table III ENGLISH CONSONANT SOUNDS CLASSIFIED BY PLACE AND MANNER OF ARTICULATION

Place of Articulation

		LABIAL	LABIO-DENTAL	DENTAL	ALVEOLAR	ALVEO-PALATAL	PALATAL	VELAR	GLOTTAL
Stops	Vl	p (pear)			t table			k cook	
	Vd	b (bear)			d dog			g good	
Fricatives	Vl		f five	θ thin	s sing	š sugar			h
	Vd		v very	ð this	z zoo	ž measure			house
Affricates	Vl					č child			
	Vd					j Just			
Nasals	Vd	m ap			n ame			ŋ song	
Liquids	Vd				lamp / l, r robe				
Glides	Vd	w ell					y yes		

(handwritten marginal note: Manner of Art.)

You will notice that the stops, fricatives, and affricates of English (with the exception of *h*) occur in pairs—one voiced, and the other voiceless.[2] The prevalence of this distinction in English indicates its importance in

---

[2] Some linguists classify the nasals as "stops" because the flow of air through the mouth is blocked in their production. For them, it would be necessary to modify this statement to exclude the "nasal stops."

the system.* You cannot feel your vocal cords vibrating in the same direct way that you can feel your lips move. However, you can feel the difference between voicing and voicelessness by putting your fingertips against your Adam's apple and saying first *zzzzzzzzzz* and then *sssssssssss*. The sensation that you feel with your fingertips during the prolonged *z* is the vibration of your vocal cords for voicing; you will feel no such vibration during the *sssssssssss* sequence.

*Note: This group is called *obstruents;* the others, including the vowels, are called *sonorants.*

VOWELS

We can now move on to the articulatory classification for the vowels of English. Vowels are the least constricted of all sounds. They are never produced by cutting off the flow of air, or by touching the tongue blade to the teeth or to the alveolar ridge. In English there are no voiceless vowels, nor any that demand friction in their production.

Table IV   THE VOWEL SOUNDS OF ENGLISH

		FRONT (unrounded)			CENTRAL (unrounded)			BACK (rounded)	
High	TENSE	i	(b*ee*t)				TENSE	u	(b*oo*t)
	LAX	I	(b*i*t)				LAX	U	(b*oo*k)
Mid	TENSE	e	(b*ai*t)				TENSE	o	(b*oa*t)
	LAX	ɛ	(b*e*t)	LAX	ʌ	(b*u*t)			
				LAX	ə	(sof*a*)			
Low	LAX	æ	(b*a*t)	LAX	a	(f*a*ther)	TENSE	ɔ	(l*a*w)

Note A: English also has three sounds which are called *diphthongs*, and which can be described as a sequence of a vowel and a following glide. They are *ay* (as in *bite*), *aw* (as in *house*), and *oy* (as in *boy*).

Note B: The symbol ʌ is called *tent*; the ə immediately beneath it is called *schwa*. They are both mid central unrounded vowels; tent occurs when the vowel is stressed, and schwa occurs in unstressed syllables, as in the examples shown. However, it is traditional in English phonology to use different symbols for the stressed and unstressed variants.

In order to describe and classify vowels adequately we must consider three things. First, we need to know whether the lips are rounded for the production of the vowel or not. Second, we are concerned with the height of the body of the tongue in the mouth. Finally, as the tongue bunches up toward the roof of the mouth, it assumes a position either toward the back or the front of the mouth (at the velum or at the hard palate), and this must be taken into consideration.

English vowels must be characterized further as either *tense* or *lax* (non-tense). The exact definition of tenseness for vowels is a matter of some dispute at the present time. It is thought that tense vowels are produced with slightly greater muscular tension in the vocal tract and with the tongue deviating more from the neutral or rest position.

This information for the vowels of English is summarized in Table IV.

The symbols in Tables I to IV provide a notation for writing out sequences of English, which linguists call a *phonemic transcription*. The use of these symbols is necessary because each one represents a single sound and it is always the same sound. This is not true if words are simply written out using the English alphabet, as the examples in the tables make clear. (Compare *boot* and *book*, for instance.) This is further demonstrated in (6), in which the words spelled on the left are transcribed phonemically on the right.

(6)	*Alphabetic Spelling* (*Orthography*)	*Phonemic Transcription*
	cape	kep
	cake	kek
	keep	kip
	beat	bit
	field	fild
	ship	šɪp
	nation	nešən
	nature	nečər
	bird	bʌrd
	read (present)	rid
	read (past)	rɛd

Notice that the phonemic transcriptions in the right-hand column correctly show the English speaker's awareness that the vowel which appears spelled three different ways in *keep, beat, field,* is the same sound. Similarly, the sound spelled as *t* in *nation* is the same as the first sound in *ship*; the phonemic transcription accurately reflects this fact. We will return to the question of sound versus spelling later in this chapter.

THE PHONEME

If a particular language has twelve meaningful sounds, it is said to have twelve *phonemes*. A phoneme is a sound of a given language that native speakers agree is just one segment, and which enables them to recognize differences of meaning between words. Rules may apply to phonemes and bring about changes in their phonetic manifestation—that is, their pronunciation. In addition, as you have already seen, the spelling system of a language may be in conflict with its phonemic representation. Since all three of these matters must be written about using symbols that are very much alike, the following notation is used to prevent confusion:

- a. A symbol that represents a phoneme will appear between two slashes, like this: /p/
- b. A symbol that represents a phonetic form will appear in square brackets: [p]
- c. A symbol that represents a letter of the alphabet will appear either in italics or set off by quotation marks.

In English /e/ and /ɛ/ are two vowel phonemes. If we substitute /ɛ/ for the /e/ of *sale* /sel/, the speaker of English will hear a different word, *sell* /sɛl/. There are many other word pairs of the same kind; for example, *bale* /bel/ and *bell* /bɛl/; *laid* /led/ and *led* /lɛd/; *mate* /met/ and *met* /mɛt/. Pairs like these, differing in only one phoneme, are called *minimal pairs*.

In Spanish [e] and [ɛ] also occur phonetically; however, there are no pairs of Spanish words that are distinguished from one another by an /e/–/ɛ/ difference. Instead, Spanish has a single phoneme /e/, which is subject to a rule that changes its phonetic form to [ɛ] whenever it is followed by a consonant in the syllable in which it occurs. Thus, the first *e* in *desde* ('until') is pronounced [ɛ], not [e]. We say, therefore, that the Spanish phoneme /e/ has more than one possible phonetic shape, each of which is called an *allophone* of /e/.[3]

A very similar situation exists with regard to English and Spanish for /s/ and /z/. Spanish has only /s/ as a phoneme, but when it occurs before a voiced consonant it undergoes assimilation and is pronounced [z]. The three symbolizations are shown in (7).

(7) a. /desde/   Phonemic
    b. [dɛzde]   Phonetic
    c. *desde*   Orthographic

[3] It is important to keep in mind that a phoneme is unique to its particular language. Thus, the phoneme /e/ of English and the phoneme /e/ of Spanish are not exactly alike.

It may seem to you that since [z] is a part of the phonetic system of Spanish, a Spanish speaker should have no difficulty distinguishing the two English phonemes /s/ and /z/. This is false; people do not necessarily have conscious awareness of the phonological processes of their language. The Spanish speaker does not hear the [z] of [dɛzde] as different from [s], because for him they are only *one* meaningful sound—the Spanish phoneme /s/. As a result, when an English-speaking teacher says a sentence such as (8a) the Spanish-speaking student may think he hears (8b).

(8) a. Don't say *sink*, say *zinc*.
     b. Don't say *sink*, say *sink*.

In such a situation the student justifiably finds this not only confusing, but irrational.

Speakers of English are so accustomed to paying attention to the difference between voiced and voiceless sounds that they often find it hard to believe that others may have difficulty in making the distinction. A typical objection is that /s/ and /z/, for instance, are "obviously two completely different sounds" and that "anyone can tell them apart." This is not the case.

To clarify this problem let's consider a phonetic distinction of English that native speakers are unaware of because it makes no meaning difference within English. Consider the following words:

(9) pit, spit, pat, spat, pot, spot, putter, sputter

English speakers will claim that all these words have as part of their structure a single sound /p/. This accurately reflects their knowledge that English has only a single phoneme /p/. However, /p/ has more than one possible allophone. Phonetically, the *p* in *pat* is *aspirated* (written phonetically as [pʰ]) whereas the *p* in *spat* is not. Aspiration refers to the small puff of air that accompanies the production of a sound, and it is predictable in English. Any voiceless stop at the beginning of a word or before a stressed vowel will be aspirated. You can feel the difference by holding your hand right before your mouth and saying first *pat* and then *spat*. You will feel the puff of air that is present after the aspirated *p* of *pat*, but you will feel none after the *p* of *spat*.

Because aspiration never causes a meaning change in English, its presence or absence goes unnoticed by English speakers, and unless they have practiced hearing the distinction (as they might in a phonetics course) they will not be *able* to hear it. To a native speaker of Korean, however, in whose language there are many minimal pairs distinguished by aspiration, it seems obvious that "anyone can tell that these are two completely different sounds." Korean has a minimal pair, /pita/ ('cut') and /pʰita/ ('bloom'), but no pairs where a change from [p] to [b] would make a difference in meaning. Both

[p] and [b] occur phonetically in Korean, but they are allophones of the phoneme /p/; the sound [b] occurs between vowels. We can summarize the phonemic/phonetic distribution for English and Korean as follows:

	PHONEMES	ALLOPHONES
English	/p/	[p] [pʰ]
	/b/	[b]
Korean	/p/	[p] [b]
	/pʰ/	[pʰ]

English has thirty-six separate phonemes, each having one or more allophones. Then there are sounds which do occur in English speech but are not meaningful. For example, if you say "Uh-oh!" you pronounce a sound between the *uh* and the *oh* which is called a *glottal stop*. This sound, written ʔ, is a consonant phoneme of many languages, but not of English. If you were asked to pronounce a glottal stop before the English vowel /a/, as you pronounced /m/, /p/, /b/, etc. before /a/ earlier in this chapter, you would probably not be able to tell whether you were following instructions or not. An English speaker would have even more difficulty with a sound which never appears in English even accidentally, such as the Navajo phoneme /tɬʔ/. This sound is a glottalized lateralized voiceless dental affricate, and it requires a good deal of vocal tract gymnastics.

The consonant and vowel sounds of a language are known collectively as its *segmental phonemes*. We cannot account for the entire sound system in terms of segmental phonemes alone, however. Look at (10).

(10) a. conduct (*verb*)   to lead, guide, direct, manage
     b. conduct (*noun*)   behavior
     c. red cap   a cap which is red
     d. redcap   a luggage porter at a railway station or air terminal
     e. ice cream
     f. I scream

In all the example pairs in (10), the segmental phonemes are identical for each member of the pair. Nonetheless we recognize them as being different sequences with different meanings. This is due to the *suprasegmental* (or *prosodic*) phonemes called *stress* and *juncture*.

Stress is a phenomenon of sound perceived as slightly higher volume and pitch on a word or portion of a word. English has a number of verb-noun pairs in which the verb is stressed on the second syllable, while the noun is stressed on the first, as in (10a–b) and (11).

(11)   con*vert*, *con*vert; ex*tract*, *ex*tract; re*ject*, *re*ject

Stress is also involved in the differentiation of sequences of adjective followed by noun (such as *red cap*) and noun compounds having the same segmental phonemes. The compound, like *redcap*, will have a stronger stress on the first syllable. Other such pairs are shown in (12).

(12)   black board, blackboard; hot dog, hotdog; black bird, blackbird

The term used to describe our perception of the boundary between words (written #) is *juncture*. Examples 10e–f when written in phonemic transcription look like this:

(13) $/\#ays\# \#krim\#/$ ice cream
       $/\#ay\# \#skrim\#/$ I scream

There is no sound segment represented by this # symbol, but we are aware of its presence.

Stress and juncture, together with variations in pitch, all work together to give sentences the pattern called *intonation*. English does not have phonemic tone, in which otherwise identical words spoken at different pitches are understood to have different meanings. The African language Nupe does have phonemic tone, as shown in (14).

(14)   [bá]   high tone, *to be sour*
       [bā]   mid tone, *to cut*
       [bà]   low tone, *to count*

But we are aware of consistent pitch patterns such as the characteristic rising of the voice at the end of English yes/no questions. You will also remember from the semantics chapter the discussion of the problem of explaining why pairs like (15) mean different things.

(15)   a. John called Mary a good sport, and then she insulted him.
       b. John called Mary a good sport, and then *she* insulted *him*.

The only perceptible difference between (15a) and (15b) is a difference in intonation, caused primarily by the presence of emphatic stress on *she* and *him* in the second sentence. Such examples have led many linguists to conclude that we cannot claim that semantics is a separate component of the grammar with no access to phonological (and syntactic) information. Others would maintain the separation of components and propose surface rules of semantic interpretation. Substantial arguments exist for both proposals, and the issue remains unsettled.

The intonation patterns of a language give it its characteristic melody. Children typically learn these patterns some time before they begin to actually speak their language, and produce sequences that their parents feel they *ought* to be able to understand, even though they may contain not one recognizable word. And it is often intonation that is responsible for speakers of a language perceiving someone as having a "foreign accent," even when that individual is otherwise very fluent and is making no "mistakes" in pronunciation.

PHONOLOGY RULES
AND THEIR FORMAL NOTATION

It would not be impossible for English to have a phonological rule which specified that the negative prefix discussed at the beginning of this chapter had the form *im-* before all sequences starting with /p/, /b/, /m/, /θ/, and /k/. However, the five sounds listed would be a strange set. /K/ is pronounced at the velum, and /θ/ requires that your tongue touch the edge of your upper teeth. Neither of these characteristics applies to /p/, /b/, or /m/, nor do /k/ and /θ/ have much else in common beyond the fact that they are both consonants.

The set composed of /p, b, m/, on the other hand, has far more shared characteristics than it does unshared ones. All three sounds require that you press both lips together, none requires that your tongue do anything in particular, and all three cut off the flow of air through your mouth. They are therefore what linguists refer to as a *natural class*, and it is not surprising to find rules that apply to the entire group, such as the prefix assimilation rule.

In order to capture explicitly the notion of natural class, as well as to show the phonetic parameters of individual phonemes, phonologists make use of *distinctive features*. As in syntax and semantics, these features are binary, specifying each phoneme as either plus or minus the feature in question.

Table V shows a distinctive feature matrix for the vowels of English.

Table V DISTINCTIVE FEATURE MATRIX FOR ENGLISH VOWELS

	i	ɪ	e	ɛ	æ	a	ʌ	(ə)	u	ʊ	o	ɔ
HIGH	+	+	−	−	−	−	−		+	+	−	−
LOW	−	−	−	−	+	+	−		−	−	−	+
BACK	−	−	−	−	−	+	+		+	+	+	+
ROUND	−	−	−	−	−	−	−		+	+	+	+
TENSE	+	−	+	−	−	+	−		+	−	+	+

A particular vowel can then be defined in terms of its set of features, as in (16).

(16)

$$/e/ \begin{bmatrix} -\text{HIGH} \\ -\text{LOW} \\ -\text{BACK} \\ -\text{ROUND} \\ +\text{TENSE} \end{bmatrix} \qquad /u/ \begin{bmatrix} +\text{HIGH} \\ -\text{LOW} \\ +\text{BACK} \\ +\text{ROUND} \\ -\text{TENSE} \end{bmatrix}$$

Other features, for example [VOICE] and [NASAL], are needed to specify the English consonants.

In contemporary linguistic literature, phonologists often refer to a sound segment or a class of segments in terms of their feature specifications. This formal notation is particularly useful for writing phonological rules. We will not discuss the notation further in this introductory text, except to offer an example of a hypothetical rule for your examination in (17).

(17)

$$\begin{matrix} V \\ [+\text{LOW}] \end{matrix} \rightarrow [+\text{NASAL}] \quad / \underline{} \begin{matrix} C \\ [+\text{NASAL}] \end{matrix}$$

This rule refers to the class of low vowels and states that all such vowels become nasalized when they occur before a nasal consonant. The underscore is used to indicate the position of the segment undergoing the rule, and the slash stands for 'when it occurs'. (This rule would of course be another example of assimilation.)

UNDERLYING REPRESENTATIONS

A major problem for phonologists is that of deciding upon the correct underlying representation of a morpheme. If we consider once again the three negative prefix allomorphs composed of /ɪ/ and a following nasal, we run into this question: Is /ɪn/, /ɪm/, or /ɪŋ/ the underlying form from which the other two allomorphs are derived? One piece of evidence to help us answer this question is shown in (18).

(18) inability, inexperienced, inimitable, inoperable, inurbane

The data shows that when *no* consonant follows the prefix it is /ɪn/; therefore, this can be chosen as the basic underlying form, and the variants /ɪm/ and /ɪŋ/ are derived by the rule assimilating /n/ to the place of articulation of the following consonant.

The application of phonological rules to language sequences often obscures their underlying structure and makes them appear to be "irregular." Look at the following Navajo examples:

(19) a. *Naashnish.*   I am working.
      b. *Nanilnish.*   You are working.
      c. *Naalnish.*   He is working. (*Or* she, it, they two are working.)

There are two phonological rules of Navajo which apply to this set of forms. One is a rule that deletes the phoneme /l/ whenever it occurs between two consonants. The other rule, which must take *morphological* information into account, applies to the Navajo morpheme *na-*, a verb prefix meaning roughly 'around', and states that its vowel becomes long whenever there is no other vowel present in the verb between *na-* and the verb stem. This rule does not apply to just any vowel /a/ in Navajo—only to the one appearing in the morpheme *na-*.

If we break up the three Navajo forms into their component morphemes and give them their underlying representations, they will look like this:

ADVERBIAL PREFIX	SUBJECT PRONOUN PREFIX	CLASSIFIER	STEM
na	š	l	nɪš
na	nɪ	l	nɪš
na	∅	l	nɪš

If no phonological rules applied to any of these forms, the surface forms would be *nashlnish*, *nanilnish*, and *nalnish*. However, only the second form is correct. To make this clear, we can apply the two rules discussed above to the underlying forms.

'I am working.'

#na	š	l	nɪš#	Underlying representation
#na	š	∅	nɪš#	/l/-rule applied
#naa	š	∅	nɪš#	*na*-rule applied
Naashnish.				Surface representation

'You are working.'

#na	nɪ	l	nɪš#	Underlying representation
#na	nɪ	l	nɪš#	/l/-rule does *not* apply
#na	nɪ	l	nɪš#	*na*-rule does *not* apply
Nanilnish.				Surface representation

'He is working.'

#na	∅	l	nɪš#	Underlying representation
#na	∅	l	nɪš#	/l/-rule does *not* apply
#naa	∅	l	nɪš#	*na*-rule applied
Naalnish.				Surface representation

There are many similar verb sets in Navajo, all undergoing these two rules.[4] When the derivations are examined, the apparent surface regularity disappears, and the second person 'you are working' form supplies evidence for the correctness of the analysis. It is then not necessary to state, for example, that first person singular Navajo verbs of this type are irregular because they do not contain a classifier morpheme. The first person singular *does* have a classifier in its underlying representation; it simply is deleted by a phonological rule. The rule itself is a natural one. Without it the Navajo word for 'I am working' would contain a three-consonant cluster—[šln]— which would be very difficult to pronounce. Such clusters are extremely rare in human languages.

Just as native speakers will reject semantically or syntactically un-acceptable language sequences, they will reject sequences which violate the phonological rules of their languages. You know which phonemes are part of the total phonemic inventory of your language, whether you can list them or not; if English is your native tongue you will refuse to accept as a possible English word any sequence containing a click as one of its phonemes, because you know English has no clicks in its sound system. Furthermore, you know

[4] In phonology as in syntax it is sometimes necessary to investigate the relative ordering of rules. For the two Navajo rules discussed here, however, no ordering is necessary. Whichever rule you apply first, the results will be the same.

which combinations of phonemes into morphemes are allowed by your language and which are forbidden. Like the speaker of Navajo, you would reject a proposed word that contained the cluster [šln], such as *shlnip*, or *meshln*.

English is very particular about three-consonant clusters at the beginning of a word, so particular that only the following is possible:

(20) *The first phoneme must be* /s/, *the second must be a voiceless stop, and the third must be a liquid.*

Thus, you might accept as possible names for a new candy bar all three hypothetical words in (21a), but you would not allow any of those in (b).

(21) a. Streep, Splate, Skripple
    *b. Ktreep, Szlate, Skmipple

You do not have to be consciously aware of Rule (20) in order to recognize that each of the sequences in (21b) violates one of the three conditions of that rule.

PHONOLOGY AND
ENGLISH ORTHOGRAPHY

In reading this chapter, you have no doubt been aware of the conflict between English pronunciation and spelling. The following questions have probably crossed your mind:

   a. When the pronunciation of a phoneme is changed by the application of a rule, why doesn't the spelling of the word it appears in change, too?
   b. Why do so many words have silent letters?
   c. Why are there so many different ways of spelling a single vowel, such as the phoneme /i/?
   d. Why has nothing been said about the contrast between long vowels and short vowels in English? Don't phonologists care about this distinction?

These are reasonable questions, and hundreds more like them would arise if you compared spelling systems and writing systems the world over. The questions raised above can be reduced to a single question: Why is there so much difference between English orthography and English phonology?

Many people think that an ideal writing system—which, like many ideals, may be impossible to achieve—would be one in which every sound had just one symbol to represent it and that symbol was *always* the same one. When you hear someone say that "the alphabet of _____ is completely phonetic" you are running squarely into the problem of widespread misinformation about this matter. It is common to hear people say that the Spanish language (or some other one) is "completely phonetic," and it is true that the degree of mismatch between sound and writing is less in Spanish than it is in English. However, the "completely phonetic" claim is false. Remember that although Spanish has no /z/ phoneme, the Spanish phoneme /s/ becomes voiced when it occurs before another voiced consonant. The *s* in *desde* ('until') is pronounced [z], just as the *s* in the English word *bells* is, but the spelling of the word does not change to *dezde*.

Spanish has /b/, /d/, and /g/ in its phoneme inventory, and they are written *b, d, g*. However, when any one of them occurs between two vowels or as the last phoneme in a word, it is not pronounced as a voiced stop. Instead, it becomes the corresponding fricative, while its spelling remains unchanged. The last sound in the word *verdad* ('true') is much closer to English /ð/ than it is to a *d* of any kind.

If a writing system attempted to reflect pronunciation changes precisely, each time a phonological rule altered the phonetic shape of a word its spelling would have to change. Notice what this would mean for a set of related words like that in (22).

(22) a. photo   [foto]
      b. photograph   [fotəgræf]
      c. photographer   [fətagrəfər]
      d. photography   [fətagrəfi]

It is unlikely that a phonetic representation would lead to any less complexity in the spelling system of any language. Such a representation is also completely unnecessary, since native speakers of a language already know what changes a word must undergo as various rules apply to it. This is not conscious knowledge, any more than the knowledge the native speaker has of syntactic derivations is conscious knowledge, but it is part of every native speaker's linguistic competence.

The English spelling system has long been looked upon as chaos, full of inexplicable irregularities and exceptions. Demands for spelling reform are as common as demands for tax reform. However, although the system is flawed, it is not so chaotic as it appears to be, and the chaos that does exist is not wholly without explanation. The seemingly bizarre spelling phenomena of English can be divided into four major categories which cast a lot of light on the orthographic darkness.

First, many spellings are simply historical relics. People once spelled English pretty much as they pleased. (Shakespeare spelled in a way that would bounce him instantly into a "remedial" class today; sometimes the same word is spelled several different ways on a single page.) Then spelling began to be standardized, and although the language went right on changing, as is normal for languages, the spelling system did not. All of the silent letters in the words below were, at some earlier stage of English, pronounced.

(23) a. *k*nee, *k*nife, *k*nave, *k*now
      b. s*w*ord, t*w*o
      c. bou*gh*, *k*nig*h*t, throu*gh*, weig*h*t

It is in just such relic spellings that we do sometimes see a movement toward reform, as in the current tendency toward *nite* for *night* and *thru* for *through*, at least in advertisements and informal contexts.

Historical facts also account for much of the astonishing variety in the spelling of English vowels. During one stage of the history of English, a massive change occurred in the pronunciation of vowels called the Great Vowel Shift. (We will return to this in Chapter Nine on historical linguistics.) The shift affected many English vowels in a number of different ways, but their spellings did not change systematically to reflect this fact. For example, *bite* [bayt] was at one time pronounced [bit], while *beet* [bit] was pronounced [bet] and *boot* [but] was pronounced [bot].

A second category of seeming irregularities is the result of phonological rules of the type discussed in this chapter, particularly as they interact with English morphology.

The silent *g* in *sign, resign, benign, malign,* for instance, is the result of a phonological rule that forbids any English word to end in a stop followed immediately by a nasal. When the *g* is not in this forbidden position, it isn't silent, as shown by the related words *signature, resignation, benignant, malignancy.* It is clear that the *g* in these words corresponds to a phoneme /g/ that is present in their underlying representations, but which is subject to a rule that may or may not allow it to appear in the pronounced form. (This is not true of the strictly historical irregularities; for example, the *k* of *knee* is not present in the underlying representation of the word in Modern English, which is simply /ni/.)

Into this same category fall the pronunciation of *t* as [š] in *nation* and *national* and as [č] in *nature* and *natural.* (The International Teaching Alphabet, widely claimed to be flawlessly phonetic, retains *t* in these words, also.) Although this may create problems for the speller, it is a source of useful morphological information. The fact that *electric, electrical, electricity,* and *electrician* are spelled identically up to the suffix, despite the varying pronunciation, helps the reader of English by clearly indicating the close relationship of meaning among these words.

The third category is one in which English uses letters of the alphabet to accomplish what many other languages do with *diacritics* (accent marks, nasal markers, umlauts, etc.). This is perfectly reasonable, in view of the fact that we must make only twenty-six letters serve for thirty-six different phonemes. English has many pairs of words which differ in their spelling only by the presence or absence of a "silent *e*," as shown in (24).

(24) a. bit, bite; sit, site; mit, mite
       b. hat, hate; bat, bate; mat, mate
       c. not, note; rot, rote; rob, robe
       d. cut, cute; hum, Hume

The function of the *e* at the end of the second member of each pair is to indicate that the preceding vowel is tense. We could just as well have done this by using a set of accent marks, as French does in a similar situation; the effect of the silent *e* is precisely the same.[5]

Pairs like those in (24) are traditionally described as containing "long *i*" and "short *i*," "long *a*" and "short *a*," etc. This statement accurately demonstrates the perception that native speakers of English have of the regular alternation of tense and non-tense vowels, but it's important to realize that the description is phonetically misleading. As shown in (25), such pairs do *not* contain the same vowel, differentiated only by length.

(25) a. *met*, /mɛt/; *mete*, /mit/
       b. *hat*, /hæt/; *hate*, /het/
       c. *not*, /nat/; *note*, /not/

Another example of this kind, again used to indicate the proper pronunciation of vowels, is sets such as those in (26).

(26) hopping, hoping; robbing, robing; filling, filing

English orthography doubles a consonant (unless already double, as in *fill*) for diacritic purposes. The vowel contrast involved is again the tense/lax distinction, with the doubled consonant indicating that the preceding vowel is not tense. The second consonant is silent.

Finally, there is a fourth category of words which are genuine exceptions, such as the words *women* and *one*. This group frequently contains words that English has borrowed from other languages, or has coined from

---

[5] Words like *love* and *live* ([lɪv]) are exceptions; they fall under an orthographic rule that prohibits any English word from ending with the letter *v*.

Greek or Latin roots in combination. All the words in (27) are true exceptions, and the only way to learn their spelling—especially for those that radically violate the rules of English—is to memorize them.

(27) pizza, gestalt, chaise longue, choir, lieutenant, sergeant, colonel, pneumonia

By no means does this four-way classification solve all the problems of English spelling; it is not intended to do so. However, it should demonstrate at least the following facts about our spelling system:

   a. It is not nearly so irregular as it seems at first glance or as it has traditionally been claimed to be.
   b. It frequently reflects the underlying representation of English words in a way that preserves valuable information.
   c. Except for the elimination of the historical oddities, none of the proposals for spelling reform would be likely to improve on the system we now have.

EXERCISES AND PROBLEMS

1. Write out the following lists of words in phonemic transcription, using the symbols provided in this chapter.

   (a) bad, feed, mast, knock, foul, fowl
   (b) bun, bright, knife, bids, church, press
   (c) climb, glide, grief, grieve, brown, threat
   (d) power, number, again, follow, machine, client
   (e) telegraphy, omnipotent, thundering, philosophy, marvelous

2. The rule for the regular English plural is usually stated as "add -*s* or -*es* to the end of the noun." Notice, however, that the pronunciation of English plurals does not always follow the rule, as shown in the following examples:

   bead, [bid]; beads, [bidz]
   beach, [bič]; beaches, [bičɪz]

One way to state the facts would be to say that the regular English plural has three allomorphs: /s/, /z/, and /ɪz/. If this is true, it must mean that the native speaker of English has to memorize, for every English noun, the form of its plural. Look at the data below and try to determine whether there is a systematic reason for the choice of plural allomorph or not. You should begin by writing the words in phonemic transcription, so that the spelling will not be a distraction.

(a) beets, books, caps, trips, gnats, bets, slips, cats, hips
(b) beds, clubs, bags, fans, bells, crimes, furs, things, bugs
(c) judges, peaches, masses, fezzes, pieces, passes, crashes, garages, badges, lodges, causes

3. Using the symbols in this chapter, find a minimal pair to support the existence of each phoneme of English. Two examples have been given to start you off.

bad/bag   show the phonemes /d/ and /g/
bad/sad   show the phonemes /b/ and /s/

4. There is a Boston dialect of English which shows a pattern for the use of /r/ in word-final position that differs from the standard usage. The sentences below have been written to reflect the dialect; look at the data and state the rule.

(a) My car is right by the tree.
(b) That idear is ridiculous, Fred.
(c) My cah needs to be repaired.
(d) That ideah bothers me, Fred.
(e) The house was built neah the bridge.
(f) I was very near Ann when she screamed.
(g) This doah seems to be stuck.
(h) The door and the window both refuse to open.
(i) A cah that looks like that couldn't be Fred's.

5. People reading aloud from material they have not seen before sometimes produce sentences with very strange intonation patterns. For example, radio newscasters are frequently heard saying things like this:

(a) In nineteen-seventy-five the production of cars was significantly higher. In nineteen-*seventy*-six economists saw an entirely different tendency developing.
(b) When ecologists first observed this mountain peak, they saw fifty-three hawks. Last year, however, they counted only *twenty*-nine.

Can you identify the factor that makes the intonation in these examples seem so odd? How should the sentences be read to eliminate the problem?

6. Below is a list of the singular and plural forms of a set of verbs in Kumeyaay, a Native American language of California. (Data from Douglas Walker.) The letter *L* represents a voiceless lateral fricative. Examine the data and state the rule for pluralization of these verbs.

	Singular	*Plural*
(a)	Lyap	Lyaap
(b)	muL	muuL
(c)	čuupul	čuupuul
(d)	saaw	saw
(e)	šuupit	šuupiit
(f)	mewas	mewaas
(g)	wir	wiir

7. The rule for Kumeyaay plural formation illustrated in Exercise 6 is only one of a number of complex rules. Another is shown in the data below. State this rule.

	Singular	*Plural*
(a)	maa	maač
(b)	iimaa	iimaač
(c)	kwaa	kwaač

Now look at one more example. What essential fact does it tell you about this pluralization system?

   Singular: sii   *Plural:* sič

8. The set of forms below is written in phonetic transcription, somewhat simplified. Some of these forms could be English words, but others could not. Identify all members of the set which could not possibly be part of English.

   rıkt, mboyt, pınsz, sbayt, grʊ, strayč, pokb, gdan, blog, klup, ppıd, pıd, sk, drɛb, klen, ngop, mə

9. English has a number of negative prefixes, one only of which was discussed in this chapter. Use a dictionary to find at least three more. Then decide whether the following is a rule of English phonology and state the reason(s) for your decision:

   Any English negative prefix which ends in a consonant must undergo assimilation to make its final consonant agree in place of articulation with the first consonant following it.

10. In Exercise 2 you worked out a rule to account for the phonetic shape of the English regular plural morpheme spelled -es. Does this rule apply only with reference to the plural morpheme? Or does it apply more generally to the entire language? Look at the data below and decide which is the correct formulation of the rule.

   bases, basis, laces, crisis, vicious, vices, nooses, noises, lysis, majesty, wishes, gorgeous, gorges

11. You also found a rule to account for the phonetic difference between the plural morpheme of *backs* and that of *bags*. Examine the data below and determine whether this rule is a general fact about English phonology or restricted to the plural morpheme.

    laps, lapse, cops, copse, badge, batch, match, Madge, collapse, labs, astrolabes, soft, saved, depict, picked

12. Do you see any evidence of an *orthographic* rule of English in such pairs as laps/lapse, cops/copse, dens/dense?

13. You will now have identified two rules which are needed to account for the surface forms of regular English plurals. Use these two rules to work out the derivations of the three words below and determine whether the ordering of the rules is important. Assume that the underlying representation of the plural morpheme itself is /z/.

    beaches, badges, bushes

14. Just as the phonetic shape of the English plural varies according to rule, there are rules which account for the phonetic shape of the regular past tense marker spelled *-ed*. Look at the data below and determine the rules.

    tripped, rubbed, waited, rapped, nodded, looked, watched, judged, begged, kicked, knocked, sagged, breathed, recanted, yelled, learned, cried, played, nailed, pinched, blessed

15. Children enjoy using "secret languages" produced by systematic changes in their real language. Pig Latin is probably the most familiar example of such a secret language. Using the examples below and the cartoon on p. 101, write the necessary rules to convert an English word into its correct form in Pig Latin.

    (a) *tree* becomes *eetray*
    (b) *dog* becomes *ogday*
    (c) *mother* becomes *othermay*

16. As pointed out in this chapter, a natural class of sounds is one in which the members of the class have a number of common characteristics. The set of English voiceless stops is a natural class, as are the English back vowels. Using Table III, look at the lists of phonemes below and decide which could be termed a natural class for English. State your reasons in each case.

© THE WIZARD OF ID by permission of
Johnny Hart and Field Enterprises, Inc.

Note: The jailer in the cartoon has made one mistake. What is it?

   (a) /m/, /n/, /ŋ/
   (b) /b/, /d/, /g/, /θ/
   (c) /p/, /t/, /k/, /b/, /d/, /g/
   (d) /s/, /z/, /č/
   (e) /p/, /b/, /m/, /w/
   (f) /m/, /n/, /ŋ/, /l/, /r/, /w/, /y/, /h/

17. This problem is about a hypothetical language in which the verb tenses are formed by adding a suffix to the verb stem. A list of future forms is given below. For each one, decide what the verb stem must be. Then write any rule (or rules) that would be necessary to derive the past tense forms of the same verbs given in the second column.

Future Tense	Past Tense
patakan	patala
didan	dila
neritan	nerila
amapan	amala
derikan	derila
sobahan	sobala
badaasan	badala
forisan	forila
bataakan	batala
amiipan	amila

18. The following is an articulatory chart for the vowels of Spanish:

SPANISH VOWELS

	FRONT (unrounded)	CENTRAL (unrounded)	BACK (rounded)
High	i		u
Mid	e		o
Low		a	

Now prepare a distinctive feature matrix for the Spanish vowel phonemes like the one for English shown in Table V in this chapter. As in Table V, assume that both central vowels and back vowels are included in the feature [BACK].

SUGGESTED READINGS

ARTICLES

BOWEN, J., and R. STOCKWELL. 1955. "The Phonemic Interpretation of Semi-vowels in Spanish." *Language* 31:236–40.

CAIRNS, C. 1969. "Markedness, Neutralization, and Universal Redundancy Rules." *Language* 45:863–85.

CAMPBELL, L. 1974. "Phonological Features: Problems and Proposals." *Language* 50:52–65.

CHAFE, W. 1968. "The Ordering of Phonological Rules." *International Journal of American Linguistics* 34:115–36.

CHOMSKY, C. 1970. "Reading, Writing and Phonology." *Harvard Educational Review* 40:287–309.

CHOMSKY, N., and M. HALLE. 1965. "Some Controversial Questions in Phonological Theory." *Journal of Linguistics* 1:97–138.

FERGUSON, C. 1966. "Assumptions about Nasals: A Sample Study in Phonological Universals." In J. GREENBERG (ed.), *Universals of Language*. M.I.T. Press, Cambridge, Mass.

FLANAGAN, J. 1972. "The Synthesis of Speech." *Scientific American* 228:48–58.

FROMKIN, V. 1971. "The Nonanomalous Nature of Anomalous Utterances." *Language* 47:27–52.

———. 1973. "Slips of the Tongue." *Scientific American* 229:110–16.

GEORGE, I. 1970. "Nupe Tonology." *Studies in African Linguistics* 1:100–22.

GREENBERG, J. 1972. "Is the Vowel-Consonant Dichotomy Universal?" *Word* 18:73–81.

HALLE, M. 1954. "The Strategy of Phonemics." *Word* 10:197–209.

———. 1962. "Phonology in Generative Grammar." *Word* 18:54–72.

HARMS, R. 1973. "How Abstract Is Nupe?" *Language* 49:439–46.

HOARD, J. 1971. "Aspiration, Tenseness, and Syllabification in English." *Language* 47:133–40.

HOOPER, J. 1972. "The Syllable in Phonological Theory." *Language* 48:525–40.

HYMAN, L. 1970. "How Concrete Is Phonology?" *Language* 46:58–76.

KROHN, R. 1972. "Underlying Vowels in Modern English." *Glossa* 6:203–24.

LADEFOGED, P. 1964. "Some Possibilities in Speech Synthesis." *Language and Speech* 7:205–14.

LYONS, J. 1962. "Phonemic and Non-Phonemic Phonology: Some Typological Reflections." *International Journal of American Linguistics* 28:127–34.

PIKE, K. 1947. "Grammatical Prerequisites to Phonemic Analysis." *Word* 3:155–72.

READ, C. 1971. "Pre-school Children's Knowledge of English Phonology." *Harvard Educational Review* 41:1–34.

SCHANE, S. 1971. "The Phoneme Revisited." *Language* 47:503–21.

———. 1972. "Natural Rules in Phonology." In STOCKWELL and MACAULAY (eds.). *Linguistic Change and Generative Theory*. Indiana University Press, Bloomington.

 STANLEY, R. 1967. "Redundancy Rules in Phonology." *Language* 43:393–436.

BOOKS

DENES, P., and E. PINSON. 1973. *The Speech Chain*. Anchor Books, New York.

HYMAN, L. 1975. *Phonology: Theory and Analysis*. Holt, Rinehart and Winston, New York.

LADEFOGED, P. 1971. *Preliminaries to Linguistic Phonetics*. University of Chicago Press, Chicago.

MAKKAI, V. (ed.). 1972. *Phonological Theory: Evolution and Current Practice*. Holt, Rinehart and Winston, New York. (This is an anthology and contains many of the articles listed above.)

SCHANE, S. 1973. *Generative Phonology*. Prentice-Hall, Englewood Cliffs, N.J.

———, and B. BENDIXEN. 1978. *Workbook in Generative Phonology*. Prentice-Hall, Englewood Cliffs, N.J.

FIVE

Sociolinguistics

Up to this point the phenomena of language have been discussed primarily as abstract concepts. Although the semantics chapter touched briefly on the problems of analyzing real language, most of our discussion has centered on sets of constructed examples. We have paid little attention to such factors as the people who are speaking, the way their lives are influenced by their language, or how their language is in turn affected by their lives. This approach has been necessary in order to lay the basic foundations of terminology and concepts, in much the same way that it has been necessary to maintain artificial boundaries between phonology, syntax, and semantics. By now, however, it will have become apparent that you cannot really cut language up into uniform chunks and subject it to dissection in isolation. This approach is limited and arbitrary, and the time has come to move beyond it. Consider the following example:

> What I did today—Johnny, cut that out, would you?—I mean, have you noticed how every time you start to do something important just about every blasted thing imaginable happens? And some that aren't imaginable?

Anyway . . . where was I? Oh, yeah, I was going to tell you what I did this morning. Not that I *planned* it, you understand, this was strictly one of those days that just *falls* on you, you know what I mean? Well, anyhow, it was about eight . . . or maybe closer to eight-thirty, 'cause the milkman had already been here, and suddenly . . . .

It's humbling to consider that example, because it represents the way most of us talk. We may not like to think so, but except for occasions when we feel that we are somehow "performing" and therefore switch to hyper-correct speech, the paragraph above is typical real-life language.

Now consider the problem of the linguist who tries to base his or her study of language upon such actual samples. Can a theory be developed for such speech, with tidy rules and formal notations to bring some sort of order out of the apparent surface chaos?

In the early days of generative transformational linguistics this question was essentially ignored. Analysis of language was based almost exclusively upon individual example sentences (or lexical items) considered in isolation. Linguists were still doing field linguistics,[1] particularly if they specialized in as yet unwritten languages. But the vast majority of the sentences which students in linguistics were presented with for study were sentences con-structed for the occasion. The professional literature written by linguists followed the same pattern, and the very tricky question—"How does anyone know *when* to say *what?*"—was never raised.

Today linguists have begun to devote much more time to the study of the language of real people in the real world. This area of specialization is called *sociolinguistics*.

William Labov has said (1969) that "the social situation is the most powerful determinant of verbal behavior," and there is no reason to believe that his statement is an exaggeration. We need only consider the failure of American education—over the course of two hundred hard-working years—to produce a single homogeneous Standard American Spoken English.

SOME ESSENTIAL TERMS IN SOCIOLINGUISTICS

Every individual who speaks (or signs) a language does so in a way unique and different from that of anyone else. Even a single speaker is unlikely to produce two examples of the same utterance that are absolutely identical phonetically. The particular and idiosyncratic manner of speech of any

---

[1] Field linguistics is the study of a language directly from contact with a native speaker or speakers, rather than from a book or in a formal classroom situation.

individual is called his or her *idiolect*, and no two idiolects will ever be exactly the same in every respect.

However, when the idiolects of a given group of speakers are so alike that their own feeling is that they all "talk the same way" in a particular language, we can usually refer to their manner of speech as a *dialect*. Dialects, like idiolects, differ; and their differences can be systematically described in terms of the presence or absence of particular rules, or differences in the formulations of those rules. Later in this chapter we will discuss examples of specific characteristics that differentiate major dialects in the United States today. For now, what matters is to keep firmly in mind that everybody, without exception, speaks some dialect of some language. The popular conception of the term "dialect" as meaning "an odd or comical or substandard way of talking or writing" is not what the word means in linguistics.[2] For the linguist a dialect is simply the set of rules associated with the verbal behavior of a group of native speakers of a language.

When a number of different dialects have so much in common that their speakers all consider themselves to have a shared medium of speech, we define that set of dialects as a *language.*

It is not always easy to decide whether two dialects belong to a single language or not, or even if they should be treated as two separate units. Nor is it easy to determine exactly where the line between dialect and language should be drawn. These matters account for the varying opinions about the precise number of languages spoken in the world today. Estimates range from about three thousand to as many as six thousand separate languages, depending on how a given linguist makes the divisions. In general terms, if the speakers of two dialects can understand one another in ordinary conversation, we can say that their dialects constitute subdivisions of a single language. However, there are countries where this definition is not satisfactory—for example, mainland China, where many dialects are *not* mutually intelligible, and people from one part of the country may be completely unable to understand the speech of people from another. Nonetheless, where Chinese is concerned, the historical evidence, the common written language, and the literary tradition of centuries, make it possible to say that all these dialects are part of a single language.

Navajo and Apache, on the other hand, are ordinarily treated as two separate tongues, even though there is ample historical evidence that they share a common ancestor in the Athabaskan language family, and speakers of the two languages can sometimes communicate with one another in a rough fashion.

When a single speaker is truly fluent in more than one language, he or

---

[2] Some linguists use the term *variety* rather than *dialect*, in order to avoid this problem of negative connotations.

she is said to be *bilingual,* or (if more than two languages are involved) *multilingual.* Similarly, a speaker may be *bidialectal* or *multidialectal.* These terms, along with *bicultural* and *multicultural,* have been used so loosely in the past—particularly in education—that linguistics is now going through a painful process of establishing more precise definitions so that we may all know what we are talking about when we use them. The term *bilingual,* in particular, is in need of clarification.

Perhaps because we have only a single official language in the United States, the truly bilingual American speaker is rather unusual. True bilingualism means that the speaker uses both languages with equal competence, would not be judged "foreign" by native speakers of either language, and can switch from one to another without hesitation in any situation whatsoever. Typically this sort of ability is only to be found in speakers who have been constantly exposed to both languages from birth, in their own homes and neighborhoods.

When a speaker acquires a native language as a small child, and then in later life learns a second language, he may or may not become fluent in that language, and the degree of fluency achieved will vary with the circumstances and from speaker to speaker. In such cases, except with very young children, it is almost always true that even though the speaker may be able to use both languages with ease, one is dominant over the other, and some language behaviors will be more difficult for the speaker in one language than in the other.

The typical individual in the United States who has learned English as a child, and then taken two to six years of a second language in high school and/or college, is unlikely ever to achieve anything approaching true bilingualism unless he or she has a constant opportunity to use the second language in conversation with native speakers of that language.

Idiolects, dialects, and languages are all closely related concepts, and the three terms refer to the speech medium used by a given individual, usually in correlation with nationality, ethnic heritage, or the geographic location of the speaker during the period of language acquisition. The term *register* also refers to the mode of language used by a particular individual, but it differs slightly from the other terms. A *register* is a style of speech or writing which can be demonstrated to be firmly linked to a particular social role or situation. It is common, for example, for an urban seventh-grade student to have one speech style for use in the classroom, a second style for use in the home, and still a third style for use with his or her peer group on the city streets. The following sequences illustrate this difference in registers:

(1)   a. Goodbye, Mr. Martin.
       b. See ya later, Mom!
       c. Okay, man, I gotta split.

"NOW HERE'S A WORD THAT'S *GUARANTEED* TO MAKE EVERBODY STOP TALKIN' AND *LOOK* AT YOU."

DENNIS THE MENACE by Hank Ketcham,
© Field Newspaper Syndicate.

One of the most amazing things about the linguistic competence of speakers is their ability to move back and forth among languages, dialects, and registers with ease, as demanded by the social situation or their own inner necessities. This skill is called *code-switching*.[3] In the United States today, especially in academic and business situations, the ability to code-switch is clearly a survival skill.

In earlier chapters we have briefly referred to the difference between grammaticality and acceptability, as well as to the fact that neither can be an either/or matter. To determine whether a given sequence is grammatical

---

[3] This same term is often used in a restricted sense to describe language sequences in which lexical items from different languages are mixed within single sentences. Here the term is used in a much broader sense.

and/or acceptable we must know if that sequence is *appropriate* for the real-world situation in which it is used. Someone who is highly skilled at code-switching will also be highly skilled at determining appropriateness, since the choice of code ordinarily depends upon that factor. Consider the following example:

(2)   I ain't got no idea.

There are a number of English dialects in which (2) is fully grammatical in the sense that it is acceptable to all speakers of those dialects. Certainly, no matter what dialect of English you may speak, the sentence is completely meaningful. But if it used by a graduate student taking his or her oral examinations for a Ph.D. in British Literature, and is the student's response to a question such as "What is the major distinguishing characteristic of the metric patterns of the poetry of Tennyson?" it is utterly and overwhelmingly *inappropriate*. The student who persists in such responses will almost certainly fail the examination.

It is a real-life fact that students suffer if they lack the skill of code-switching between their native dialects and the Standard Academic English (especially Standard *Written* Academic English) required for term papers, examinations, essays, and the like. Although the media, especially television, have begun to make inroads into the traditional prejudices against differing *spoken* dialects, the resistance to any variety of written English except the Standard shows no sign of relaxing in the foreseeable future. Whether such relaxation would be an improvement or a disaster is one of the major issues in education in this country today. In the chapter on Applied Linguistics we will return to this question and discuss it in detail.

THE MULTILINGUAL NATION

The multilingual nation will always be beset with sociolinguistic problems. The severity of these problems will vary with such factors as the size of the country, its wealth, its technological sophistication, its educational situation, and whether one or more of the languages spoken within its borders is considered to have greater prestige than the others. As Robbins Burling says (1973):

> By our language we define the groups to which we belong. We define certain people as inside the group, and we leave others out. Language comes to be an accurate map of the sociological divisions of a society.

Switzerland, a small and relatively wealthy nation, seems to manage nicely with a population which has as its languages French, German, Italian, and

Romansch. In other countries, however, things do not go so smoothly. In recent years we have seen riots and bloodshed in various parts of the world over the question of which of two or more languages is to be used in both formal situations and in daily life. In Canada the strife in the French-speaking province of Quebec has been severe enough to interfere with that country's air transportation system; in South Africa there has been rioting against the enforced use of Afrikaans in the schools; in Belgium, Flemish militants have fought with mounted police over the issue of equal language rights for Flemish, claiming that Flemish speakers are suffering discrimination from French speakers in that country. In the United States, choice of language has not been a specific issue, but questions of bilingual education have been the subject of Supreme Court suits, and seem likely to be a source of major discord for many years to come. In addition, differences that are language-based are closely linked with many of our other socioeconomic problems.

Social problems based upon language typically arise in the following situations:

a. where a very large population (as in India) speaks such a variety of different languages that neighboring towns sometimes speak mutually incomprehensible languages or dialects;

b. where a dominant political and economic group (as in almost any colonial situation) attempts to impose its own language by force upon a native population;

c. where a particular language becomes a symbol of national pride and identity (as with the Gaelic language in Ireland);

d. where a powerful national or ethnic group gains economic control of some area, and it becomes desirable for the population originally living in that area to speak some approximation of the language of the dominating group, at least for business purposes.

There are a number of things that may happen in these and related situations. We will begin our discussion of possible outcomes with the basic concept of the *lingua franca*.

When the Crusaders went off to the Holy Land, they came from many different countries and spoke many different languages. In order to solve their communication problems they used as a common language the "French language," by which they meant Provençal, the speech of an area of southern France. From this came the term *lingua franca*, now used to identify the various kinds of languages that may be used when diverse linguistics groups must find a common medium of communication.

A lingua franca may be a natural language, that is, the native language spoken at some time by some group of people. Both Greek and Latin have served in this way in the past, and Swahili seems likely to do so in much of Africa today. However, this is not the most usual solution, since it isn't easy either to agree upon any one language for this purpose or to induce everyone involved to learn it rapidly enough.

It is more common for a lingua franca to be what is known as a *pidgin* language. The definitions and uses of the term *pidgin* vary in the literature; in this book, however, it will be defined as a mode of speech that is not anyone's native language, but which can be demonstrated to have developed from at least two such languages. Typically, a pidgin retains a large portion of the vocabulary and phonology of a language, but simplifies its morphology and syntax. Such things as grammatical gender distinctions, elaborate compound verb tenses, and complicated systems of pronouns are frequently eliminated in pidginization.

When people speaking a pidgin are for one reason or another isolated from other language communities, it may happen that a new generation will be born which acquires no other language except the pidgin. A language like this, which has been a pidgin but has become a native language, is called a *creole*. Obviously, the exact point at which a pidgin stops being a pidgin and becomes a creole may be difficult to determine.

Métis is a language spoken in northern Canada which appears to be the result of extensive contact between French and the Cree Indian language. It is difficult to say whether Métis is a pidgin or a creole, but it offers some excellent examples of the results of such language contact.[4]

French has an impressive array of interrogative and relative pronouns, among which are *qui, que, quoi*, and a host of others. These pronouns take part in a complicated system of grammatical distinctions. The speakers of Métis have bypassed most of this complexity by choosing the single French pronoun *quoi*, which never varies its form. The following sentences show the standard French and the equivalent sequence in Métis.

(3) French: Vous voyez *ce que* je veux dire.
     Métis: Vous voyez *quoi*   je veux dire.
              'You see *what* I mean.'

(4) French: *Qu'est-ce que* c'est?
     Métis: *Quoi*   c'est?
              '*What* is it?'

In these sentences Métis has simplified the syntax of French, while at the same time keeping a vocabulary item from the French lexicon.

---

[4] For the material on Métis I am indebted to Robert Papen.

Another Métis example shows a process which is not a matter of syntactic simplification, but rather of the imposition of Cree syntax upon French lexical items. Cree has a mechanism for indicating the possessive which produces expressions translatable literally as "John-his-hat" or "Mary-her-car." The effect of the interaction of this pattern and the French vocabulary in Métis is shown in (5).

(5) French: *les neveux de Maman*
the nephews of mama

Métis: *Maman ses neveux*
mama her nephews

Pidgins will disappear quickly if the need for their existence does, since they are always only a supplement to the speaker's native language, and frequently a hated one. Creoles, on the other hand, may endure long after the need for a lingua franca is past, particularly if the native speakers are isolated in some way from the rest of the population. This is what has happened with the English-based creole called Gullah, which is spoken by the population living on the Sea Islands off the coast of South Carolina. The natural isolation imposed by island living, as well as that imposed on minority groups in general, has prevented Gullah from dying out.

Standard English maintains a gender distinction for the third person singular personal pronouns. In Gullah this distinction has disappeared, leaving behind only the forms *him*, *im*, and *e*—all derived from the English masculine forms. In addition, although the first person pronouns in Gullah remain *I*, *me*, *my*, *we*, the pronoun *us* does not occur. Finally, the Gullah form for *you*, both singular and plural, is the word *un*, which does not exist at all in English.

People have always agreed that it would be useful, given all the difficulties of international and intranational communication, to have one language that *everybody* spoke. This language would serve as a lingua franca for the world, and in the abstract there seems to be no dispute about its desirability.

In practical terms, however, the consensus disappears when it comes to the point of actually agreeing upon such a language. The problem is of course *which* language? Human egos being what they are, the immediate response is "*my* language," whatever that language may be.

One frequently suggested way of getting around this problem (which is not likely to go away by itself) is the so-called "international auxiliary language," which would not be anyone's native language but would be constructed for the express purpose of serving as a lingua franca. A number of such artificial languages have been proposed, the best-known being Esperanto, a language devised by Ludwig Zamenhof.

Estimates of the number of Esperanto speakers today range from a minimum of several hundred thousand on up. There is an Esperanto head-quarters—the Universal Esperanto Association in Rotterdam—with member associations in more than one hundred countries. There are more than thirty thousand books available in Esperanto, and the language now has a large original literature as well as the expected translations. In a number of countries (for example, Italy, Austria, and the Netherlands), Esperanto is taught in the schools as a foreign language on a basis similar to that of any other foreign language. Vatican Radio now transmits a weekly program in Esperanto over six separate frequencies, three in Europe and three to Africa. Esperanto has been extremely popular in Japan and China, and even in the United States there is a large and active Esperanto association which holds frequent conventions. After only two hours of instruction, adults begin to use Esperanto with amazing ease; and children who have had half a dozen Esperanto lessons can begin corresponding with children all over the world through the international correspondence exchange called *Granoj en Vento.*

Given all these seeming advantages, what is keeping the people of the world from unanimously adopting Esperanto as an international language? Look at the following brief selection from *El Afriko*, an Esperanto children's book:

(6)   Preskaŭ 40 milionoj da homoj loĝas en la baseno de la rivero Nilo. Dum miloj de jaroj, la bonstato de tiuj egiptoj kaj sudanoj dependis de la fluo de la Nilo. Dum sezonoj, kiam la pluvofalo en la sudaj montoj estis granda, la "nilanoj" prosperis.

(Almost 40 million people live in the basin of the river Nile. For thousands of years, the well-being of every Egyptian and Sudanese has depended on the flow of the Nile. During seasons when the rainfall in the southern mountains was heavy, the "people of the Nile" prospered.)

The source of the barrier to Esperanto should be immediately obvious. Although it is proposed as an international language, it is based entirely upon the Indo-European languages. Its vocabulary is almost transparent if you can read French or German or Spanish or English, or even Russian—all these languages being represented among the Esperanto lexical items. But what if you are a native speaker of Samoan or Cherokee or Swahili or Thai? For you, Esperanto will still be the foreign language of a dominant social and political group.

Just what the fate of Esperanto will be is not easily determined at this point. It is seeing a slow but steady gain in popularity, and appears to be gaining in prestige to some extent. The January/February 1977 newsletter of the Esperanto League for North America reported that at the Modern

Language Association's 1978 meeting, the two-hour session on Inter-linguistics would be conducted one hour in English and one hour in Esperanto.

It is interesting to note that there are now a number of people who spoke Esperanto as their *first* language, rather than as an auxiliary tongue. This has happened in cases where the parents spoke different languages and the only shared language in the home was Esperanto. Such speakers are called *denaska* (from-birth) Esperantists. This development may cause the sociolinguists to turn their attention to Esperanto, since it raises many new questions. For example, if Esperanto can serve as a native language, has it become a kind of creole? And what happens when speakers of many different languages, with radically differing native presuppositions and rules for appropriateness (not to mention different phonologies), all gather at a lengthy conference and speak only Esperanto? What is the impact of Esperanto, or any other artificial language, in a country where it is widely used?

Two clear principles arise from the broad range of problems (and attempted solutions) related to dialect and language diversity throughout the world. First, it is clear that the ethnic identity of an individual, and his or her personal self-image, is tightly bound to the speech medium which is used; to ask people to give up their native language is to ask them to surrender a part of their heritage and of their identity as a people. (That this should lead to discord ought not to surprise anyone.) For this reason, attempts to legislate the use of language usually fail in the long run, and where they succeed at all are ordinarily confined to highly restricted environments such as universities, courtrooms, and conference halls. Secondly, before any group of people can be persuaded to learn a second language or dialect in addition to their native one, and to do so in a manner that will be useful for something more than just passing an end-of-term examination, they must see the second speech medium as one that has prestige and status when it is used. Otherwise, all such efforts will be futile, no matter how much money and expertise are placed behind them.

DIALECT DIVERSITY IN THE UNITED STATES

Within the space of this text it would be impossible to discuss a representative selection of the dialects of English spoken in the United States today, even if the discussion were confined to those dialects characteristic of relatively large numbers of speakers. There are Black dialects, Chicano and other Latino dialects, Asian-American dialects differing as widely as the languages upon which they are based, a similar span of American Indian dialects, and

Polynesian dialects. There is a broad variety of Anglo dialects; consider Brooklyn, New Orleans, Boston, and Nashville, for example. In addition, within these dialects there are sub-dialects. The Chicano dialect of New Mexico is not the same as the Chicano dialect of East Los Angeles, and both differ from the Cuban-based dialect of Miami Latinos and the Puerto Rican dialect of New York City. In all this multitude of types of English, none of which shows any disposition to follow the melting-pot prescription and blend into a Standard Spoken American, it is hard to know where to begin such a discussion.

Rather than attempt the impossible, we will examine briefly three major dialects with which the author is personally familiar: Urban Black English, Southern California Chicano English, and Ozark English. In the suggested readings for this chapter you will find a number of sources for more detailed analyses on a wider range of dialects.

Urban Black English

In the phonology chapter we mentioned a rule of English which states that no English word is allowed to end with a stop followed by a nasal. This rule accounts for the "silent *g*" in words such as *sign, malign, benign, resign.* Urban Black English (UBE) has this rule in common with the Standard. In addition, it has a rule of the same type, not found in SE:

(7)   *No word is allowed to end in a fricative followed by an alveolar stop.*

Just as the SE rule results in "silent letters" in surface forms of words, so will the rule in (7). For example, any word ending in the fricative /s/ followed by /t/ or /d/ will now have a "silent" final letter. Look at the examples in (8).

(8)	test	will become	[tɛs]
	best		[bɛs]
	last		[læs]
	past		[pæs]
	passed		[pæs]

This rule will mean that the number of homophonous pairs (words which are spelled differently but sound alike, such as *reed* and *read*) will be much larger in UBE. Notice that the phonetic sequences on the right in (8) are homophonous with the words listed in (9).

(9)   Tess, Bess, lass, pass, pass

The set *pass, past, passed* will constitute a homophonous triplet.

It is easily demonstrated that, like the *g* in *sign*, the final *t* or *d* sounds are really present in the deep structure of these words. The speaker of UBE will say *testing* or *tested*, where the /t/ is followed by a vowel, with a pronounced /t/, just as all English speakers say *signature* with a pronounced /g/. The /t/ and /d/ sounds are only deleted when they occur in the environment specified by the rule in (7).

It should be pointed out that the deletion of the final consonant sound by this rule can have consequences which go beyond a mere pronunciation difference. Since the marker of the simple past tense in English is regularly /t/ or /d/, application of the rule will very often result in the deletion of the past tense marker on the verb. This may result in speakers of UBE writing sentences like "John pass the exam yesterday" in which the *-ed* marker is absent in the written sequence as the /t/ would be in the corresponding spoken one. Since the "pastness" of the verb is expressed by the word *yesterday* this does not interfere with the meaning of the sentence, but it will be treated as an error.

There are also a number of syntactic differences between SE and UBE. Exercise 8 of the syntax chapter raised the following as a theoretical question: What is the source of the verb *be* which appears in English sentences whose predicates do not contain a constituent that can be marked for tense? Let's assume, for the purposes of the discussion below, that Standard English has a rule of *Be*-Insertion as stated in (10).

(10) *Whenever the predicate of a sentence is not a true verb, insert a form of be as the first element of that predicate.*

This rule would ensure that a deep structure such as #John in the kitchen#, and having past tense indicated as part of the deep structure meaning—in the form of a feature on the predicate, for example—would appear as the surface structure "John was in the kitchen."

It happens that this rule is not obligatory in UBE, so that the sentences of (11) are all fully grammatical in that dialect.

(11) a. She a professor at the university for six years now.
      b. My uncle in San Diego all winter long.
      c. Harry a lot taller than Tom now.
      d. The meeting at seven o'clock sharp next Tuesday.

When this pattern is transferred to written English, it again results in sentences that are considered grammatically incorrect. But the situation is even more complicated than it appears at first glance. Not only does UBE differ from SE in not having *Be*-Insertion as an obligatory rule, it also has a totally different rule of *Be*-Insertion which is used to express a difference of aspect.

Unlike the SE rule, this rule inserts only the word *be* without changing its form either for tense or to agree with the subject of the sentence in person or number. That is, it will always insert *be*, never *am*, *is*, *was*, or *were*.

If, in SE, you want to indicate that a particular action or state is a habitual one, you must add something to your sentence to convey that information, as in (12).

(12) a. Some people are always complaining.
     b. We always have hamburgers on Friday.
     c. Every time I see Martha, she's busy.

The same additional constituents may appear in UBE if the speaker wishes to include them, but the information on habitual aspect can be conveyed by *be* alone. Look at (13).

(13) STANDARD ENGLISH
     a. My brother is always busy.
     b. We spend every Tuesday afternoon in Philadelphia.
     URBAN BLACK ENGLISH
     a. My brother be busy.
     b. Tuesday afternoons we be in Philadelphia.

The UBE sentences are fully equivalent to the SE ones, and the consequences for communication are rarely of any great importance. As with examples of ambiguity, the context or the real-world situation takes care of any potential problem of this kind. The social consequences for the student or employee, however, can be very serious, since both the absence of the Standard obligatory rule and the use of the non-Standard one will be viewed as errors of grammar. The reaction to sentences such as "He busy" and "He be busy" is predictable for Standard speakers; the nonstandard forms are stigmatized. The fact that the two differences involved both relate to the use of *be* only multiplies the possibilities for misinterpretation and confusion, especially in academic situations.

Southern California Chicano English

Chicano speakers, unlike speakers of Urban Black English, are usually partly bilingual as well as bidialectal, and in many cases Spanish is their dominant language even when their English is extremely fluent. This means (among other things) that they may apply the phonological rules of Spanish to their pronunciation of English lexical items. You will recall from the phonology chapter that English has twelve separate vowel phonemes, while Spanish has only the five shown in Table I.

Table I THE VOWEL PHONEMES
OF SPANISH

	FRONT	CENTRAL	BACK
High	i		u
Mid	e		o
Low		a	

In addition, none of the four front/back vowels of Spanish has the /y/ or /w/ off-glide that follows its closest equivalent in English.

These major differences in vowel phonemes bring about a correspondingly major difference in the pronunciation of English in the two dialects being compared. We will consider only one of these effects—the fact that the Chicano speaker will ordinarily use the Spanish phoneme /i/ to pronounce both the English phoneme /i/ and /ɪ/, leading to a set of homophonous forms like those shown in (13).

(13)　ship　　will be pronounced like　　sheep
　　　slip　　　　　　　　　　　　　　sleep
　　　bid　　　　　　　　　　　　　　bead
　　　lip　　　　　　　　　　　　　　leap
　　　dip　　　　　　　　　　　　　　deep

This means that a single sound sequence like *ship* is, technically speaking, ambiguous in this Chicano dialect, since it could mean either *ship* or *sheep*. In real life terms, this kind of ambiguity occurs as rarely as any other. You are unlikely ever to encounter a single real sentence in which you do not know whether the person you are speaking with is talking to you about ships or sheep.

The transformational rules of Spanish and English are not identical, of course. Since two different languages are involved, this typically means that the Chicano speaker has a non-Standard dialect in both Spanish and English. We will not consider the deviations from the hypothetical Standard Spanish here.

In Spanish a negative sentence will ordinarily have the Spanish word *no* before the verb, no matter how many other negatives appear later in the sentence. When this syntactic pattern is carried over into English, the result is sentences like those in (14).

(14)　a. I no want nothing.
　　　b. We no buy no more groceries at that store.

These sentences not only violate the traditional English rule against "double negatives"; they also fail to apply the English rule of Negative Placement which moves the basic negative marker of the English sentence to a position after the first auxiliary. Furthermore, the sentences do not contain the auxiliary *do*, which would be present in any SE negative sentence which contained no other auxiliary. When all these differences appear in a single sentence, the resulting sequence sounds very "foreign" indeed to the speaker of Standard English.

The formation of yes/no questions is also different in Spanish and English, leading to a pattern in Chicano English which is both syntactically and semantically different from the hypothetical Standard English. In Spanish, an ordinary declarative sentence pronounced with a rising intonation is a yes/no question. Unlike English, no movement rule or other alteration is obligatory in the sentence. Thus, the Chicano speaker frequently uses sentences like (15) as English yes/no questions.

(15)   The coffee is ready?

Although (15) *is* an English question, it is not a question for which just *yes* or *no* is appropriate as an answer. It is a special type of question used in one of two situations: when you can hardly believe what you just heard someone say, and you are asking for confirmation; and when you didn't hear or understand what was said and you are asking for a repetition of the sequence. (This second situation is usually referred to as an "echo" question.) Thus, the situations described in (16) show appropriate uses of (15) as an English question.

(16)   a.   You're backpacking at an altitude at which it takes water at least twenty minutes to boil. You have only been in camp for five minutes. Your backpacking companion disappears behind your tent for a few seconds and then emerges saying, "The coffee is ready." Your proper response is an astonished "The coffee is ready?"

   b.   You live right on a freeway and with your windows open, it's very noisy. Your companion calls out to you from the kitchen something that sounds vaguely like a statement about coffee. You can't really hear and aren't positive what was said, but you *think* it was that the coffee is ready. Since you don't want to leave the work you are doing for nothing, you repeat (echo) "The coffee is ready?"

Because Chicano speakers do from time to time hear non-Chicanos use these interrogative forms, since Spanish does allow the formation of yes/no questions in this way, and because context ordinarily makes it clear that a yes/no question is intended, it isn't surprising that this particular dialect difference has become systematic.

It is interesting, and typical of the interactions of speakers in multi-lingual areas, that the Chicano pattern now appears to be influencing the non-Chicano speakers of Southern California. Many of these speakers, especially the younger ones, are beginning to adopt this pattern for ordinary yes/no question formation and are surprised to learn that it is not part of Standard English.

Ozark English

The Ozark dialect (often referred to as Midland English, and closely related to Appalachian English) is spoken throughout Kentucky, Tennessee, Arkansas, parts of Oklahoma, and much of Missouri. In addition, there are pockets of this dialect in the Southwest in areas where people settled after heading out of the Dust Bowl during the early 1900's. In Ozark English the three vowel phonemes /ɪ/, /æ/, and /e/ have merged before the nasal /ŋ/, all three being pronounced as /e/. Some examples of the effect of this merger on pronunciation in Ozark are shown in (17).

(17) pink   is pronounced   [peŋk]
      things   [θeŋgz]
      spank   [speŋk]
      bank   [beŋk]

This merging of vowels, unlike the phonological rules described above for Urban Black English, does not create large numbers of homophonous pairs. Joseph Foster (1977) has pointed out, however, that it does have a minor grammatical consequence for verbs such as *sing* and *ring*. Look at (18).

(18) STANDARD ENGLISH
      a. I walk, I walked, I have walked.
      b. I sing, I sang, I have sung.
      OZARK
      a. I walk, I walked, I have walked.
      b. I sing, I sung, I have sung.

Notice that the past participle of the verb is clearly distinguished in both SE and Ozark by the presence of *have* immediately before it. And in SE the simple present and simple past forms of *sing* are distinguished from one another by the different vowels /ɪ/ and /æ/. In Ozark, on the other hand, because of the vowel merger, the two forms *I sing* and *I sang* would be pronounced exactly alike. Many English verbs have a paradigm in which the simple past and the past participle are identical, but both are different from the simple present; Ozark has adopted this pattern for verbs of the *sing* type, as shown in (19).

(19)   a. I think, I thought, I have thought
      b. I work, I worked, I have worked
      c. I sing, I sung, I have sung

Example (19c) is of course considered an error of grammar in Standard English.

There are many differences between the syntax of Ozark English and that of the standard dialect. For example, you will remember the rule of Question Formation that was discussed in the syntax chapter of this text. This rule, which moves the first auxiliary to the left of the subject NP, is applied in SE only when the question is *not* embedded in another sentence. For example:

(20)   a.   Will the train leave on time?
      b.   I wonder if the train will leave on time.
      c.   *I wonder if will the train leave on time.

Ozark allows the rule of Question Formation to apply to *all* questions, embedded or not; in addition, the *if* that begins the embedded question is deleted. The Ozark equivalent of the sentences of (20) is shown in (21).

(21)   a. Will the train leave on time?
      b. I wonder will the train leave on time.

Finally, we will examine a semantic difference which is found in the Ozark dialect in a much stronger form than in the standard.

English has two forms of the passive, one called the *Be*-Passive and the other the *Get*-Passive; examples are shown in (22).

(22)   a. He was run over by a truck.
      b. He got run over by a truck.

The difference between these two forms was at one time considered to be only a matter of style, with the *Get*-Passive looked upon as an informal version of the *Be*-Passive. Research in the past few years has made it clear, however, that even in SE there are pairs of sentences where the difference is much more than a stylistic matter. For example:

(23) a. Eileen was arrested on purpose.
      b. Eileen got arrested on purpose.

For most speakers the *on purpose* in (23a) refers to those doing the arresting, while in (23b) it refers to Eileen. The two sentences can be roughly paraphrased as in (24).

(24) a. Somebody arrested Eileen on purpose.
      b. Eileen deliberately went out and got herself arrested.

In Ozark English this distinction goes much farther and is maintained even in sentences with no obvious additions such as *on purpose* or *deliberately*. For example, look at the pair of sentences in (25).

(25) a. I was kept in after school.
      b. I got kept in after school.

Sentence (25a) means that the child did nothing wrong and has been punished unfairly. In example (25b) the child is admitting that the punishment was justified. Example (25a) is therefore a complaint, while (25b) is a confession; the difference is substantial. In Ozark the following pair (and others like it) is always synonymous unless real world facts would make synonymy impossible.

(26) a. I got arrested.
      b. I got myself arrested.

It should be pointed out that (26) does not necessarily mean that the speaker deliberately went looking to be arrested. It may mean that it was carelessness or bad luck or just being in the wrong place at the wrong time. The speaker is, however, accepting responsibility for what happened, even if indirectly.

METHODS FOR SOCIOLINGUISTIC INVESTIGATION

Since a major interest of sociolinguists is real speech in natural social contexts, the methods they use to study such speech are plagued by potential problems. Obviously, if someone knows that his or her speech is the subject of investigation by a linguist, it is hard for that person to speak naturally. On the other hand, it is difficult for the linguist to carry out a study under scientific conditions without informing the subjects that it is going on, even when there may be no ethical considerations involved.

William Labov in 1962 devised an ingenious way out of this dilemma, with extremely interesting results. He wanted to investigate the use of /r/ after vowels by New York City speakers of English. Numerous investigations of this phenomenon had indicated that the presence of post-vocalic /r/ was considered a mark of linguistic prestige in New York.

To check this hypothesis, Labov conducted a study in three New York department stores: S. Klein's (lower-priced merchandise), Macy's (average), and Saks Fifth Avenue (high-priced). The prestige ranking of the stores themselves was already well established. Labov's hypothesis was that the lower the prestige rank of the store, the more speech a linguist would find in which post-vocalic /r/ was absent.

The technique used was for the sociolinguist to assume the role of a customer and approach a salesperson with the question "Excuse me, where are the women's shoes?" The answer would be "Fourth floor." The linguist would then say "Excuse me?" as if there had been a problem of understanding, and the usual response would be a more careful and emphatic "Fourth floor." (The question used *on* the fourth floor was "Excuse me, what floor is this?").

Labov (1972) points out that:

> As far as the informant[5] was concerned, the exchange was a normal salesman–customer interaction, almost below the level of conscious attention, in which relations of the speakers were so casual and anonymous that they may hardly have been said to have met. This tenuous relationship was the minimum intrusion upon the behavior of the subject; language and the use of language never appeared at all. . . . From the point of view of the interviewer, the exchange was a systematic elicitation of the exact forms required, in the desired context, the desired order, and with the desired contrast of style.

Not only did the results of the study show that the absence of post-vocalic /r/ was greater at Macy's than at Saks, and greatest of all at S. Klein's, Labov also discovered that the language behavior varied from floor to floor as well. Thus, use of post-vocalic /r/ was significantly greater on the luxurious upper floors of Saks than on the ground floor.

---

[5] Until recently the word *informant* was used by linguists to refer to an individual providing the linguistic investigator with examples of language. Today the word has taken on a meaning synonymous with *informer*. To avoid the unsavory connotations of *informant*, therefore, most linguists now use the term *consultant*.

Studies like this one are very different from the classic interviewer-with-a-tape-recorder setting of the traditional linguistic investigation. They offer strong support for the concept of the *variable rule*: that is, the idea that a speaker's use of a given rule is not an either/or matter, but varies systematically with the setting in which the speech occurs. The salesperson on Saks's fourth floor who always pronounces /r/ after vowels there may show much less frequency for the same characteristic at home or when shopping on S. Klein's budget floor, even though natural speech is being used on both occasions. We cannot therefore say that this speaker does or does not "have" the rule in question in his grammar—it depends.

The data from the Labov study is clearly far more reliable than any that could be obtained by asking subjects to read aloud a list of phrases such as *fourth floor* or *park the car* in a laboratory setting. Natural speech can rarely be obtained under such unnatural conditions.

We have now looked at a few brief examples of some characteristic differences among dialects found in contemporary American speech. Because these differences have educational and socioeconomic repercussions completely out of proportion to their linguistic significance, it is extremely important that they be carefully analyzed and described, and that the descriptions be made available to teachers, employers, members of the various service and health professions, and so on.

Unfortunately this cannot be done quickly. It is a long and difficult process to work out the systematic differences between dialects, and it requires both skill and patience to make the description of such differences either interesting or clear to the reader who is not a linguist. To make a serious problem even worse, the only way to be certain that such descriptions are really accurate is for them to be prepared by *native speakers* of the dialects in question, who have native intuitions about the sequences of language they are discussing.

At the present time the trained linguists who can do this sort of work and who are also native speakers of nonstandard dialects are in very short supply. This is one of the educational and socioeconomic effects mentioned above, making the situation both self-perpetuating and circular. Until we see Ph.D.'s in linguistics coming in substantial numbers from the ethnic groups which speak Urban Black English, Chicano English, Ozark English, and all the rest, there will continue to be a shortage of adequate descriptive and explanatory materials on nonstandard dialects.

It should be clear from the preceding section that all too frequently the very language differences that characterize the nonstandard dialects are responsible for keeping their speakers out of the graduate schools. This is a major problem of sociolinguistics in the United States, and one for which there do not appear to be any easy solutions.

1. In 1975, during the period of the Vietnamese refugees' arrival in this country, the *Los Angeles Times* published an Interlandi cartoon showing a freeway scene with a large sign beside the road. The sign read as follows:

WELCOME TO
CALIFORNIA
SE HABLA VIETNAMESE

Can you explain the significance of the cartoon?

2. For Ozark English speakers who have the strong semantic difference between the *Be*-Passive and the *Get*-Passive, the following sentences present a problem:

(a) The cheese got eaten during the night.
(b) The tree got blown down.
(c) My purse got stolen on the train.

Speakers are very unlikely to use such sentences, and will instead use forms like those shown below. (They would use the *Be*-Passive only in very formal situations.)

(a) Something ate the cheese during the night.
(b) Something blew the tree down.
(c) Somebody stole my purse on the train.

Explain why the second set of sentences would be preferred to the first in this dialect.

3. In many languages there are special forms used to make absolutely clear the degree to which participants in a conversation are on terms of different or equal status. A number of languages have more than one form for the word "you" (as English once had *you* and *thou*) in order to assist in this process. Titles such as *sir* and *Miss*, or special terms called *honorifics*, are also involved here. Keeping all this in mind, answer the following questions:

(a) Does the lack of a pair of different "you" forms in English make it difficult to determine the relative social status of speakers in conversation?
(b) What other linguistic devices are there in English which can be used to convey the same kind of information once conveyed by *you* and *thou*?

(c) What is the effect of having only a single *you* form with regard to *commands* in English? If this causes problems, can you describe some solutions?

(d) Do the following sequences fit into the problem we are discussing, and if so, how?

$$\text{Hey, there,} \begin{Bmatrix} \text{kid} \\ \text{lady} \\ \text{boy} \\ \text{you} \\ \text{Miss} \end{Bmatrix} \text{—where do you think you're going?}$$

(e) Would the following sentence be acceptable to speakers of English? (Explain your answer.)

Hey, there, Sir—where do you think you're going?

4. Certain words and expressions can be considered as "trigger" words, in the sense that they evoke an emotional reaction that may be completely out of proportion. When such words are obvious insults, ethnic labels, or obscenities, the reason for the reaction is easily understood. However, it is not so simple to explain a sharp reaction to the word *intellectual* or *housewife*. Can you clarify this? Are there any words which "trigger" you personally, but do not appear to affect English speakers in general as they affect you? Give examples.

5. In the various media, differing registers can be noted. For example, the speech of an announcer on a radio station playing only classical music is clearly different from that of a disc jockey playing rock records, and both appear to be using a different mode of speech behavior from that of the television anchorman. The sports announcer has yet a different register. Choose one media speaker for this exercise and observe his or her language behavior carefully over a period of time sufficient to allow you to answer the following questions:

(a) Is there a specific register associated with this person's speech?

(b) What characteristics can you list as part of the description of the register? (If you have chosen a television speaker, consider also nonverbal behavior such as gestures, facial expressions, etc., in addition to speech.)

(c) Do the characteristics of the register appear to be primarily matters of vocabulary, or do they involve other areas such as intonation, syntax, pronunciation, and so on? Cite specific examples.

6. The following data illustrates another area in which the syntax of Urban Black English differs systematically from that of Standard English. Consider the data and state the difference.

SE: John is in the kitchen.   UBE: John in the kitchen.
      John's in the kitchen.
      I know John is here.   I know John here.
      I know John's here.
      That is John's hat.   That John's hat.
      That's John's hat.
      Bill knows where John is.   Bill knows where John is.
      *Bill knows where John's.   *Bill knows where John.
      I'm going if John is.   I'm going if John is.
      *I'm going if John's.   *I'm going if John.

7. Rules of appropriateness often come into play in the United States when strangers share an elevator ride. Propose some informal rules for language behavior (verbal and nonverbal) in the following situations:

(a) Two adult males, of the same ethnic group and dressed in business suits, ride seven floors together.

(b) Situation (a), plus one elderly male in overalls and a work shirt.

(c) Situation (a) plus four teenagers of mixed sexes.

(d) Situation (c) plus two elderly women dressed rather formally, as if for an expensive lunch.

(e) Situation (d)—but reduce the number of women to one.

(f) One adult male and a seven-year-old boy.

(g) Two adult females and that same seven-year-old boy.

Remember that all these individuals must be strangers to one another. After looking over all your rules, can you propose any tentative generalizations about appropriate language behavior under these conditions?

8. A common situation in which the phenomenon of register difference becomes very apparent in adults is in the doctor/patient relationship. (This is especially true if the doctor and the patient are of different sexes.) Consider your own language behavior, as well as the doctor's, in your usual visit to his or her office, and answer the following questions:

(a) Do you talk to the doctor any differently in the consulting or examination room than you would if the meeting had taken place at a cocktail party?

(b) Does the doctor seem to have an "office register" that differs from the way he or she would talk to you if you were (a) the office nurse; (b) a person selling medical supplies?

(c) Is there a difference between the way the doctor talks to you (or you to the doctor) in the preliminary conversation in the office, as compared with your conversation in the examining room?

HERMAN

©1976 Universal Press Syndicate

"Who's going to have their injection?"

(d) If you see a doctor of the opposite sex, do you use a "patient" register in speaking to him (or her)? Is it different from your manner of speaking to other men (or women)? List specific differences and explain them.

9. Decide what ethnic group you belong to. (For this exercise, and for all practical purposes, *everybody* belongs to some ethnic group, just as everybody speaks some dialect.) Pay close attention to your speech over the course of one week, as compared to the speech of the instructor of your linguistics course. State any systematic dialect differences that you notice. (If your dialect happens to be the same as your instructor's, choose someone else for comparison.)

10. Make a collection of at least 30 insults—preferably from actual observation of real speech. For each one, answer the following questions:

(a) Why is the item an insult?

(b) Is it always an insult, or is it insulting only in specific contexts?

(c) How would you classify the insult on a scale of Mild, Annoying, Disgusting, Unbearable?

(d) Do any socioeconomic factors enter into your classification?

(e) What information about the culture of the speaker can be gained from a consideration of the insult?

Now group your insults into the four categories: Mild, Annoying, Disgusting, Unbearable, defining your categories and giving your reasons for putting each item into a particular class. Finally, select ten of your items and rewrite each in the styles or registers of the other three categories. For example, if you classified one as Unbearable, rewrite it to be Mild, Annoying, and Disgusting.

11. In the examples below, try to identify the speakers by age, sex, and/or profession.

(a) Well! Now that we've put on our pretty gown, why don't we comb our hair?

(b) Be very careful not to color outside the lines.

(c) It is with deep regret that I come before you today to make this announcement.

(d) I can understand when I read the book, but the minute you start talking I lose the whole thing.

(e) I wonder if I might share my perceptions with you for a moment.

(f) There is no excuse whatsoever for your disgusting attitude.

(g) Isn't she a cute little thing?

(h) When I get here I expect to find my dinner on the table, and I don't expect to have to listen to any complaints or excuses. Is that clear?

(i) Why *can't* I borrow the car? I'm not going to wear it out, you know.

(j) The alleged suspect was reportedly apprehended immediately after the incident.

Compare your answers with those of others in your class. Does the decision as to the sex of the speakers in the examples seem related in any way to the sex of the student doing the exercise?

12. In medical books, magazines, and articles on medicine in the professional journals, the patient is ordinarily referred to as *he* or one of the other masculine pronouns. However, in discussions of psychosomatic illness or emotionally-induced illness, one frequently finds sentences like: "The patient should be reassured that her symptoms do not reflect any underlying organic disease." What sociolinguistic fact about American culture does this suggest?

SUGGESTED READINGS

ARTICLES AND EXCERPTS

BASSO, K. 1970. "To Give Up on Words: Silence in the Western Apache Culture." *Southwestern Journal of Anthropology* 26:213–30.

BRIGHT, J., and W. BRIGHT. 1965. "Semantic Structures in Northwestern California and the Sapir-Whorf Hypothesis." *American Anthropologist* 67:249–58.

*CASSELL, E. et al. 1976. "A Preliminary Model for the Examination of the Doctor-Patient Communication." *Language Sciences* 43:10–13.

DILLARD, J. 1974. "Lay My Isogloss Bundle Down: The Contribution of Black English to American Dialectology." *Linguistics* 45:5–14.

ELGIN, S. 1972. "The Crossover Constraint and Ozark English." In J. KIMBALL (ed.). *Syntax and Semantics*, Vol. I, pp. 265–75. Academic Press, New York.

FASOLD, R. 1970. "Two Models of Socially Significant Linguistic Variation." *Language* 46:551–63.

FISHMAN, J. 1968. "Sociolinguistic Perspective on the Study of Bilingualism." *Linguistics* 39:21–49.

FOSTER, J. 1977. "On Natural and Unnatural Dialect Differences: When the Standard is the Deviant." *Language Today* 2:46–56.

———. 1979. "Agents, Accessories and Owners: the Cultural Base and Rise of Ergative Structures, with Particular Reference to Ozark English." In *Ergativity: Toward a Theory of Grammatical Relations*, Frans Planck (ed.). Academic Press, New York.

*HALL, E. 1960. "The Silent Language of Overseas Business." *Harvard Business Review* 39:87–96.

*HOUSTON, S. 1973. "Black English." *Psychology Today*, March 1973.

KEY, M. 1972. "Linguistic Behavior of Male and Female." *Linguistics* 43:15–31.

*KOLIN, P. 1973. "The Language of Nursing." *American Speech* 48:192–210.

*LABOV, W. 1962. "Academic Ignorance and Black Intelligence." *Atlantic Monthly*, June 1962.

———. 1963. "The Social Motivation of a Sound Change." *Word* 19:273–309.

———. 1969. "Contraction, Deletion, and Inherent Variability of the Copula." *Language* 45:715–62.

———. 1972. "The Social Stratification of (r) in New York City Department Stores." *Sociolinguistic Patterns*, W. LABOV (ed.). University of Pennsylvania Press, Philadelphia.

LAKOFF, R. 1971. "Passive Resistance." *CLS-7*, D. ADAMS et al. (eds.).

———. 1972. "Language in Context." *Language* 48:907–27.

*———. 1974. "You Are What You Say." *Ms.*, July 1974.

LAMBERT, W. 1967a. "A Social Psychology of Bilingualism." *Journal of Social Issues* 23:91–109.

———. 1967b. "The Use of *tu* and *vous* as Forms of Address in French Canada: A Pilot Study." *Journal of Verbal Learning and Verbal Behavior* 6:614–17.

LAMBERT, W. et al. 1966. "Judging Personality Traits Through Speech: A French-Canadian Example." *Journal of Communication* 16:305–21.

*LONGFELLOW, L. 1970. "Body Talk: The Game of Feeling and Expression." *Psychology Today*, October 1970.

McDAVID, R. 1948. "Postvocalic *r* in South Carolina: A Social Analysis." *American Speech* 23:194–203.

———. 1966. "Sense and Nonsense about American Dialects." *Publications of the Modern Language Association* 81:7–17.

*MILLER, C., and K. SWIFT. 1972. "One Small Step for Genkind." *The New York Times Magazine*, April 16, 1972.

NASH, R. 1970. "Spanglish: Language Contact in Puerto Rico." *American Speech* 45:223–33.

———. 1971. "Englañol: More Language Contact in Puerto Rico." *American Speech* 46:106–22.

NIDA, E., and H. FEHDERAU. 1970. "Indigenous Pidgins and Koines." *International Journal of American Linguistics* 36:146–55.

*RICHARDS, H. 1970. "Trinidadian Folk Usage and Standard English: A Contrastive Study." *Word* 26:79–87.

SACKS, H. et al. 1974. "A Simplest Systematics for the Organization of Turn-Taking for Conversation." *Language* 50:696–735.

SLOBIN, D. 1963. "Some Aspects of the Use of Pronouns of Address in Yiddish." *Word* 19:193–202.

SMITH, R. 1974. "Research Perspectives on American Black English." *American Speech* 49:24–39.

UNDERWOOD, G. 1976. "How *You* Sound to an Arkansawyer." *American Speech* 48:208–15.

BOOKS

ALLEN, B., and G. UNDERWOOD (eds.). 1971. *Readings in American Dialectology.* Appleton-Century-Crofts, New York.

BAILEY, R., and J. ROBINSON (eds.). 1973. *Varieties of Present-Day English.* Macmillan Company, New York.

BIRDWHISTELL, R. 1970. *Kinesics and Context: Essays on Body Motion Communication.* University of Pennsylvania Press, Philadelphia.

BURLING, R. 1970. *Man's Many Voices: Language in Its Cultural Context.* Holt, Rinehart and Winston, New York.

BURLING, R. 1973. *English in Black and White*. Holt, Rinehart and Winston, New York.

BENTLEY, R., and S. CRAWFORD (eds.). 1973. *Black Language Reader*. Scott, Foresman, Glenview, Ill.

DILLARD, J. 1972. *Black English: Its History and Usage in the United States*. Vintage Books, New York.

——. 1975. *All-American English: A History of the English Language in America*. Random House, New York.

FISHMAN, J. 1968. *Readings in the Sociology of Language*. Mouton, The Hague.

——. 1970. *Sociolinguistics: A Brief Introduction*. Newbury House Publishers, Rowley, Mass.

GUMPERZ, J., and D. HYMES. 1972. *Directions in Sociolinguistics*. Holt, Rinehart and Winston, New York.

HERNANDEZ-CHAVEZ, E. et al. (eds.). 1975. *El Lenguaje de los Chicanos*. Center for Applied Linguistics, Arlington, Va.

HYMES, D. (ed.). 1971. *Pidginization and Creolization of Languages*. Cambridge University Press, London.

SAMOVAR, L., and R. PORTER (eds.). 1976. *Intercultural Communication: A Reader*, 2nd ed. Wadsworth Publishing Company, Belmont, Calif.

WOLFRAM, W. 1974. *Sociolinguistic Aspects of Assimilation: Puerto Rican English in New York City*. Center for Applied Linguistics, Arlington, Va.

——, and D. CHRISTIAN. 1976. *Appalachian Speech*. Center for Applied Linguistics, Arlington, Va.

SIX

Psycholinguistics

Psycholinguistics, like sociolinguistics, is a rapidly growing subfield of the discipline, and one in which there has been a flood of recent research and publication. Psycholinguistics can be most simply defined as the study of the relationship between human language and the human brain. (Even in animal communication research, a subject of great interest to psycholinguists, human language must be used as a reference point and a basis for comparison.) Simplicity stops at the definition, however, because the human brain is a new frontier characterized by a limitless territory. One of the things we know with greatest certainty about the workings of the human brain is that we know very *few* things with certainty.

Given the size and scope of the field, it will be useful to list a representative sampling of the kinds of questions that psycholinguists are attempting to answer.

1. How do human beings learn their native languages?
2. There are four activities involved in what is called *verbal processing*: speaking, understanding, reading, and writing. How does this

processing happen? How does it work, in terms of cognition, perception, and physiology?

3. How do human beings learn foreign languages? In what way does such learning resemble—or differ from—the learning of a first (native) language?

4. What is verbal learning and how does it take place? This question necessarily involves the problem of memory, and all the additional questions that entails.

5. Is there any evidence for the psychological reality of the models of grammar proposed by generative transformational linguistics?

6. What can we know with certainty about the location of the various language functions in the brain? Is it possible to localize such functions or are they spread throughout the entire brain without distinction?

7. When something goes wrong with human language ability, as a result of such factors as disease, injury, or congenital malformation, how can we describe and explain these disorders and what can we do about them?

8. Is the traditional assumption that language is uniquely restricted to human beings a correct one? If not, where else in the animal kingdom should we look for language and what are we to do about the prospect?

9. How is the vast amount of new knowledge about questions 1 to 8, which is being amassed almost daily by psycholinguists, to be made known to specialists in related fields (particularly education and therapy) where it is needed?

All these questions are interesting; all of them have implications for every one of us that make them far more than mere questions of theory. However, to attempt to discuss all of them, even superficially, is not possible within the scope of this text. The discussion in this chapter will therefore be limited for the most part to questions (1) and (2). The suggested readings at the end of the chapter will refer you to sources of supplementary material relating to the questions not taken up here.

LANGUAGE ACQUISITION

If you were asked how children acquire their native language, you might say something like "They learn it by imitating their parents and other people around them." This is a logical conclusion to come to, and one that appeals strongly to the intuitions of anyone who has been around little children as they learned to talk. It is also essentially the content of one of the two major competing positions in contemporary psycholinguistics with regard to this issue: the theoretical position associated primarily with the work of B. F. Skinner and known as the *behaviorist hypothesis.*

According to the behaviorist hypothesis the mind of the newborn infant is linguistically a blank slate. The child imitates speech around it, using a process of trial and error. It is reinforced in these imitations, or discouraged from them, by the degree of success it achieves in communicating. This is a standard stimulus-and-response, positive or negative reinforcement approach, and finds support in such undeniable facts as that a child who asks for candy and gets it will have a strong tendency to produce the word *candy* correctly thereafter. Language, then, for the behaviorists, is learned behavior that occurs as a result of this process.

In contrast to the behaviorist hypothesis, a second theory, called the *innateness hypothesis,* has developed out of generative transformational grammar. It is associated with the work of Chomsky and Lenneberg (among others).

The innateness hypothesis proposes that the ability to acquire a human language is part of the biologically innate equipment of the human being, and that an infant is born with this ability just as he or she is born with two arms, two legs, and a beating heart. It also claims that the innate language-learning ability is linked in some manner to physiological maturation, that it is strongest in the very small child, and that some degree of decay in this function begins around the time of puberty. The evidence for the innateness hypothesis is very strong, primarily because first language learning in the normal child shows almost none of the characteristics of learned behavior in the Skinnerian sense.

First, no matter what language a child hears, it will begin to speak that language at about 18 months of age, and will have learned its grammar by about the age of 5. This does not mean that the kindergarten child has the vocabulary or performance skills of the adult speaker, of course; it means that he has mastered the basic grammar rules of whatever language he has been exposed to. The child can make statements, ask and answer questions, give and respond to commands, make sentences negative, form plurals and tenses, and so on. He is capable of carrying on a conversation in just the same way as an adult, although not on the same scale.

There are of course exceptions to this time-table. Many of us have known or heard about a child who began speaking very early or very late. But the number of exceptions is far too small to be of any statistical significance, and the 18 months to 5 years span is universal.[1] This sort of

---

[1] It should be pointed out that this universality of acquisition demonstrates that no language is *inherently* any more "difficult" than any other. If such differences in difficulty existed, the children learning those languages would learn them more slowly, begin to speak them later, and so on. This does not happen.

invariability is not characteristic of learned behavior. If language were acquired by trial-and-error, stimulus-and-reinforcement, we would expect to find marked variations in age and speed relative to language learning, depending upon the individual child's learning situation. This is precisely what we do not see.

If you take a baby as soon as it can be propped up in an infant seat and you provide it with daily language lessons from the finest experts, it will begin to speak at about 18 months and learn its grammar by about the age of 5; if you do nothing at all, except go about your daily life, precisely the same thing will happen. Compare this to what you would expect if you provided a child with lessons in music, sports, art or similar activities, and the difference here should become clear.

If the behavioral hypothesis were true, we would expect to find variations in the learning time-table correlated with such factors as the amount of language exposure, the speech style of the speakers around the child, the child's intelligence, and the like. Again, this is not borne out by the facts. Some children are raised in homes where there is a great deal of language activity, while others grow up in far less verbal environments; we see variations in their language acquisition only in such extreme cases as those of children who have spent their infancy in understaffed institutions, or some similarly unusual situation, and have therefore had almost no exposure to human speech. The same thing is true with regard to intelligence; it is only at the extreme end of the scale, in cases of severe mental retardation, that any significant difference in language acquisition can be demonstrated.[2]

Children learn their languages easily, without ever taking lessons, and can learn two or more languages at once without any significant lag in the pattern of acquisition. A child growing up in a truly bilingual or multi-lingual home acquires his or her languages without any sign of foreign accent in any one of them, and although occasional confusion between the languages occurs during the acquisition period, this is a transient phenomenon and causes no long-term difficulty. Contrast this with the typical example of the adult foreign-language learner, who does take lessons, often for years and years, or who spends most of his adult life in a foreign country in constant exposure to its language. Very rarely does such an adult learn the second language with native or near-native fluency, as does the child; and it is in no way unusual to find adults who have spoken a second language in their daily business and household lives for thirty years or more, but are still speaking it

---

[2] This mention of intelligence should not be understood as an endorsement of the traditional IQ figure attached automatically to children by our educational system. The debate over what, if anything, the IQ tests measure is being hotly waged by scholars in many fields. However, the signs of severe mental retardation of the type and degree that actually interfere with language acquisition can be readily observed without the need for tests.

with a marked accent. Whether such an accent in the adult is considered charming (as with Zsazsa Gabor), intellectual (as with Henry Kissinger), or a handicap (as with a teenage job applicant from Mexico) is a matter of fashion and historical accident. What is quite certain is that children below the age of 5 or so acquire their languages without any foreign accent whatsoever. (It is curious that we respond to this fact by initiating foreign-language teaching at the secondary and college level.)

A crucial claim of the behaviorist hypothesis is that children imitate the speech of those around them; however, it is not accurate to say that this describes what is going on. For example, children acquiring English as a native language go through a speech stage during which they form questions like the following:

(1)   a. Why he is leaving?
      b. Who she is kissing?
      c. Where the truck is going?
      d. Why the baby is crying?

The characteristic intonation of these questions is a strong rising stress on the initial question word, as well as a rising intonation at the end.

In these examples, the obligatory rule of Question-Formation, which inverts the auxiliary verb and the surface subject NP, has not been applied. No child ever hears questions of this form from any adult, yet every English-speaking child uses such questions. The child has not as yet mastered the rule of Question-Formation, and his or her grammar differs in this respect from the adult grammar. This is a systematic, not a random difference, and it cannot be accounted for on the basis of imitation.

That children follow definite rules of grammar is obvious to anyone who observes their language behavior. Every adult has heard children say things like "I goed," "Mary singed," and so on. Some children, when faced with an adult's demand for *went* rather than *goed*, respond—very logically—with *wented*. They do this long before anyone has ever formally said to them anything like "the sign of the English simple past tense is the suffix *-ed*, which is pronounced as either /t/, /d/, or /əd/." They have observed the facts about *-ed* for themselves, and as a productive strategy they apply it to all verbs. They must then be taught the irregular forms which, paradoxically, are the "correct" ones.

A similar example in English language acquisition is seen in the forms which small children use for the reflexive. They have heard a number of sets like those shown in (2).

(2)   a. my shoes, your shoes, his shoes, her shoes, our shoes, your shoes, their shoes
      b. my toys, your toys, his toys, her toys, our toys, your toys, their toys

When the child subsequently hears the words *myself* and *yourself*, it generalizes the pattern in (2) and produces—according to the rule perceived—the set in (3).

(3)   myself, yourself, hisself, herself, ourselves, yourselves, theirselves

This does not happen because the child has heard others saying *hisself* and *theirselves*. It is just as inevitable in children from homes where the adults never use such forms and carefully shield their offspring from all exposure to them as it is anywhere else.

If the child is *not* doing all this by trial and error and imitation, how are we to describe native language acquisition? In the innateness hypothesis framework, the psycholinguist would make the following statement:

> Young children have the innate ability to extract from raw language data—even very disorganized and sporadic data—the grammatical rules of the language, and then to use those rules productively and creatively. The child has the ability to internalize the grammatical system independently and use it to generate his or her own language sequences.

The distinction between learning by internalization and learning by memorization is probably best explained by an analogy. Consider two boys who are interested in music. The first has learned to play, note by note, two musical compositions on the piano. They may well be extremely complicated compositions, and he may play them flawlessly. The second boy may not be able to play anything as complicated as these two selections, but he can play many different songs. Not only that, if you ask him to play something he has never heard before and it is not beyond the limits of his performance skill, he will say "I don't know it, but if you can hum it I'll follow you."

Only the second individual described can be said to have internalized the system we call "playing the piano" and to really know how it is done. Parrots and mynah birds memorize sequences of human language, but they do not internalize them, and a bird that could recite the Gettysburg Address and one chapter of a Spanish novel would *not* be a bilingual (or even monolingual) bird.

The capacity children have for language acquisition appears to be sharply curtailed in adults, who probably accomplish most of their second-language learning through memorization and according to the behaviorist model. We cannot be certain if this difference is due primarily to physical maturation, or if it involves other factors such as cultural attitudes, the stages of cognitive development proposed by Jean Piaget, etc. Undoubtedly the typical self-consciousness of the adolescent must be taken into account. But it is beyond question that language learning in the very young child and in the adult differ greatly, whatever the reasons.

At this point the innateness hypothesis splits into a weak and a strong version. In the strong version the human infant's language-learning capacity represents a kind of biological pre-programming specifically for the acquisition of human languages. In the weak version the claim is that the child has a set of innate cognitive and perceptual strategies for learning, together with a specific ability to *apply* these strategies to the learning of human languages. The weak version does not require that these strategies be defined as separate from those which children use in other learning, but recognizes that their application to language acquisition is somehow linked to maturation, just as in the strong version.

You will remember that the set of possible characteristics which a human language can have is surprisingly small and quite severely constrained. This concept, which is called the *universal grammar hypothesis*, is closely linked to the innateness hypothesis, since it is far easier to understand how all children acquire their native languages with such uniformity if it is true. Children acquire *generative* grammars for their languages, which means that they are able to produce sequences which they have never encountered before, by applying the grammar rules creatively. As Noam Chomsky (1972) has stated:

> Assuming the rough accuracy of conclusions that seem tenable today, it is reasonable to suppose that a generative grammar is a system of many hundreds of rules of several different types, organized in accordance with certain fixed principles of ordering and applicability and containing a certain fixed substructure, which, along with the general principles of organization, is common to all languages. (*Language and Mind*, pp. 75-76.)

It is important to remember that these rules will apply not just to syntax, but also to phonology, semantics, and all other aspects of language behavior.

Linguists now have some evidence that more of the language learning ability remains after puberty than had been thought possible. If this proves to be true, it is a discovery of great importance both for those who are involved in the treatment of language disorders and for those who are attempting to teach foreign languages to normal adults.

VERBAL PROCESSING

The term *verbal processing*, as used in this text, is meant to include all four language activities—speaking (or signing), understanding, reading, and writing. It is meant, therefore, to include both the production aspect of processing and the processing of the language output of others. That is, to speak or write is to produce a sound sequence; to understand is its converse, the processing of a sequence spoken or written by someone else.

Linguists are sometimes quoted as saying that reading and writing are secondary activities, and this is then taken to mean that they consider the skills of reading and writing unimportant.[3] This misunderstanding is much like that in which the linguistic term *nonstandard* applied to a dialect is taken to mean *substandard* rather than simply *different from the hypothetical standard form*. What the linguist means by calling reading and writing secondary to speaking and understanding is that although every human society develops speech and the understanding of speech (because communication is necessary to survival), many have never developed a form of their language for use in reading and writing. All four activities are intimately related, however, since written language is the symbolic representation of spoken language, and reading is the understanding of that symbolic record.[4]

Verbal processing is an intricate system of activities. One human being produces a sequence of noises or gestures, or sets down on a page a sequence of marks, with the intention of conveying meaning. Another human being is then able to perceive those sounds, gestures, or marks, and understand that intended meaning. This is called communication, and is something that we usually take for granted without much appreciation of either its complexity or its almost miraculous quality. Only when the process breaks down and communication does not take place do we ordinarily pay it much attention. As with language acquisition, the big question is—how does it all work?

A number of proposals, based upon meticulous psycholinguistic experimentation, have been brought forward as explanations. At the moment all of these proposals are simply that—hypotheses, proposed tentatively, and still subject to modification as more and more evidence is obtained. In order to present here a brief discussion of some of this material, we will be forced to do some radical simplification. The easiest way to do that is probably to restrict the discussion to one process—reading—and use it as an illustration of all four. Look at example (4).

(4)   Uxdxrnxxth txx pxrxh I sax xxven xiny xxppixs xx x bxx.

Can you read (4)? Unless you are not a native speaker of English, you can, and with very little difficulty. And yet twenty of its letters, almost 50 percent of the total, are missing. It cannot be true, therefore, that you read the sentence by looking at and recognizing each letter in a word until you have

---

[3] See, for example, the article "Why Johnny Can't Write," in *Newsweek*, Dec. 8, 1975.

[4] It is of course usually true that, except for quoted speech, the written register differs a good deal from the spoken one.

recognized the entire word, and then combining them. Nor can it be true that you are looking at each individual word and recognizing it—upon the basis of its spelling or its shape, for example—and then combining all those words to arrive at the meaning of the sentence. If all that you had to work with was the individual letter, or the individual word, you would be able to read the sequence in (5) with similar ease.

(5) xx x bxx

If you compare this sequence with that in (4) you will notice that the unreadable (5) is identical to the last three units of (4), which you had no problem at all in understanding as "in a box." Where does the difference lie, then? Kenneth Goodman (1967) puts it as follows:

> Reading is a process in which the reader picks and chooses from the available information only enough to select and predict a language structure which is decodable. It is not in any sense a precise perceptual process. . . . It is not a process of sequential word recognition. A proficient reader is one so efficient in sampling and predicting that he uses the least (not the most) available information necessary.

When you looked at "xx x bxx" in (5), you did not have enough information to allow you to *select and predict* a sequence from among all the possible sequences that it might represent. Just a few of the possibilities are shown in (6).

(6) in a box
      on a bus
      to a boy
      by a bed
      if I buy
      or I beg
      or a bat
      to a bee

In example (4), however, because of the information provided to you by all the preceding sequences, this multiplicity of choices was reduced to just three: *in a box, on a box, by a box.* Adding to that what we know about tiny puppies and the real world, the first alternative becomes the most obvious choice.

In the processing of written information, you are able to reduce the number of possible meanings that a sequence could have by using everything that you know about the language you are reading, from the most superficial level of all, the graphic one represented by letter shapes, to the broadest—the pragmatic level that must include the real world context. Much of this is what linguists call *redundant*; that is, there will be not just one reason to make a particular choice, but a number of different reasons that reinforce one another. You know that the last word of (4) is *box* because it is a three-letter word beginning with the letter *b*, because the sequence before it must be either *a* or *I* (there being only those two one-letter words in the entire English language), because a box is an appropriate place for puppies to be found, and so on. Frank Smith (1971) explains redundancy in reading as follows:

> All information acquisition in reading, from the identification of individual letters or words to the comprehension of entire passages, can be regarded as the reduction of uncertainty. Skilled reading utilizes redundancy —of information from a variety of sources—so that, for example, knowledge of the world and of language will reduce the need for visual information from the printed page. (*Understanding Reading*, p. 12.)

When you are considering whole sentences, the number of possible choices of meanings to be assigned to a particular string of letters may be large, and will vary from sentence to sentence. It is easy to grasp the concept of "reduction of uncertainty" in reading, however, if you consider what it would mean for recognizing a given letter. The set of possible English letters is not infinite; there are only 26 possibilities. The number of possible choices is then theoretically 26, for any letter that you look at. However, if you notice that the letter is one which includes a downstroke below the horizontal base of the printed line, you have immediately reduced the number of possibilities to five, since the only English letters of that form are *g, j, p, q,* and *y*.

You carry out this process without being consciously aware that you are continually making guesses (predictions) and choices, selecting and discarding upon the basis of your linguistic competence. This is one reason why proofreading is so hard to do well. If you are reading a line of print in which "thx United States" appears, you will not ordinarily be aware of having perceived *thx* at all. You will have processed *thx* as the word *the*, which it clearly has to be. A proofreader must in fact learn to ignore redundancy and actually look, however fleetingly, at every symbol on the page. This is utterly different from ordinary reading.

It should be obvious that since in reading you do not perceive and recognize every letter, or even every word, you are not even in the sense of a *model* somehow transferring the graphic representation into your mind, converting it to its phonetic representation, and converting that to yet another level until at last you reach the semantic representation which is the *meaning*. All of the available evidence on this matter indicates that, whatever the precise details of the process may be, reading is a matter of extracting the meaning directly from the written words. If you hand a paragraph of material to an adult to read, and afterward ask him or her what that paragraph said, you will be given in oral form the *meaning*, not the exact words that were written on the page. Except for children in elementary school, people almost never go through a process of converting a graphic sequence to a sound sequence by reading aloud; if they did, they would be arbitrarily restricted to reading at the speed of oral language, which is about 250 words per minute.[5]

To summarize, you are able to process written language so well because you know so much about it. You know, given some parts of words, what the restricted set of other possible parts can be. Given parts of phrases and sentences, you are able to make highly informed guesses about what *their* missing parts must be. It is because languages are so structured, so systematic, and so redundant, and because you know so much about all three of those parameters, that you were able to read (4) with ease.

In the processing of speech, as in the processing of writing, meaning is determined by predicting possibilities based upon knowledge of the language and choosing among them. Just as you are able to read written language even when many of the letters are missing, or when the print is blurred or distorted, you are able to understand spoken language on the basis of an astonishingly small amount of data. When you listen to someone speaking your language under difficult conditions (for example, at a party where there is a lot of competing noise, or when the speaker is a foreigner and the sound sequences are substantially different from those of native speech) you do precisely the same thing that you do in reading. From the limited information given to you perceptually, plus your knowledge about the possible alternatives that might make up all the different or missing pieces, you are able to extract the meaning, and communication takes place.

No one would want to claim that this process is perfect. It may be true that we *never* understand the *full* meaning of a language sequence. Certainly it is an unusual individual who cannot remember many instances when he or she was misunderstood, or understood only to a very limited extent. The distinction between competence and performance is fully operative in conversation and in reading. However, for the practical purposes of everyday life, if the two participants in a conversation or a written exchange speak the same language and either the same dialect or closely related ones, enough of the meaning will be transmitted by the operations of verbal processing to allow us to get by.

The model of verbal processing presented in the discussion above is

---

[5] If a child reads well, reading aloud can become a source of much frustration, precisely because it is so slow and so artificial. Such a child, having read aloud "I was walking through the woods" for the printed "I was walking through the forest" will resent the illogic of being told that he or she has made an "error."

HERMAN

©1976 Universal Press Syndicate

**"Exchanging beads for gold is a fantastic idea.
We'll go and get our beads."**

called the *analysis-by-synthesis* model. As with most models in linguistics, its formalization is made difficult by real world considerations. For example, this model proposes that when a listener hears a spoken sequence, he or she begins generating guesses about the content of that sequence. If we remember that the set of potential sentences of any human language is infinite, and that any sentence at all can always be made longer by adding "and" plus additional material, a major problem with the model becomes immediately apparent. That is, the set of potential *guesses* is also—formally speaking—infinite. If this fact had any real-world validity, none of us would ever get beyond the very first sentence we attempted to understand. Since we do manage to communicate with one another, there has to be a difference between the formal description of the model and its real-world analogue. There must be some way, or perhaps many ways, in which the listener or reader can restrict the number of possible interpretations of a sequence to a finite number that can be managed efficiently.

No one would claim that this concept is an easy one to grasp. It may help somewhat to consider an analogous situation that is familiar to most of us. Consider what you do as you are driving along in the rightmost lane of a freeway and come to a spot where traffic is merging into your lane from an onramp. There are cars all around you, in your own lane and in the lanes beside you. You notice three cars approaching from the onramp, and now you must do one of four things: slow down, speed up, maintain your speed, or change lanes. How do you decide among these alternatives? You do it by making guesses, very rapidly, as to where your car will be—and where those other cars will be—in the next few seconds. You use all the information from your previous experience in merging traffic situations, your perception of the speed of the three cars you are watching and the other cars around you, your perception of the speed of your own car, and so on. You must make your choice very quickly and make it correctly or you are likely to end up in the hospital—which is highly motivating for your choice. One of the things you learn very early in this sort of situation is what information you do *not* need to pay attention to. For example, it makes no difference what color the three cars joining your traffic lane are, or what their radiator ornaments are like, or whether they are carrying any particular number of people. Just as in reading, where the fact that an *a* was written slightly above the line of print would not have to be considered in your identification of the letter as an *a*, you know what you must notice and what you can ignore.

The term *heuristic* is very important in describing how this is done. A heuristic is a guess, in a way; but it is not a random guess. It is a guess based upon information, experience, and common sense.

Consider a very common situation, in which you have misplaced some object in your bedroom. There is a formal way of finding that object which will always work,[6] and that is to begin at any point in the room and examine every other point until you come across whatever you have lost. In real life, if you always used this procedure when you had misplaced something, you would spend a ridiculous amount of time looking for things, and you do not proceed in this way. Instead, you reduce the set of possible places where the lost object might be to a manageable number, based upon information that you already have. This is guessing, since you do not have any assurance that the object will be in one of those places, but it is *heuristic* guessing. You do not resort to the formal procedure of looking everywhere there is to look until the heuristic procedure has failed you and you have no other choice.

Some of the heuristics of verbal processing for which substantial evidence from psycholinguistic research exists are listed in (7).

---

[6] A formal procedure of this kind is called an *algorithm*.

(7) a. The processor analyzes a sequence of language into its underlying sentences by identifying the deep structure predicates that it contains, assigning to each of these predicates its related noun phrases, and determining what relationships exist among them.

b. The processor takes advantage of all the things that he or she knows about constraints on the environments in which particular items or sequences can appear.

c. The processor makes maximal use of all the surface markers in a sequence that provide clues to deep structure relationships, such as relative pronouns, complementizers, etc. These markers help greatly in the sorting of surface structure into deep structure sentences.

d. The processor makes maximal use of what he or she knows to be the most *usual* configurations of the language used in the sequence.

e. Finally, the processor will take into account all possible clues to the meaning of the sequence that can be found in its written or real world context.

We can take a single sentence, "Evelyn wanted to leave," as an example, and show in (8) how each of the heuristics in (7) applies to that sentence.

(8) HEURISTIC (7a)
There are two predicates in "Evelyn wanted to leave"—*wanted* and *leave*. There is only one subject NP, however. The processor knows that it is Evelyn who wants something, that it is Evelyn who will be leaving if her desire is realized, and that the two Evelyns are one and the same. The sequence can therefore be identified as composed of two sentences (sometimes called *sentoids*) in underlying structure, each of which has Evelyn as its subject.

HEURISTIC (7b)
In English the only constituent that can follow a sequence like *want to* or *need to* or *have to* is a verb, or a manner adverb followed by a verb. Thus the processor must include guesses such as *wanted to leave* and *wanted to quickly leave* but can rule out sequences like *wanted to New York* or *wanted to between*. (It is true that *wanted to quickly leave* is traditionally a split infinitive and is frowned upon. However, split infinitives are too common in real language for any processor to safely ignore them.)

HEURISTIC (7c)
In English the presence of *to* immediately before a verb signals that its deep structure subject has been deleted or moved. The processor therefore knows that *leave* has to have been part of a deep structure sentence containing a subject and a predicate of its own.

HEURISTIC (7d)

The most common form for an English declarative sentence is either a subject followed by an intransitive verb, or a subject followed by a transitive verb followed by a direct object. Many other kinds of declarative sentences exist, but they are less common. The processor assumes that the sentence is composed of subject plus verb—and perhaps an object—until he or she has some reason to assume the contrary. In "Evelyn wanted to leave" the assumption will prove to be correct.

HEURISTIC (7e)

The processor may know that Evelyn was at a cocktail party, and that she considers all cocktail parties to be a waste of valuable time that could be better spent in doing something useful. Such knowledge makes the likelihood of the sentence much greater than it would be if Evelyn were known by the speaker to be someone who enjoys cocktail parties very much and is always the last to leave.

Keep in mind that we are still discussing a *model*. No linguist would suggest that any speaker of a language literally follows each transformational rule in order through the derivation of a sentence, in the way that a cook follows each step of a recipe. This fact is sometimes obscured by the terminology of psycholinguists, who are forever speaking and writing of "input" and "output" and "processing" and the like. Similarly, linguists make no claim that anyone deliberately and consciously follows through each of the steps listed in (7) and (8) in the order that they are presented. It just happens that there is no other way to discuss things in written English except in linear order, top to bottom, left to right.

It may be that the heuristics described are all applied at once, for example, or that their order of application is exactly the opposite of that given here. This is a limitation of surface description that may have no counterpart whatsoever in the brain, for all we know.

In psycholinguistics we are only just beginning to learn, but the new information has a potentially enormous application to many areas of our daily life and many problems that now plague our society. Psycholinguistics, like sociolinguistics, has little of the "ivory tower" about it.

EXERCISES AND PROBLEMS

1. One area of psycholinguistic investigation is the comparison of linguistic development and behavior in monolinguals versus that of bi- or multilinguals. Lerea and LaPorta (*Language and Speech*, April 1971) describe an experiment of this kind, in which they gave subjects lists of Hebrew

words to memorize, each containing the phoneme /x/. Subjects included both monolinguals and bilinguals, but none knew any language which had /x/ as one of its phonemes. The lists of words were first presented visually, and memorization was tested in writing; then a second list was presented aloud, and was orally tested. The results of the experiment indicated that monolingual subjects learned the visual lists faster than bilinguals. Bilinguals, however, learned the vocal lists faster than the monolinguals. Can you suggest any explanation for the results of this experiment? Can you think of any factors which might account at least in part for the results?

2. Thomas Bever has done a number of experiments with sets of English sentences like the following: "The horse raced past the barn tripped." In his experiments Bever found that subjects tended to hear such sentences as if they had contained a conjunction. That is, they would claim that they had heard the following sentence: "The horse raced past the barn and tripped." Here are some more examples of sentences of this kind:

(a) The soldiers marched by the students blushed.
(b) That woman shoved through the screen door shrieked.
(c) The horse jumped by the child whinnied.
(d) The girl whirled past the entrance wept.
(e) The ball rolled down the road went into a ditch.
(f) The man thrust through the crowd was ignored.
(g) The child dragged down the stairs complained.
(h) A cow pushed past the dogs kicked the farmer.

Examine the data and decide what is causing the difficulty that subjects have in processing these sentences. State what conditions such a sentence must meet in order to be a member of this set. Consider also which of the processing heuristics described in this chapter might be interfered with by the structure of the example sentences.

3. Although it is clear that no inherent connection exists between the phonological shapes of words and their meanings, linguists are interested in the occasional manifestations of sound symbolism in language. In *Language and Speech* (April 1971) Christine Tanz reports a study showing that in six different language families many languages have sets of words for "here" and "there" containing an /i/ phoneme for the word signifying nearness and an /a/ phoneme (or in some cases /o/) for the words signifying distance. Can you think of any similar phenomena in your own language or one with which you are familiar?

4. The neurophysiology of language has some curious aspects. For example, perceptual input to the left ear goes directly to the brain's right hemisphere. Input to the right ear goes directly to the left hemisphere. The two hemispheres are divided by a membrane called the *corpus callosum*. Since language processing is done in the left hemisphere, a word presented to the left ear only (as can be done with earphones, for example, or by whispering) must go first to the right hemisphere and then cross over to the left hemisphere; it cannot go to the left hemisphere directly. There are a few individuals for whom medical conditions have made it necessary to separate the two hemispheres of the brain surgically, via the corpus callosum. If such an individual (known as a *split-brain subject*) closes his or her eyes and has a pencil placed in his left hand, although he knows what the object is he will not be able to say its name. If he opens his eyes and looks at the object, this difficulty will no longer exist. Can you explain why opening of the eyes should solve the problem?

5. A number of studies have been done in animal communication using chimpanzees as subjects. Those in which attempts were made to teach vocal speech failed. However, recent experiments by scientists using either sign language or a set of physical tokens of language as a communication medium have been much more successful. (The vocal tract of the chimpanzee is not suited for production of human speech, but the chimps have great manual dexterity.) If it is possible to teach chimps to communicate in this manner, does this mean that we should assume that they, like the human infant, have an innate language learning capacity? Explain your reasoning carefully.

6. One of the identifying characteristics of human language usage, as opposed to that of a parrot or mynah bird, is creativity. The bird may have excellent pronunciation, but can never produce any sequence that it has not been explicitly taught. Human beings, on the other hand, constantly produce unique sequences. The chimp Washoe had been taught the sign for *bird* and the sign for *water* and used them consistently and accurately. She had never been taught any sign for *duck*. However, upon seeing a duck swimming she immediately signed *water bird*. Does this strike you as evidence of a kind of linguistic creativity?

7. By various kinds of experiments it is possible to demonstrate that some sequences of language are more difficult to process than others. For example, subjects may be asked to listen to sentences and repeat them or write them down; or they may be given sequences to memorize and then tested on their ability to do so. In the data below (based on experiments by Epstein, Fodor and Garrett, Weksel and Bever, and others), the (a) sentence in each pair was proved *easier* to process than the (b) sentence.

(a) The yigs wur vumly rixing hum in jegest miv.
(b) The yig wur vum rix hum in jeg miv.
(a) The man that the girl knew got sick.
(b) The man the girl knew got sick.
(a) It surprised Max that Mary was happy.
(b) That Mary was happy surprised Max.

Compare the harder-to-process (b) sentences with the (a) ones. You should then be able to make a statement about at least one factor that is *not* a reliable indicator of sentence processing difficulty. What is that factor?

8. Psycholinguists have learned that the order in which the English morphemes listed below are acquired is identical for children learning English as their native language. (There are of course individual variations, but not of any statistical significance.)

(a) *-ing*
(b) *on*
(c) *in*
(d) *-s* (plural)
(e) irregular pasts, such as *went* or *did*
(f) *-s* (possessive)
(g) forms of *be*, without contraction
(h) *a, an, the*
(i) *-ed*
(j) *-s* (third person singular)

Is this evidence for or against the innateness hypothesis of language acquisition, or it is irrelevant to that hypothesis? Why?

9. This exercise is a psycholinguistic experiment that you can do for yourself. Get a piece of cardboard and cut a narrow vertical slot in it. Then have someone take adding machine tape (or any narrow strip of paper that can be pulled through the slot in your piece of cardboard) and write on it in a continuous sequence. (It makes no difference what they write, so long as it is a comprehensible passage of your native language; for example, they might copy the first paragraph of a newspaper story, so long as you have no idea what its content is.) Now have your partner pull the written material through the slot for you to look at, at a very slow rate—say thirty words a minute. Are you able to understand and remember what is written on the paper?

10. One of the mechanisms of English grammar is that of turning adjectives or verbs into nouns (*nominalization*) by adding endings to them. Any verb can be nominalized just by adding *-ing*, as in "Swimming is fun." However, many words have special nominalizing suffixes of their own. The three most common suffixes of this kind are probably *-ment* as in *abandonment*, *-ness* as in *tenderness* and *-ion* as in *demonstration*. Linguists have not yet found any systematic way to determine why a given word takes one rather than another of these endings.

Find at least ten subjects and read to them the nonsense words written below in phonemic form. Ask them to assume that the nonsense words are verbs or adjectives and to indicate for each one whether they would nominalize it by adding *-ment*, *-ness*, or *-ion*. (You should tell them that *-ion* frequently appears as *-tion*, as well.)

(a) /blæp/, brɛb/, /plɪk/, /kran/, /dug/, /rɛl/, /mos/, /ak/, /ɪp/, /za/

(b) /tidak/, /seta/, /fɪnɪp/, /bɛda/, /lubæs/, /zɪnon/, /amnɪd/, /olyɛp/, /kuzdɪn/, /strɪnad/

(c) /akatɛp/, /fijɪšan/, /pætɪsat/, /kronɪdək/, /ilɪdrɛp/, /slænofar/, /lonodon/, /maraplɪd/, /udəgək/, /nɛktrɪfɛr/

In order to keep confusing elements from interfering with your experiment, accent the *first* syllable in all the words of group (b) and group (c). Now look at your results. Do you see any patterns at all? Do your subjects appear to have reacted any differently in their choices when the nonsense word had two or three syllables than when it had only one? Does the final sound of the nonsense word seem to have made any difference in the choice of ending? Do your subjects' choices seem to be basically random?

11. Using a different group of subjects for your experiment, repeat Exercise 10, but this time accent the *last* syllable in groups (b) and (c). Do your results differ from those you obtained the first time? Do they differ in any systematic way?

SUGGESTED READINGS

ARTICLES AND EXCERPTS

ATKINSON, R., and R. SHIFFRIN. 1971. "The Control of Short-term Memory." *Scientific American* 225:82–90.

*BELLUGI, U. 1970. "Learning the Language." *Psychology Today*, December 1970.

*———, and E. KLIMA. 1972. "The Roots of Language in the Sign Talk of the Deaf." *Psychology Today*, June 1972.

————, and S. FISCHER. 1972. "A Comparison of Sign Language and Spoken Language." *Cognition* 1:173–200.

BEVER, T. 1970. "The Cognitive Basis for Linguistic Structure." In J. HAYES (ed.), *Cognition and the Development of Language.* John Wiley and Sons, New York.

BORNSTEIN, H. 1973. "A Description of Some Current Sign Systems Designed to Represent English." *American Annals of the Deaf* 118:454–63.

BRONOWSKI, J., and U. BELLUGI. 1970. "Language, Name, and Concept." *Science* 168:669–73.

BROWN, R. 1968. "The Development of Wh-Questions in Child Speech." *Journal of Verbal Learning and Verbal Behavior* 7:277–90.

————. 1973. "Development of the First Language in the Human Species." *American Psychologist* 28:97–106.

————, and D. MCNEILL. 1966. "The 'Tip of the Tongue' Phenomenon." *Journal of Verbal Learning and Verbal Behavior* 5:325–37.

BRUNER, J. 1964. "The Course of Cognitive Growth." *American Psychologist* 19:1–15.

CAZDEN, C. 1968. "The Acquisition of Noun and Verb Inflections." *Child Development* 39:433–38.

CHOMSKY, N. 1959. "Review of B. F. Skinner's *Verbal Behavior.*" *Language* 35:26–58.

————. 1968. "Language and the Mind." *Psychology Today*, February 1968.

CURTISS, S. et al. 1974. "The Linguistic Development of Genie." *Language* 50:528–54.

DE VILLIERS, J., and P. DE VILLIERS. 1973. "A Cross-Sectional Study of the Acquisition of Grammatical Morphemes in Child Speech." *Journal of Psycholinguistic Research* 2:267–78.

————. 1973b. "Development of the Use of Word Order in Comprehension." *Journal of Psycholinguistic Research* 2:331–41.

DUNN-RANKIN, P. 1978. "The Visual Characteristics of Words." *Scientific American* 238:122–30.

FROMKIN, V. 1973. "Slips of the Tongue." *Scientific American* 229:110–17.

———— et al. 1974. "Language Development Beyond the Critical Age." *Brain and Language* 1:81–107.

GARDNER, R., and B. GARDNER. 1969. "Teaching Sign Language to a Chimpanzee." *Science* 165:664–72.

GAZZANIGA, M. 1967. "The Split Brain in Man." *Scientific American* 217:24–29.

GESCHWIND, N. 1972. "Language and the Brain." *Scientific American* 226:76–83.

*GOODMAN, K. 1964. "A Linguistic Study of Cues and Miscues in Reading." *Elementary English* 42:39–44.

*————. 1967. "Reading: A Psycholinguistic Guessing Game." *The Reading Specialist* 4:126–35.

HOLMES, D. 1971. "The Independence of Letter, Word, and Meaning Identification in Reading." *Reading Research Quarterly* 6:394–415.

INGRAM, D. 1971. "Transitivity in Child Language." *Language* 47:888–910.

———. 1974. "Phonological Rules in Young Children." *Journal of Child Language* 1:49–64.

KIMURA, D. 1973. "The Assymetry of the Human Brain." *Scientific American* 228:70–80.

KRASHEN, S. et al. 1973. "Lateralization, Language Learning, and the Critical Period: Some New Evidence." *Language Learning* 23:63–74.

LENNEBERG, E. 1969. "On Explaining Language." *Science* 164:664–72.

*LOTZ, J. 1956. "Linguistics: Symbols Make Man." In L. WHITE, Jr. (ed.), *Frontiers of Knowledge*. Harper and Brothers, New York.

MILLER, G. 1956. "The Magical Number Seven, Plus or Minus Two: Some Limits on Our Capacities for Processing Information." *Psychological Review* 63:81–97.

PENFIELD, W. 1965. "Conditioning the Uncommitted Cortex for Language Learning." *Brain* 88:787–98.

*PREMACK, D. 1970. "The Education of Sarah: A Chimp Learns the Language." *Psychology Today*, September 1970.

PREMACK, A., and D. PREMACK. 1972. "Teaching Language to an Ape." *Scientific American* 227:92–99.

RUMBAUGH, D., and E. VON GLASERFELD. 1973. "Reading and Sentence Completion by a Chimpanzee." *Science* 182:731–33.

SEBEOK, T. 1968. "Communication in Animals and in Man: Three Reviews." In J. FISHMAN (ed.), *Readings in the Sociology of Language*. Mouton, The Hague.

SEGAL, E. 1975. "Psycholinguistics Discovers the Operant: A Review of Roger Brown's *A First Language: The Early Stages*." *Journal of the Experimental Analysis of Behavior* 23:149–58.

*SLOBIN, D. 1972. "Children and Language—They Learn the Same Way All Around the World." *Psychology Today*, July 1972.

*STAFF. 1975. "A Layman's Guide to the Brain." *Saturday Review*, August 9, 1975.

*STROMEYER, C. 1970. "Eidetikers." *Psychology Today*, April 1970.

WILSON, E. 1972. "Animal Communication." *Scientific American* 227:52–60.

*"The World of the Brain." *Harper's*, December 1975.

BOOKS

BANDLER, R., and J. GRINDER. 1975. *The Structure of Magic I*. Science and Behavior Books, Palo Alto, Calif.

BAR-ADON, A., and W. LEOPOLD (eds.). 1971. *Child Language: A Book of Readings*. Prentice-Hall, Englewood Cliffs, N.J.

CHOMSKY, N. 1972. *Language and Mind*, 2nd ed. Harcourt Brace Jovanovich, New York.

DALE, P. 1976. *Language Development: Structure and Function*, 2nd ed. Holt, Rinehart and Winston, New York.

DEESE, J. 1970. *Psycholinguistics.* Allyn & Bacon, Boston.

FERGUSON, C., and D. SLOBIN (eds.). 1973. *Studies of Child Language Development.* Holt, Rinehart and Winston, New York.

FODOR, J. et al. 1974. *The Psychology of Language: An Introduction to Psycholinguistics and Generative Grammar.* McGraw-Hill, New York.

GRINDER, J., and R. BANDLER. 1976. *The Structure of Magic II.* Science and Behavior Books, Palo Alto, Calif.

HAYES, J. 1970. *Cognition and the Development of Language.* John Wiley and Sons, New York.

LENNEBERG, E. 1967. *The Biological Foundations of Language.* John Wiley and Sons, New York.

*LILLY, J. 1969a. *Man and Dolphin.* Pyramid Publications, New York.

*———. 1969b. *The Mind of the Dolphin: A Nonhuman Intelligence.* Avon Books, New York.

MOORE, T. (ed.). 1973. *Cognitive Development and the Acquisition of Language.* Academic Press, New York.

NORMAN, D. 1969. *Memory and Attention: An Introduction to Human Information Processing.* John Wiley and Sons, New York.

SAPORTA, S. (ed.). 1961. *Psycholinguistics: A Book of Readings.* Holt, Rinehart and Winston, New York.

SLOBIN, D. 1971. *Psycholinguistics.* Scott, Foresman, Glenview, Ill.

SMITH, F. 1971. *Understanding Reading.* Holt, Rinehart and Winston, New York.

———. 1973. *Psycholinguistics and Reading.* Holt, Rinehart and Winston, New York.

SEVEN

Stylistics

The word *stylistics* as it is used in this chapter refers to the application of the theory and methodology of linguistics to literary language. In reading linguistic literature you will come across a number of terms that have to do with one or another facet of stylistics; the most common are *prosody, prosodics, poetics, metrics, rhetoric,* and *literary analysis.* We will use *stylistics* as a cover term for all of these, unless otherwise indicated.

The analytical and descriptive methods of generative transformational grammar were at first applied exclusively to nonliterary language. By comparison with the quantity of writing and research relating to that language mode, literary language was almost totally ignored. Only in the past ten years have transformationalists begun to turn their attention to any significant degree toward the language of poetry and prose.

For some linguists this has no doubt been due to a lack of interest in the subject. For most, however, it has been a decision based upon the conviction that literary language is not an appropriate subject for formal analysis within the transformational model.

Two reasons are frequently offered for this decision. The first is that to analyze literature formally is to somehow devalue or debase it. This is a minor objection. Knowing what binders and pigments Picasso used does not harm his paintings. Enumerating the notes, chords, rhythms, and modulations of Beethoven's symphonies in no way lessens their greatness. The claim that written works of art are unable to withstand the same sort or rigorous analysis is probably more insulting than any analysis possibly could be.

The second reason is quite different, and deserves serious consideration. It is the claim that the methodology of transformational grammar is not *adequate* for stylistic analysis, in that literary language is beyond its effective capacity. If this is true, then it is a waste of time to attempt such analysis, much as it would be a waste of time for an astronomer to insist upon attempting the examination by telescope of a star which lay far beyond that instrument's range.

In the analysis of language the task of the linguist is essentially to demonstrate the systematic relationship that exists between the deep structures of that language (the meanings) and their surface structures. This task can be done most easily when it is restricted to carefully chosen example sentences in isolation. It becomes more difficult when the range of the data is extended to include real language as it is used by human beings in their daily life, as in contemporary sociolinguistic studies. When the data is the language of literature, the difficulty begins to appear insurmountable, and one is strongly tempted to say that the analysis cannot be done.

What lies behind this hesitancy is perhaps best summed up by the term *poetic license*, which is often interpreted to mean that in literature—and especially in poetry—there *are* no rules. This leads to the idea that the effects writers achieve are accidental, or are the result of a mysterious and seemingly random process known as *inspiration*, which may or may not be available when a writer needs it most. Richard Ohmann (1964) said: "A style is a way of writing—that is what the word means. And that is almost as much as one can say with assurance on the subject, which has been remarkably unencumbered by theoretical insights."

However, there is a serious problem with this entire manner of approaching the subject of stylistic analysis. If it is true that there is no system to be demonstrated in literary language, then how are we to explain the fact that we are able to *recognize* a particular work as having been produced by a particular writer? How are we to account for the fact that although we might not be able to identify one sequence of language as the work of Dickens and another as the work of Faulkner, we would nonetheless unhesitatingly state that two different writers were involved? And finally, how are we to explain the process of parody, in which one individual writes in the style of another for deliberate comic effect, and does so successfully? All of these must depend upon the recognition of a set of defining characteristics that, in combination, constitute someone's written style.

It is important to remember that claiming systematicity for literary language does not constitute a claim that writers are consciously aware of the steps they go through in achieving their work. Conscious awareness of the operations of a grammar is not a necessary part of speaking or understanding a language or using it for such tasks as reading directions or filling out forms. Neither is there any reason to assume conscious awareness of such operations in the process of writing literary language.

By no means does this lack of conscious awareness mean that the writer does not "know what he (or she) is doing." When you use a sentence like (1) below, you are unlikely to be able to state the rules involved, but you certainly know quite well what you are doing.

(1)   Congressman Thorpe had been expected to win by every member of his campaign committee, which made his defeat even more discouraging than it would have been if they had not been so confident.

It is complicated, but possible, for the linguist to set down very specifically the rules of phonology, morphology, and syntax that are required for the generation of sentence (1). A less precise, but commendable start can be made on the listing of the semantic rules as well. The question is whether the skills that are used in such a task are adequate to tackle a sequence of language such as James Joyce's *Finnegans Wake*, or the poetry of our modern experimental poets.

We cannot settle the question in this brief chapter. We can, however, examine a few of the possible applications of transformational stylistics to see what resources it offers us. Because of space limitations the discussion will be limited for the most part to poetry, where the poetic line can be looked upon as analogous to the sentence in nonliterary language, and will provide us with adequate examples.

First of all, we will take up the question of how we know that the language sequence we are reading or hearing *is* poetry.

RECOGNITION OF THE POETIC REGISTER

Every one of us would probably insist that we know a poem when we see one, and yet no really satisfactory definition of a poem has ever been proposed. The Second College Edition of *Websters New World Dictionary* defines *poem* as follows:

> (1) an arrangement of words written or spoken, traditionally a rhythmical composition, sometimes rhymed, expressing experiences, ideas, or emotions in a style more concentrated, imaginative, and powerful than that of ordinary speech or prose; some poems are in meter, some in free verse; (2) anything suggesting a poem in its effect.[1]

> [1] With permission. From *Webster's New World Dictionary*, Second College Edition. Copyright © 1972 by The World Publishing Company.

This definition includes almost anything, provided we are willing to consider it sufficiently "concentrated, imaginative, and powerful." It is not very helpful. The definitions of poets—such as Emily Dickinson's claim that she could recognize a poem because she felt as if the top of her head had been taken off—are more interesting, but equally unsuitable for our purposes. There is no way for you to judge whether someone looking at a sequence of language alleged to be a poem feels as Dickinson specified or not.

There are certain characteristics of poetry in English that we can list with reasonable confidence. They do not constitute a final definition, but they can be used as a beginning.

First, a poem will have a physical shape that is recognizably different from prose or other writing. It will ordinarily have a title above it, it will be surrounded by white space on the page, and its lines will not run from margin to margin but will be cut off at varying lengths. These characteristics, which we might call *recognition conventions*, are the least important part of poetry, but they represent a linguistic signal agreed upon by readers of English.

Second, a poem cannot ordinarily be paraphrased or tampered with without destroying it. This is very unlike nonliterary language, where a great deal of paraphrase is possible and the effects rarely matter to anyone. Compare the examples of (2) with those of (3).

(2)   a. I'd like you to build a house for me.
  b. Please build me a house.
  c. I'm here to ask you to build a house for me.
  d. I need someplace to live, and I'd like for you to build it.
  e. How would you feel about building me a house?

(3)   a. Build thee more stately mansions, O my soul.
                (Oliver Wendell Holmes)
  b. Build yourself bigger mansions, O my soul.
  c. Soul o'mine, how about building thee more stately mansions?
  d. Build thee statelier mansions than you've been building, O my soul.
  e. Please build statelier mansions for yourself, Soul.

It makes little difference which of the sentences of (2) is used, and many more alternatives are possible. In (3), on the other hand, each attempt to paraphrase (a) produces something utterly different from the original, and it matters.

Finally, poetry is characterized by its *deviance* from the rules of the grammar of ordinary language. This deviance may be little more than the differences of line length, capitalization and punctuation of traditional blank verse, or it may go to such extremes that a poem looks almost like a random sequence of letters and symbols, as in much of the work of E. E. Cummings.

These three characteristics—physical shape, resistance to paraphrase, and the presence of deviance—have nothing whatever to do with quality. Consider example (4).:

(4) "Spring Rain"

> the grass is wet
> and yet
> I will set
> my dog down on it . . .
> poor little pet.

This constructed example is awful, but it is—formally—a poem. No definition of poetry exists which will exclude it. It is a part of your linguistic competence that you are able to rank poems along a scale of "poeticality," as you can rank sentences on a scale of grammaticalness, but judgments of quality are the proper subject for the critic, not the linguist.

Once a sequence of language has been recognized as poetic, then what? How is it to be handled by the grammar?

A much-analyzed line by E. E. Cummings will help us at this point: "he sang his didn't he danced his did."[2] We all know that this line, even if we were to add a comma or the word *and* after *didn't* to link its two clauses, could not be an acceptable sequence of nonliterary English. The clauses seem to be structurally parallel to the sentences of (5), all of which are allowed by the phrase structure grammar rules in (6).

(5) a. He launched his ship.
b. He cooked his lunch.
c. She painted her house.

(6) a. S → NP VP
b. NP → (Det) N
c. VP → V (NP)

The Cummings line, however, violates the rule in (6b), since the words *did* and *didn't* which follow the determiner *his* are not nouns.

Two ways of approaching this issue have been proposed in transformational literature. One suggestion is that there is a grammar of ordinary English, which contains the rules in (6), and a separate grammar of literary English, which contains (7).

(7) NP → Det V

[2] From "anyone lived in a pretty how town," *Complete Poems 1913–1962* by E. E. Cummings (New York: Harcourt Brace Jovanovich, Inc., 1972).

Another suggestion is that the poem by Cummings should be considered a different *dialect* of English, with a grammar of its own, and that the rule in (7) is contained in the grammar of that dialect.

So long as the separate grammars proposed in these two alternatives include the rule that allows the contraction of an auxiliary verb and a following *not*, (7) will allow the generation of both "he danced his did" and "he danced his didn't."

The point of both alternatives is, of course, to prevent the language of poetry from having an unwanted effect upon the nonliterary grammar. Formally speaking, if linguists say that "he danced his did" is grammatical, without adding any restriction, then the same claim must be made for a potentially infinite number of sequences such as those of (8) in ordinary speech.

(8)   a. She screamed her wouldn't.
      b. I don't think he remembers his can't.
      c. None of us hammered our shouldn't.

This problem is only a formal one, since it is very unlikely that speakers of English would ever use such sentences. Part of their linguistic competence lies in the knowledge that sequences like those in (8) are not appropriate to ordinary language. Nonetheless, it is not a problem that can simply be ignored.

It would be a very wasteful procedure to write an entirely separate grammar for every English poem, since large portions of each such grammar would only duplicate the grammar of English as a whole. A separate grammar for all poetry is just as unsatisfactory; not only would it also have the disadvantages of duplication, but it would have to include many, many rules which might occur only in the work of a single writer or only in one or two poems.

In order to avoid these difficulties, while still maintaining the generalization that many things are allowed in poetry that are not allowed elsewhere, a compromise is needed. First, we can acknowledge the obvious fact that much of the language of poetry is generated by the rules of ordinary discourse. When an author writing in English forms a question by applying the rule of Question Formation, there is no need to say that this rule is in any way part of some separate "stylistic component." It is an obligatory rule of English syntax being used in a literary context. Not only will this happen frequently, it will happen in the majority of cases. (If a poet were to decide that he or she had a separate rule for forming questions that consisted of repeating each word in the line three times, the chances of any reader understanding the line to be a question are almost nonexistent.) The same is true if the writer obeys the phonological constraint that rules out English words beginning with *spt-* or *dlr-*; no special device is needed to indicate what has been done.

The next step is to divide the writers' deviations from the norm set by the grammar of ordinary language into two types:

a. violation of obligatory rules contained in the grammar of non-literary language;
b. the use of optional rules *not* so included, but still subject to the general constraints of the grammar of nonliterary language.

An example of the first type, and one with broad application throughout all types of literature, is the violation of selectional restrictions. You will remember from the semantics chapter that such restrictions are needed in order to ensure that the direct object of the verb *eat* will be something edible, that the noun modified by the adjective *pregnant* will not be one presupposing the feature [+MALE], and so on. We are willing to suspend these restrictions in poetry. If a friend told you that she was astonished because she had just seen a mountain swallow a locomotive and follow that up by gnashing its teeth, you would be justifiably concerned about her physical and mental condition. You would not react in that way to the hypothetical sequence of poetry in (9).

(9) I saw the mountain swallow a locomotive
     and gnash its stony teeth,
     unsatisfied;
     and I was
     astonished.

Similarly, you would accept all of the examples of (10) in poetic lines, although you would reject them in ordinary speech or writing.

(10) a. forth went proudly battalions nine
        (word order violation)
     b. the child behaved the child
        (violation of the obligatory Reflexive rule)
     c. the tower tall loomed over the plain
        (violation of the obligatory rule of Adjective Preposing)

Because a poem can be examined at leisure and pondered over for so long as the reader is willing to do so, violations such as these do not interfere with communication as they would in speech, where there would not be time to process the deviant utterance and determine its meaning.

For stylistic analysis of this kind, what is needed is not a statement that a poet has done something unique demanding the writing of a separate rule. Rather, the linguist need only note that an otherwise obligatory rule from some level of the grammar has not been applied.

A Poetic Transformation

Consider the following lines from a poem by E. E. Cummings titled "there is a here and":[3]

> ... the town is
> so aged the ocean
> wanders the streets are so
> ancient the houses enter the
> people ...

There are of course deviations in the example which are the result of violations of selectional restrictions. We do not ordinarily speak of "aged" towns; although rivers are sometimes said to wander, oceans are not; and *the people* cannot serve as direct object of the verb *enter*, particularly with *the houses* as its subject. These deviations are not our concern at the moment.

The Cummings lines are ambiguous, just as "Flying planes can be dangerous" is ambiguous. The two possible underlying structures are shown in (11) and (12).

(11) #the town is so aged that the ocean wanders the streets#
      #the streets are so ancient that the houses enter the people#

(12) #the town is so aged and the ocean wanders the streets#
      #the streets are so ancient and the houses enter the people#

For the rule that will be discussed here, it makes no difference which of these structures is the correct one. We will arbitrarily choose (11), but either choice would be satisfactory.

Notice that the two lines share an identical constituent, the noun phrase *the streets.* You will remember from the syntax chapter that one characteristic of English grammar is a resistance to repetition of identical elements in a single sentence, as shown in (12).

(12) a. *Jorge$_i$ saw Jorge's$_i$ sister yesterday.
      b. Jorge$_i$ saw his sister$_i$ yesterday.

[3] *Complete Poems 1913–1962*, by E. E. Cummings (New York: Harcourt Brace Jovanovich, Inc., 1972).

  c. *The car$_i$ the car$_i$ broke down was mine.

  d. The car$_i$ which$_i$ broke down was mine.

  e. *If Mary says she will run the university with an iron hand no matter how much resistance she encounters from the faculty, she will run the university with an iron hand no matter how much resistance she encounters from the faculty.

  f. If Mary says she will run the university with an iron hand no matter how much resistance she encounters from the faculty, she will.

Ordinarily repetition is avoided by either deleting the second of the pair of identical elements or substituting a pronoun for it.

  The same objection to repetition is true beyond the boundaries of the single sentence, especially in two sentences which are *immediately contiguous* (that is, which follow one another without any other sequence between them). Look at the examples in (13) and (14):

(13) X: She is a lying, sneaking troublemaker motivated only by her own personal desire for self-aggrandizement.

   Y: *She is not a lying, sneaking troublemaker motivated only by her own personal desire for self-aggrandizement.

(14) X: She is a lying, sneaking troublemaker motivated only by her own personal desire for self-aggrandizement.

   Y: She is not.

  In the sequence of poetic lines in Cummings' poem he has not "invented" some radically new grammatical operation. He has merely extended the process of identity deletion that is already needed for the nonliterary grammar of English. The effect of the rule is to delete the second of two identical items which are immediately contiguous to one another. As with all known identity deletion rules, one of the pair of identical items must appear in the surface structure to ensure that the deletion will be recoverable and there will be no meaning change. The rule is called Overlap Deletion.

  An example of the application of the rule within a single line is the hypothetical (15).

(15) a. #I have seen you you have seen me#

   b. #I have seen you $\emptyset$ have seen me#

   c. I have seen you have seen me

It is possible to apply Overlap Deletion to (15a) because the subject and object forms of the second person pronoun *you* are identical in English. If we try to construct an example in the third person, we will find that it is impossible, even though structurally the lines are exactly like those of (15).

(16) a. #I have seen him he has seen me#
      b. #I have seen him ∅ has seen me#
      c. *I have seen him has seen me

Certainly (16c) could occur as a line of English poetry; however, it cannot be the result of the derivation shown in (16a–b), in which the meaning of *he has seen me* has been lost.

    Overlap Deletion also cannot apply when the two items are phonologically identical but have entirely different meanings—for example, when one is a noun and the other a verb. The examples in (17) will make this clear.

(17) a. #never tell a lie lie on my shoulder#
      b. *Never tell a lie on my shoulder.

      c. #only the loving die#
          #die, but remember me#
      d. *only the loving die
          but remember me

This restriction is consistent with the nonliterary grammar, in which identity deletion (or substitution) rules will not apply to a sequence containing two instances of, say, "James Martin" if in fact they refer to two different individuals who happen to have orthographically identical names.

    Research done on Overlap Deletion has shown that it can be very precisely stated, that it is not applied in a random manner, and that it is in fact rigidly constrained. The important point is not the formal structure of the rule, however, but the fact that its use by a poet does not require anything more than an *extension* of the grammar of nonliterary English.

    For literary transformations, as for all others, there remains the primary constraint that no transformation be allowed to change meaning. It is clear that for literary language, and especially for poetry, the distinction between competence and performance is going to be highly significant. The writer of poetry is in effect deliberately attempting to introduce systematic deviance into his language and is relying upon the reader to understand his meaning nonetheless. The skill with which this is done, both in writer and in reader, will vary from individual to individual. When poetry is presented orally instead of in writing, the performance factors that may interfere with comprehension ordinarily increase still more, because the opportunity to examine the poetic sequence over and over is no longer available.

GENERATIVE PHONOLOGY
AND ENGLISH METRICS

It is probable that the phonological patterning of poetic language is the first thing we appreciate about it. Long before a child is old enough to say more than a few words, it will respond with obvious pleasure to such immortal sequences as:

(18) Pat-a-cake, pat-a-cake,
      Baker's man!

The child does not point out to us that (18) runs through the sequence of English voiceless stops twice, or that the pattern of labial consonants and alternating /æ/–/e/ vowel sounds is fascinating. It has no way of indicating whether it notices such things. But it makes its awareness of the rhythm of (18)—the *meter*—unmistakably clear, by clapping its hands or jumping up and down in time with the verse.

The meter of (18) is traditionally referred to as *trochaic*, a term used to indicate that the pattern of stressed syllables in the line is a strong syllable followed by a weak one. The opposite of trochaic meter, a weak syllable and then a strong one, is called *iambic*. These syllable groups are said to be metric *feet*, and the number of such feet in a line is indicated by more terms borrowed from Greek—*pentameter* for five feet, *tetrameter* for four, *hexameter* for six, and so on. This system appears to have worked well for other languages, but it has never been very satisfactory for English.

For most of us, our earliest experience with this system is our introduction to the iambic pentameter line, which becomes permanently enshrined in our memories in the deadly form of (19).

(19) da DA/ da DA/ da DA/ da DA/ da DA

All of the lines in (20) are examples of this pattern, which is considered to be the cornerstone of English metrics.

(20) a. I *saw* the *ships* sail *in* on *Christ*mas *day*
            (traditional carol)

      b. When *forty* *win*ters *shall* be*siege* thy *brow*
            (Shakespeare)

      c. Shall *I* com*pare* thee *to* a *Sum*mer's *day*
            (Shakespeare)

These lines are flawless examples of (19), and very pleasant; but if perfect iambic pentameter goes on for more than a few lines, it becomes unbearably tedious. Furthermore, it is unusual for it to do so, which means that English poetry is everywhere filled with lines that we feel are somehow the same rhythmic type as those in (20) but which are very different from the presumed pattern in (19). For example:

(21) a. Full many a glorious morning have I seen
       Flatter the mountain-tops with sovereign eye
                       (Shakespeare)

    b. And that one talent which is death to hide
       Lodged with me useless, though my soul more bent
                         (Milton)

Many attempts to explain this have been made over the years, usually in the form of listing all the multitude of "exceptions" that are allowed in an iambic pentameter line. For instance, it has been customary to state that it is permissible to invert the first da DA and make a DA da out of it, as in the second lines of both examples in (21).

As the list of exceptions grew longer and longer, however, it began to look as though it would have been simpler to describe an iambic pentameter line as one that must not extend for more than three inches on the page, or something of the kind. Obviously some generalization was being missed.

The problem is that stress in English is not absolute; a syllable cannot be specified as weak or strong in the way that Greek syllables could be specified absolutely as long or short. As Otto Jespersen pointed out long ago, it is the *relative* weakness or strength of syllables that is important to English verse; that is, the strengths of syllables in comparison with one another. Jespersen (1966) said that "Verse rhythm is based on the same alternation between stronger and weaker syllables as that found in natural everyday speech."

Morris Halle and Samuel Keyser, following Jespersen's lead, proposed a system for the characterization of iambic pentameter based upon the concept of the *stress maximum*, which they defined as follows:

A stress maximum is a syllable which is more heavily stressed than the syllables flanking it on either side.

This means, of course, that neither the first nor the last syllable of a line could ever constitute a stress maximum, whatever their degree of strength or weakness, since they have a flanking syllable on only *one* side rather than both.

To this definition Keyser and Halle added the following two rules, here somewhat simplified:

An iambic pentameter line consists of ten slots which can potentially be filled by syllables.

A stress maximum may occupy only even-numbered *slots, in the line, but not all such slots have to be filled.*

Example (22) is an ordinary iambic pentameter line chosen from those in (20). The positions within the line are filled by numbered syllables, and those which constitute stress maxima have been outlined.

(22) I saw the ships sail in on Christmas Day.

I	saw	the	ships	sail	in	on	Christ-	mas	Day
1	2	3	4	5	6	7	8	9	10

If you read the line aloud to yourself you will notice that each of the outlined syllables is more strongly stressed than either of the syllables which flanks it on the right or on the left. This line contains four stress maxima, which means that every possible position for a stress maximum is filled. Now consider the following hypothetical example:

(23) Look at the ships sail in on Christmas Day.

Look	at	the	ships	sail	in	on	Christ-	mas	Day
1	2	3	4	5	6	7	8	9	10

In this line it is true that the first word, *look*, is more strongly stressed than the word *at* which follows it. Remember, however, that to constitute a stress maximum a syllable must have a weaker-stressed syllable on *both* sides. Therefore, this line contains only three stress maxima.

There are times when two syllables may count as one *metric* syllable, in English. This is possible, for instance, when two syllables are separated only by a nasal, as in (24).

(24) I sat in a tree and watched the day go by.

I	sat	in a	tree	and	watched	the	day	go	by
1	2	3	4	5	6	7	8	9	10

The two syllables of *in a* are made up of two vowels separated by a single nasal consonant and therefore can fill a single metric position; the line has four stress maxima. The same thing has been done in Shakespeare's line "Full many a glorious morning have I seen," which would traditionally be "irregular" because it contains—in strictly orthographic terms—eleven syllables. The second syllable of the word *many* and the following word *a* fill only one metric position, not two.

All of the examples above have been heavily filled. The more stress maxima there are in a line, the more insistent the rhythm will be, but a succession of lines with four stress maxima quickly becomes doggerel rather than verse. An important part of the pleasure we get from poetry is its unexpectedness and its difference, and there is simply nothing unexpected about dozens of uninterrupted repetitions of perfect iambic pentameter in the traditional sense. It is common for English iambic pentameter lines to have only two stress maxima, or even only one, per ten positions.

The stress maximum concept has had exciting results for English metrics. It is now possible to explain much more precisely why a line is felt by the English-speaking reader or listener to be iambic pentameter even when it varies markedly from the formula based upon the totally *non*-English concepts of traditional metric feet.[4]

Joseph Beaver (1968) pointed out that the stress maximum was clearly extendable to other metric patterns. He suggested that the tetrameter line be looked upon as eight potential syllabic slots, in which the stress maxima would be allowed to occur only in odd-numbered positions. Again, not every potential position would have to be filled. Look at (25).

(25)   Mary, Mary, quite contrary

Ma-	ry	Ma-	ry	quite	con-	tra-	ry
1	2	3	4	5	6	7	8

This line contains three stress maxima, the highest number possible for a tetrameter line. The rhythm is therefore very strongly felt. Most nursery rhymes, jump-rope rhymes, and game rhymes are written with the full utilization of all possible stress maxima.

The stress maximum theory is an important contribution to English stylistics; but it is no more than an extension of the principles of stress that are already essential to the phonology of nonliterary English. Therefore, there is no need to consider it a separate phonological phenomenon requiring its own "literary" grammar.

---

[4] It would seem reasonable to discard the non-English terminology along with the concepts. The battery of terminology from metrics—*iamb, trochee, spondee, anapest, septameter*, etc.—has never served to do much more than convince English speakers that metrics is a mystery to be avoided if possible. However, no new terminology has yet been proposed to replace the old.

POTENTIAL APPLICATIONS

Given the concepts that have been developed in this chapter, what can be said about the possibilities for their further use?

One of the most important applications of these ideas is to the characterization of style. Style is something we all feel, whether we are able to talk about it or write about it or not. If we read a great deal of the work of some particular writer there comes a time when we can pick up a story and know, without looking at the by line, that it is his or her work. We develop for the style of particular poets and prose writers the same feeling of recognition that we have for the voices of people we talk to frequently. This feeling that we have, this recognition of the writer's "voice," lies behind the art of literary criticism.

There are as many styles of literary criticism as there are styles in the works being criticized. Sometimes it approaches the metaphysical: "He writes and one hears the roar of the open sea and is sucked into the vortex of a powerful imagery that carries all before it." Sometimes it is statistical: the "Did Melville use more *w*'s than Twain?" approach. And sometimes it is brilliant—fine literature in its own right.

For the work of the linguist, however, the traditional methods of literary criticism are not appropriate. The goal of the linguist is to discover, describe, and—if possible—explain systematic pattern. It is traditional to refer to Hemingway's style as "masculine," but what does that mean, precisely? Is there any way to determine whether what the critic means by "masculine" is the same as your concept, as reader, of that term? Words like "powerful," "overwhelming," "limpid," "fresh," "piercing," have meanings that may vary widely from one person to another. It is here that linguistics may be of significant use.

First the linguist can examine the work of a given writer to see how and to what extent he or she employs the nonliterary transformations of English which are not obligatory. If Writer X uses the rule of Topicalization a great deal, but Writer Y almost never uses it, then that constitutes a specific fact about the difference between the two styles. If a writer makes very frequent use of a particular deletion transformation, the linguist can point this out; something is then being said about the writer's style that is subject to empirical verification and that means the same thing for all speakers of English.

At this point it is important to clarify a potential source of confusion. The natural tendency is to say, "Why is it any better to know how many Topicalizations a writer uses than it is to know how many *w*'s he uses?" The two seem at first to be parallel.

But this is a mistaken impression. When a writer uses the various members of the inventory of optional transformations, he effects actual changes, or refrains from making such changes. Suppose that he begins with the following tree:

(26)

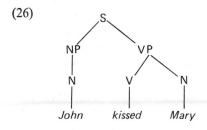

From this single underlying structure it is possible for all of the following sentences to be derived:

(27) a. John kissed Mary.
　　b. Mary was kissed by John.
　　c. It was John that kissed Mary.
　　d. It was Mary that was kissed by John.
　　e. What John did was kiss Mary.

When a writer chooses one of these alternatives rather than another, it shows nothing at all, if it happens only once or twice. But when a consistent preference for one type of surface structure over the others can be shown, then this constitutes a definite characteristic of his style.

The writer is not in quite the same situation with regard to the choice of letters. The letters that make up English words are not a matter of relatively free choice. It is almost impossible for a writer not to use many, many *e*'s, because *e* is by far the most frequent letter in English orthography.

What the writer *can* do, and does very frequently in poetry, is show a definite preference for particular patterns of sounds, by choosing sets of words which contain them. If you are eating dinner and someone at the table with you says "Pass the peas, please," it is almost certainly a coincidence that three of the four words in the sequence begin with /p/ and that the last two are a perfect rhyme (and, of course, that all four are monosyllabic words). When this happens in a poetic line, on the other hand, it is reasonable to assume that the poet has done it on purpose. "Could I have some more of those peas?" would do as an alternative sequence of language in the dinner table context; it would completely destroy the phonological patterning of the same sequence as a line of poetry. This sort of choice becomes far more unlikely in prose, where the number of instances of a specific letter or sound is usually dictated by the vocabulary that the text requires. One of the characteristics most likely to trigger a description of someone's prose as "poetic" is a tendency to sound-patterning beyond that which we are accustomed to encountering outside of poetry.

Once a writer's patterns of preference for optional transformations have been noted, the linguist can move on to look for the two types of deviations discussed earlier in this chapter: deliberate violations of obligatory rules, or extensions of processes already in the grammar but not acceptable outside the literary context. When all this has been done, the linguist should be able to say something like "We know of this writer that she consistently uses the optional transformations A, B, and E; that she almost never uses optional transformation D; and that she has extended transformations S and Z in ways that can be systematically described." This is rather different from stating that so-and-so's style is "masculine." If enough detailed transformational descriptions of this type could be put together and compared, we might begin to see larger patterns that would enable us to understand more clearly why the style of Hemingway is viewed as masculine and the style of someone else is not.

In poetry the linguist will note the poet's use of stress maxima. Is there a marked preference for filling all possible stress maximum positions? Does the poet show a low incidence of fully utilized lines? Is there a consistent pattern of alternation such as a line with only one stress maximum, then a line with three, then another line with one?

It should be possible to characterize not only the styles of various individual writers, but also those amorphous things known as "schools" of writing. For example, Donald C. Freeman (1970) notes that:

> The shift in metrical style during the sixteenth century from the stiffly formal pentameters of Gascoigne and Grimald to the more flexible verse of Marlowe and Kyd can be characterized . . . as a shift in the metrical ideal from a line with four actualized stress maxima to a line with three. (*Linguistics and Literary Style*, p. 448.)

There is no reason why the use of certain transformations, or certain patterns of stress maxima, should not be as subject to fashion as the decline and fall of such poetisms as *o'er* and *ope*.

Finally, there is the possibility of looking for literary universals. This seems a bit premature at the moment, since we have only the embryonic beginnings of an understanding of the literary structure of our own language. However, certain things are known about universal stylistics even at this early stage. First, there is no human society that is *without* a literary language. Second, there is no language which lacks rhythmic devices for its literature, although their forms may vary radically from one language to another. Just as every language has a means of indicating negation, although the words and patterns used may be very unlike, so does every language have a way of indicating rhythmic pattern, even though the surface realizations are not the same.

We know something about the recognition conventions of other languages. We know, for instance, that literature cannot be recognized by its status as printed material on a page in a culture which has no written form for its language. In such cultures there will be an oral literature, the most common characteristic of which is likely to be a high frequency of repetition. (This repetition allows the listener a chance to consider the material at leisure in a manner analogous to that which print offers the reader.) It may be that the literary language is reserved for use on special occasions, or for use by specific persons, such as priests or shamans. In some cultures the language itself may be different from that of daily discourse not only in its syntax but in its phonology as well. The Navajo have a large literature of religious songs and chants which show systematic differences from the phonology of ordinary Navajo; for example, a Navajo word which in daily speech contains a nasal vowel will almost always be found in songs and chants with an oral vowel followed by a nasal consonant.

The rule of Overlap Deletion was discussed in this chapter as a device specific to English literary language, particularly English poetry. However, it is interesting to note that this transformation is also common in a language as widely removed from English as Japanese, where it is in fact less constrained than it is in English. There is no reason in principle why it should not turn out to be the case that this transformation is a universal process of literary language.

As linguists work with literary texts, applying to them the principles of linguistic theory, we will learn more and more about literary language. We are just at the beginning of this area of research, and some of the unsolved problems are monumental. For example, no one has had much luck in precisely characterizing the rhythms of free verse, or the rhythms of prose, although we all know that they exist. However, the theory of linguistics gives us some scientific tools with which to tackle such problems, and to begin proposing solutions for them.

EXERCISES AND PROBLEMS

1. Underline the stress maxima in each of the following examples.

(a) Peter, Peter, Pumpkin Eater
Had a wife and couldn't keep her;
Put her in a pumpkin shell, and
There he kept her very well.

(b)   *Sonnet LXV*

Since brass, nor stone, nor earth, nor boundless sea,
But sad mortality o'ersways their power,
How with this rage shall beauty hold a plea,
Whose action is no stronger than a flower?
O, how shall summer's honey breath hold out
Against the wreckful siege of battering days,
When rocks impregnable are not so stout,
Nor gates of steel so strong, but time decays?
O fearful meditation! where, alack!
Shall Time's best jewel from Time's chest lie hid?
Or what strong hand can hold his swift foot back?
Or who his spoil of beauty can forbid?
     O none, unless this miracle have might
     That in black ink my love may still shine bright.
                                   (William Shakespeare)

(c)   *Loving in Truth*

Loving in truth, and fain in verse my love to show,
That she, dear she, might take some pleasure of my pain,
Pleasure might cause her read, reading might make her know,
Knowledge might pity win, and pity grace obtain,
I sought fit words to paint the blackest face of woe;
                                      (Sir Philip Sidney)

(d)   *Broom, Green Broom*

There was an old man and he lived in a wood,
     And his trade it was making of broom, of broom,
And he had a naughty boy, Jack, to his son,
     And he lay in bed till 'twas noon, 'twas noon,
          And he lay in bed till 'twas noon.
                                           (Anonymous)

In doing this exercise, did you notice any other ways that a potential syllable slot in a line can be filled besides those discussed in this chapter?

2. Choose any brief English poem you like that is reasonably regular rhymed and metered verse. Then transcribe it phonemically, using the set of symbols provided in the phonology chapter. What advantage does this transcription give you in the analysis of its sound patterns?

3. The data for this exercise is a poem by Elgin which will serve as a representative example of contemporary free verse. Read the poem and then do the following tasks:

(a) List as completely as you can the deviations which the example shows from the grammar of nonliterary English. Consider orthographic deviations, and lexical or morphological deviations, as well as those types discussed in this chapter.

(b) Rewrite the poem in such a way that you "correct" all the deviations that you found, so far as that is possible without changing the meaning.

(c) Compare the original poem and your revision. Is the latter still recognizable as literary language? Is it still a poem? Explain your answer.

Extraperceptory Sensation

in this web
we BE
where
we ARE
star-anchored
we are angered by
those
who will not join the dance

(ah, friend,
bend to my touch,
touched, lend me your mindtips)
here, hear more
than all that you have heard

heretofore
in this ruled random
where lovepulses leap tenderly
tracing
(is such sin taxing?)
from connection beloved to connection,
the irritants wear
(while we ARE)
their handy deafcaps blithely
saying
"See! Man ticks slowly . . ."
. . . .
mindtwined allterms are defined
behind the eye

4. In Japanese poetry Overlap Deletion can be applied to items which are only parts of words. A comparable example from English would be the derivation of *friendshipmate* from a sequence consisting of *friendship* followed immediately by *shipmate*, which does not work because, for one thing, the *-ship* of *friendship* and the *ship-* of *shipmate* differ in meaning. But even examples which avoid this restriction do not seem plausible in English, except for over-obvious compounds such as *quicksandpile* from *quicksand sandpile*. The examples below, however, *do* seem to be successful, in that no part of the overlapped sequences is lost. Can you explain why?

   (a) A stitch in time saves ninety-
       nine men on a dead man's chest
   (b) Love me, love my doggedly
       she wandered on
   (c) Read me no star-crossed loverse
   (d) One and one are toothless,
       three and two are five;
       nine and one are tentative,
       six is argumentative.

5. There is a hybrid form of poetry which has not been common in English, called the *prose poem*. Prose poems lack one of the primary recognition conventions of English poetry, because the lines run all the way from margin to margin just as they do in a chemistry textbook. Can you suggest how—short of simply naming them "Prose Poem on Such-and-Such-A-Subject"—a poet could make sure that the work would be recognized as poetry rather than prose?

6. Stan Kenton once wrote a song called "Celery Stalks at Midnight." This deviation can be expressed in feature notation by marking the word *stalks* both [+NOUN] and [+VERB]. Construct at least four more examples of this kind.

7. A *pun* is deliberate systematic ambiguity, with the intention of conveying both possible deep structures at one time. Collect or construct ten examples of puns; if you have trouble finding good ones, look for them in advertisements. Write out the two underlying sequences that have been collapsed to produce the pun, paraphrasing as extensively as you need to. Here is an example to get you started:

   An insurance company uses the slogan "Our policy is serving you." The underlying sequences are:

(a) The insurance policy that our firm writes is serving you.
(b) It is the standard business policy of our firm to serve you.

8. English is not an unwritten language; however, we do have an oral literature in the form of political speeches and sermons, in which the total effect of the language is dependent on the skill of listening. There is no time for an audience to go over and over the sequences of a political speech, and yet the speaker would usually like to think that the speech will be memorable. In order to achieve this result, political speakers use systematic processes that differ from ordinary language. Look at three speeches (or sermons, if you prefer) and try to describe at least one such process. (The sermons of Martin Luther King, or the speeches of John F. Kennedy, are excellent sources of data for this exercise.)

9. One of the examples in Exercise 4 contains a "sloppy identity" as defined in Chapter Three, Exercise 10. Which example is the sloppy one?

10. Although it is customary in every other area of linguistics for linguists to construct hypothetical examples to illustrate the points they are making, this writer frequently encounters objections to constructed examples of poetry on the grounds that they are not "really" poetry. Do you think this position can be defended? Why or why not?

11. Choose an example of free verse that you like; it should be at least twenty lines long, in order to provide you with enough data. Identify all the stress maxima in your selection. Does it seem to you that the stress maximum is useful as a tool for analyzing free verse? Compare your results, and your answer to the question, with the responses of others in your class. Are you in agreement with one another?

SUGGESTED READINGS

ARTICLES AND EXCERPTS

AARTS, J. 1971. "A Note on the Interpretation of 'he danced his did'." *Journal of Linguistics* 7:71–73.

BAMGBOSE, A. 1970. "Word Play in Yoruba Poetry." *International Journal of American Linguistics* 36:110–16.

BANFIELD, A. 1973. "Narrative Style and the Grammar of Direct and Indirect Speech." *Foundations of Language* 10:10–39.

BEAVER, J. 1968. "A Grammar of Prosody." *College English* 29:310–21.

BOLINGER, D. 1950. "Rime, Assonance and Morpheme Analysis." *Word* 6:117–36.

CHATMAN, S. 1957. "Linguistics, Poetics, and Interpretation: The Phonemic Dimension." *Quarterly Journal of Speech* 43:248–56.

———. 1967. "Stylistics: Quantitative and Qualitative." *Style* 1:29–43.

EATON, T. 1970. "The Foundation of Literary Semantics." *Linguistics* 62:5–19.

ELGIN, S. 1975. "The Language and Structure of Poetry." *Pouring Down Words*, Chap. 8. Prentice-Hall, Englewood Cliffs, N.J.

ELLIS, J. 1970. "Linguistics, Literature, and the Concept of Style." *Word* 26:65–78.

FISH, S. 1970. "Literature in the Reader: Affective Stylistics." *New Literary History* 2:123–62.

———. 1973. "What Is Stylistics and Why Are They Saying Such Terrible Things About It?" *Approaches to Poetics*, S. CHATMAN (ed.). Columbia University Press, New York.

FOWLER, R. 1966. "Structural Metrics." *Linguistics* 27:49–64.

HALLE, M., and S. KEYSER. 1966. "Chaucer and the Study of Prosody." *College English* 28:187–219.

HAYES, C. 1966. "A Study in Prose Styles: Edward Gibbon and Ernest Hemingway." *Texas Studies in Literature and Language* 7:371–86.

———. 1968. "A Transformational-Generative Approach to Style: Samuel Johnson and Edward Gibbon." *Language and Style* 1:39–48.

IKEGAMI, Y. 1969. "A Linguistic Essay on Parody." *Linguistics* 55:13–31.

———. 1965. "Semantic Change in Poetic Words." *Linguistics* 51:11–33.

IVES, S. 1950. "A Theory of Literary Dialect." *Tulane Studies in English* 2:137–82.

LEECH, G. 1965. "'This Bread I Break': Language and Interpretation." *Review of English Literature* 6:66–75.

LEVIN, S. 1963. "Deviation—Statistical and Determinate—in Poetic Language." *Lingua* 12:276–90.

———. 1964. "Poetry and Grammaticalness." *Proceedings of the 19th International Congress of Linguists*, H. HUNT (ed.). Mouton, The Hague.

———. 1965. "Two Grammatical Approaches to Poetic Analysis." *College Composition and Communication* 16:256–60.

———. 1965a. "Internal and External Deviation in Poetry." *Word* 21:225–37.

———. 1966. "Literature as Sentences." *College English* 27:261–67.

———. 1968. "Review of W. Koch, *Recurrence and a Three-Modal Approach to Poetry*." *Language* 44:436–42.

LOEWENBERG, I. 1975. "Identifying Metaphors." *Foundations of Language* 12:315–38.

MERRILL, T. 1969. "'The Sacrifice' and the Structure of Religious Language." *Language and Style* 2:275–87.

MESSING, G. 1971. "The Impact of Transformational Grammar upon Stylistics and Literary Analysis." *Linguistics* 66:56–73.

NIST, J. 1964. "The Word-Group Cadence: Basis of English Metrics." *Linguistics* 6:73–82.

OHMANN, R. 1964. "Generative Grammar and the Concept of Literary Style." *Word* 20:424–39.

RUSSELL, W. 1971. "Linguistic Stylistics." *Linguistics* 65:75–82.

SASTRI, M. 1974. "Deviance and Poetic Style." *Language Sciences* 31:11–12.

THORNE, J. 1965. "Stylistics and Generative Grammars." *Journal of Linguistics* 1:49–59.

————. 1969. "Poetry, Stylistics and Imaginary Grammars." *Journal of Linguistics* 5:147–50.

WELLEK, R. 1961. "The Main Trends of Twentieth-Century Criticism." *Yale Review* 51:102–18.

WHEELWRIGHT, P. 1940. "On the Semantics of Poetry." *Kenyon Review* 11:263–83.

BOOKS AND MONOGRAPHS

CHATMAN, S. 1965. *A Theory of Meter*. Mouton, The Hague.

———— (ed.). 1971. *Literary Style: A Symposium*. Oxford University Press, New York.

————, and S. LEVIN (eds.). 1965. *Essays on the Language of Literature*. Houghton Mifflin, Boston.

DEUTSCH, B. 1969. *Poetry Handbook: A Dictionary of Terms*. Funk and Wagnalls, New York.

DOLEŽEL, L., and R. BAILEY (eds.). 1969. *Statistics and Style*. American Elsevier, New York.

EMPSON, W. 1962. *Seven Types of Ambiguity*. Penguin Books, New York.

ENKVIST, N. 1973. *Linguistic Stylistics*. Mouton, The Hague.

FREEMAN, D. (ed.). 1970. *Linguistics and Literary Style*. Holt, Rinehart and Winston, New York. (Many of the articles cited above are collected in this volume.)

GIBSON, W. 1966. *Tough, Sweet, and Stuffy*. Indiana University Press, Bloomington, Ind.

GROSS, H. 1964. *Sound and Form in Modern Poetry*. University of Michigan Press, Ann Arbor, Mich.

LEVIN, S. 1962. *Linguistic Structures in Poetry*. Mouton, The Hague.

MILIC, L. 1967. *A Quantitative Approach to the Style of Jonathan Swift*. Mouton, The Hague.

MINER, E. 1968. *An Introduction to Japanese Court Poetry*. Stanford University Press, Stanford, Calif.

SEBEOK, T. (ed.). 1960. *Style in Language*. M.I.T. Press, Cambridge, Mass.

THOMAS, O. 1969. *Metaphor and Related Subjects*. Random House, New York.

TUFTE, V. 1971. *Grammar as Style*. Holt, Rinehart and Winston, New York.

ULLMANN, S. 1962. *Semantics: An Introduction to the Science of Meaning*. B. Blackwell, Oxford, England.

————. 1964. *Language and Style: Collected Papers*. B. Blackwell, Oxford, England.

————. 1973. *Meaning and Style: Collected Papers*. B. Blackwell, Oxford, England.

WELLEK, R., and A. WARNER. 1956. *Theory of Literature*. Harcourt Brace Jovanovich, New York.

EIGHT

Applied Linguistics

The term *applied linguistics* has received a wide variety of interpretations, particularly in the United States, where it has become entangled with the bilingual/bidialectal education controversies. The basic definition of the term is simply the application of the principles and theory of linguistics to other areas of knowledge. There is of course a sense in which such fields as psycho-linguistics, sociolinguistics, and the like are part of applied linguistics. But these fields have grown to such an extent that they are now full-fledged separate disciplines and must be treated as such. Fields of study that fall within the broad definition of applied linguistics include at least computer languages, speech and hearing therapies of several kinds, mathematical linguistics, mechanical translation, some types of animal communication research, and a number of other highly specialized activities. Like the line between a pidgin and a creole, the line at which a particular linguistic specialty ceases to be part of applied linguistics and becomes a separate sub-discipline is hard to draw and is bound to be squabbled over.

In this chapter no attempt will be made to settle this definitional quandary (which may never be resolved). Instead, the discussion will be confined to the specific area of applied educational linguistics, which is one of the largest subdivisions of the field and is in a stage of rapid development.

APPLIED EDUCATIONAL LINGUISTICS

The term "applied linguistics" has become fashionable in the field of education in recent years, and, as often happens with pedagogical fads, has been used so broadly and so loosely that it has almost ceased to have any real meaning at all. The book market has been flooded with "applied" materials of all kinds, especially in language arts, foreign language teaching, and the area of bilingual/bidialectal education. This has sometimes led to serious problems, particularly since many of these materials confuse structural linguistics and generative transformational linguistics and offer products based upon that confusion. When these materials fail to "work" in the classroom, the tendency is to blame linguistics, which is not really either fair or accurate. A brief historical discussion may be of some help here.

The first wave of published work actually *called* applied linguistics probably can be said to have begun with Leonard Bloomfield's attempt to establish a "linguistic method" for the teaching of reading. This first wave reached its peak in the 1950's with the publication of the pedagogical materials of Charles Fries, Archibald Hill, John Carroll, and others. It continued into the 60's (and continues today), primarily in the area of foreign language teaching, where the work of scholars such as Eugene Lado and Robert Politzer dominates the field.

These studies were written within the theoretical framework of either traditional or structural linguistics, and they presented many useful techniques and concepts upon which the generative transformational model of applied work has built. We are indebted to this stage of applied linguistics for the first nontechnical writings (that is, writing intended for the non-linguist) which expressed in pedagogical terms the following important points:

1. That *prescriptivism* in language—the idea that there is one and only one "correct" way of saying or writing anything in a particular language—does not reflect the facts of the real world and cannot be used as the entire basis for teaching in the language arts.

2. That language is systematic and patterned, and that the native speaker of a language, or the individual learning a foreign language, can be helped by the demonstration and analysis of these patterns and by practice in their use.

3. That the internalized patterns of one language may profitably be compared and contrasted with the patterns of others; and that this process (called *contrastive analysis*) can be extremely useful not only for providing information to students but also for predicting areas in which learning difficulties may be anticipated.

During the first flush of this stage of the field, there was a feeling that education was going to be completely shaken up and drastically changed by the linguistic work going on. This was reflected in statements like the following from "Revolution in Grammar," an article by W. Nelson Francis:

A long overdue revolution is at present taking place in the study of English grammar—a revolution as sweeping in its consequences as the Darwinian revolution in biology. It is the result of the application to English of methods of descriptive analysis originally developed for use with languages of primitive people.[1] To anyone at all interested in language, it is challenging; to those concerned with the teaching of English (including parents), it presents the necessity of radically revising both the substance and the methods of their teaching. (*Quarterly Journal of Speech*, Oct. 1954.)

Although this statement was written over twenty years ago, the "long overdue" revolution mentioned is still forthcoming, and is no longer even the same revolution Francis was referring to. *His* revolution has perhaps finally begun to take hold today, in schools which in 1954 would have had little or no tolerance for the advice of linguists in their classrooms. Students frequently ask why this is so, and it is difficult to answer the question satisfactorily.

Perhaps a major reason why the entity popularly known as the "educational establishment" is so reluctant to undergo major change is that previous experience has been so negative that its members now fear the fire. Ask any fourth-grade teacher nearing retirement age how many "new grammars" and "new maths" and "new reading methods" have come his or her way, over the years. Ask that same teacher what the usual experience with the "new" things has been, and you will hear that it went like this:

a. glowing promises of wondrous gains in learning;
b. chaos and confusion as teachers attempted to adjust to the "new" method;
c. little demonstrable evidence of the promised advantages for the students;

---

[1] A linguist writing today would be unlikely to use the phrase *primitive people* in this sense; it was not looked upon as pejorative in 1954.

  d. chaos and confusion as teachers attempted to adjust to the mess
     created by the change;
  e. finally, the arrival of yet another "new" something or other to
     disrupt the classroom.

This has been discussed here at such length only because linguists, and others, are so quick to criticize the classroom teacher and the administrator for a seemingly inflexible determination to rely on the tried and the traditional and to resist experimentation at all costs.

The lag between the findings of research and its implementation in the elementary and secondary classroom (as well as beyond) really does exist. No doubt it contributes to some of the problems we face in education in the United States today, often with unpleasant consequences for the students. However, it is not fair to blame the situation entirely on the educators and administrators. All too often the research scholar has simply done the research, published it, and then abandoned it, the idea being that his or her contribution stopped right there. The unfortunate result has been the dissemination of materials which were rushed into print by publishers who did not understand what they were publishing, rushed into the classroom to be taught by teachers who did not understand what they were teaching, and thoroughly despised thereafter by everyone involved. Linguists who fold their hands and refuse to accept any responsibility for such messes should not be surprised when their research is not welcomed with open arms by the educational community.

Today linguists working in pedagogical research are trying to make haste somewhat more slowly. The urgency of the need for their work is great and the desire for haste—together with pressure for haste from many sources—is almost overwhelming, and difficult to resist. There are two excellent reasons for this urgency and for the pressure; they are inextricably interwoven.

First, there is the multi-ethnic mix in American education, with its tremendous problems based in great part squarely upon language, dialect, and cultural differences. Second, there is the alleged "crisis" in basic literacy skills, which is by no means confined to ethnic minority groups. The latter has created a new stereotype at the university level—The Entering Freshman Who Cannot Read Or Write A Single Coherent Sentence Of His/Her Language.[2]

Linguists, like educators, had the "haste-makes-waste" lesson driven home to them very forcibly in the late 60's and early 70's, when attempts were made to incorporate the formalism—the elaborate rule notations and tree diagrams of generative transformational theory—into such subjects as Language Arts at the elementary school level. (For example, the *Roberts*

---

[2] In eight years of college teaching I have yet to encounter even one such student; however, I continue to hear—and read—that they exist in abundance.

English Series was a paradigm case of this type of "revolution"; for all its merits in theory it failed dismally in practice.) Today, although the research and publication in these areas of linguistics clearly have broad applications for education, there is a wholesome trend towards slower incorporation of research into pedagogical literature. The word "wholesome" is accurate here, however great the need to solve the problems. It is much easier to get some "method," some set of textbooks or other curriculum materials, firmly entrenched in a school system, than it is to get it out again, although neither task could accurately be described as simple.

The major activity in applied educational linguistics today, within the generative transformational framework, can be summed up as the attempt to meet the two most critical needs in American education—the difficulties of multi-ethnic teaching and the literacy question—by developing pedagogical techniques and curriculum materials that are based upon contemporary linguistic theory and research. This effort draws from all the sub-fields of linguistics (as it obviously must), taking what is useful from each, and attempts to relate these elements to one another and to contemporary educational practice.

Clear and systematic descriptions of the differences between the Standard dialect and the major nonstandard varieties of speech are now available, particularly for Black English. Similar materials for Chicano English are beginning to appear. A detailed description of Appalachian English (Wolfram and Christian 1975) has just been published. The professional journals of education, linguistics, and psychology now contain detailed articles explaining not only the differences in the sound systems and grammatical systems of the nonstandard dialects, but also information as to what kinds of educational problems and advantages these differences can be expected to bring about in the classroom. The bookstore shelves are bulging with collections of articles on the cultural differences of American minority groups as contrasted with the familiar melting-pot image. Teachers can now take courses in Applied Linguistics in which, having first learned the basic theory and concepts of phonology, syntax, and semantics, they can learn for themselves the nonstandard/Standard differences and their educational implications.

So far, so good—in theory and on paper. At this point, however, the great debate begins, and it rages fiercely for every recognized nonstandard dialect. The teacher, assuming that he or she has a job in a school system allowing relative freedom of teaching techniques and materials, now must choose among at least the following three alternatives:

1. Use every resource available, including the new information from linguistics, in an effort to stamp out completely the nonstandard dialect and teach the student Standard English, both in speech and in writing.

2. Make no effort whatever to change the native dialect of the student; instead, change the methods and materials used in the classroom to conform with the rules of that dialect.

3. Provide a bidialectal (or bilingual) education for the student, maintaining the language skills in the native speech medium while at the same time teaching the student Standard English in order that he or she may freely use both modes.

The first alternative is the traditional one. The people arguing for it—many of whom are themselves members of linguistic minority groups—base their arguments either on conventional prescriptivism (the "one and only one correct way" of using a language), or on their conviction that only in this way can minority students be given the opportunity to compete equally for economic and professional status in the United States. Here is a statement from the NAACP periodical, *The Crisis* (April/May 1971), which is representative of this conviction:

> What our children need, and other disadvantaged American children as well—Indian, Spanish-speaking, Asian, Appalachian, and immigrant Caucasians—is training in basic English, which today is as near an international language as any in the world. To attempt to lock them into a provincial patois is to limit their opportunities in the world at large.

The advocates of this position see the advocates of bidialectalism (or of the more extreme alternative 2 above) as engaged in a deliberate educational conspiracy to exclude Black students, and all minority students, from the mainstream of American life—with all the socioeconomic penalties that such exclusion entails.

The second alternative, precisely *because* of those socioeconomic penalties, is not proposed seriously except by extremists. It is true that the meaning conveyed by "John work yesterday" and "John worked yesterday" are one and the same, and that both sequences ought to be equally acceptable in the classroom, in the office, in Congress, or anywhere else.[3] It is also true that this is real life, not Never-Never-Land, and that the individual who militantly insists upon "John work yesterday" in all situations is going to suffer an automatic downgrading in prestige. It is unjust, but it is true. If the second position is to be accepted, it entails not only a change in the methods used in the classroom, but a radical restructuring of American society as a whole.

---

[3] This is particularly true since it is not, in the vast majority of cases, the English verb that carries time information in a sentence.

The third alternative, which is a compromise position, comes in several possible versions.

a. Let the student begin school in his or her native dialect (or language), and master the essential skills of reading and writing—as well as the equally essential role skill of functioning in an academic environment—in that native speech medium. Then, at the level of perhaps the third or fourth grade, begin the shift to teaching in Standard English, while still allowing ample opportunity for the native speech medium to be used in enough areas of the curriculum to maintain competency.

b. Offer all instruction, from the very beginning, in both languages or dialects, and let the student acquire both from exposure to both, just as the native speech medium was acquired in the home and community.

c. Offer most instruction in Standard English, but provide a special ESL (English as a Second Language) class or SESD (Standard English as a Second Dialect) class for the students whose native speech is nonstandard. In addition, provide a class period in which language and other material from the native culture is actively encouraged, as in the typical Ethnic Studies course.

There are of course varying mixes of all these alternatives, particularly alternative (c), ranging from one hour a day for the native speech medium up to an approximate 50/50 split, depending upon the given school situation. All such programs have one factor in common, however else they may differ. They emphasize as strongly as possible the fact that the native speech medium of the student, and the cultural heritage that accompanies that speech medium, is equal in every way to that of Standard English—with the obvious exception of prestige.

The problem of choosing among these positions is simply that there *is* no correct choice. None of these solutions is the "right one." On the other hand, from the preschool level all the way to the university it is a rare teacher who is not forced to go daily into the classroom, face real students, and choose one of these alternatives or some variant or mixture of them. How else is any teaching to take place? The choice is not made any easier by the fact that the Standard English toward which so many are aiming does not really exist. The "Standard" of Boston is not the "Standard" of Chicago or Dallas or San Francisco or St. Louis or Nashville. Even in Written English, where the phonological differences that appear as you move about the country are neutralized, there is no solid consensus on what is "standard." If you find this hard to believe, try to get any Department of English in the country to provide you with a list of the characteristics of Standard Written English that has the endorsement of every member of the English faculty. You will find that the largest area of agreement is a negative one; for example, Standard Written English will not include the lexical item *ain't*, and it will not include the double negative, and it will not include quite a number of other things. What it *does* include is a very different question; here is a typical answer, synthesized from several dozen provided to this writer by recognized scholars in this field:

> Standard Written English is that variety of English which meets the standards of good English prose.

This is a *non*definition, since it is completely circular.

The luckiest teachers are those who are absolutely serene and secure in their own conviction that there is one and only one variety of English that is worth teaching, that they know quite well what its characteristics are, and that it is their function in life to teach that variety to their students. However, this position is becoming more and more difficult to maintain. The evidence from psycholinguistics and sociolinguistics makes the prescriptive position a tricky one to square with one's conscience. Furthermore, teachers have yet to demonstrate any significant degree of success in their attempts to achieve this homogeneous dialect goal, and they have been trying in this country for at least two hundred years; this is bound to be discouraging.

The second position—that of leaving the student's language strictly alone—runs into impossible difficulties when two separate languages are involved. The American citizen who cannot speak English at all is too handicapped in daily life to make this practicable, even for the most militantly radical teacher. Where we are dealing with two dialects of English, rather than two languages, it is probably possible—but there are severe problems. A few are listed below, and these are just the tip of the iceberg.

a. In order for this method to work, the teacher must be a native speaker of the dialect in question, or near enough native to be accepted as such by the students.

b. Curriculum materials do not exist for all the minority dialects; they are probably available to even a minimally adequate degree only in Black English, Navajo, and Chicano English. The Chicano materials are often flawed for classroom use because they are based upon the Spanish of Madrid or of Mexico City, neither of which is suitable for many Latino student groups. This means that the teacher of students who are Puerto Rican, Vietnamese, Filipino, Hawaiian, Chinese, Ozark, Sioux—and all the rest—must be able to prepare curriculum materials in the students' native speech medium for all subjects taught, and must have the facilities and budget for this process.

c. There are so many different dialects; if this is to be done for one it must, in the name of justice, be done for all. The logistics of such a task are overwhelming.

d. There must be solid support for the teacher from the students, their parents, the administration, the community, and the rest of the faculty.

e. At the end of all this, unless some way has been found in the meantime to convince all of American society to accord equal respect and prestige to all dialects, the students will have to suffer the socioeconomic penalties resulting from their teacher's convictions.

The third alternative is offensive to those who advocate either of the other two, precisely because it is a compromise. It is seen by those who advocate (a) as a debasement of standards or a racist conspiracy; it is seen by the advocates of (b) as a spineless cop-out and as a furthering of an already unbearable inequality within the system. Nevertheless, this is the alternative that is being tried, particularly in the elementary schools, and it is what most people mean when they use the phrase "bilingual education."

Unfortunately we cannot say that the only problem with this third alternative is the fact that not everyone approves of it. As with the other "solutions," there are multiple problems.

It is true that the Lau v. Nichols Supreme Court decision (which mandated educational reforms for school districts having substantial numbers of nonnative speakers of English among their students) has brought into existence a multitude of federal programs to fund such education. Unfortunately, money alone is not the answer.

The staffing problem remains unsolved. Where are we to find teachers who can teach comfortably in these other languages or dialects, or at least teacher's aides who can help the teacher unable to manage except in some version of Standard English? The problem of teaching materials continues; the market is glutted with poor materials produced in a crisis atmosphere, in an attempt to get something—however inadequate—into the teachers' hands. The choice among the various teaching approaches must still be made, with all the difficulties that entails. Where is room to be found in the already over-burdened curriculum for the special courses in Afro-American or Mexican-American Language and Culture? And how is the teacher caught in the middle of all this to get through the day, in a classroom where—as in California, for example—he or she may well face a class in which as many as three or four different minority populations are to be provided equal and equally adequate education?

The applied linguists can help here, if the teachers can be convinced to trust them. Research over the past ten years has provided results that are directly applicable to the classroom situation, and many linguists are now willing to write down those results in ways that do not require the reader to be equipped with a doctorate in linguistics.

The following is a list of fifteen things applied linguists can do that are of practical use to the teacher.

1. They can demonstrate with clear descriptive and contrastive materials that there is no dialect of English which is more logical, more simple, more inherently grammatical, more meaningful, more "correct," than any other dialect; there are only dialects that are more prestigious than others. When the teacher is able to understand and accept this, and to realize that dialects are nothing more than differing sets of rules, a major step forward will have been taken, leading directly into (2).

2. They can help the teacher overcome the tendency to make stereotypical judgments about students based upon their language differences alone, as well as the tendency to equate a differing manner of speech with a difference in intelligence, motivation, degree of "verbalness," or anything of that kind. A clear understanding of what dialect differences really are effectively undermines these tendencies.

3. They can demonstrate to the teacher that a child arrives at school already well-equipped linguistically with a superb grammar of his or her native tongue, and that this competence should be regarded with respect and looked at as a foundation upon which to build.

4. They can demonstrate to the teacher that classroom prophecies are self-fulfilling; that if the student is continually treated as if he or she will fail, failure is almost guaranteed; and that respect for the student's native ethnic heritage, both linguistic and cultural, is the first step toward preventing the self-perpetuating cycle of failure.

5. They can demonstrate to the teacher that not all students learn in the same way, and that therefore it is not sensible to attempt to teach all of them in exactly the same way.

6. They can demonstrate to the teacher that the program in the classroom must have the support of the community, of the parents and peers of the students, and of all the people who interact with them; and they can suggest methods for gaining that support.

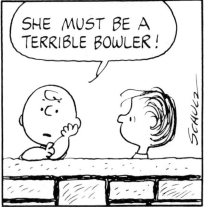

© 1976 United Feature Syndicate, Inc.

7. They can show the teacher ways to adapt existing curriculum materials to new situations, or to create new materials where none exist; and they can suggest places to go for help when faced with a totally new situation of this kind.

8. They can explain what verbal processing is really like, and how such activities as reading and writing really do take place; they can demonstrate the difference between learning by memorization and learning by internalization, and show how this difference fits into programs for teaching literacy skills.

9. They can train the teacher in the techniques of contrastive analysis, for all areas of the grammar, thus providing a technique that allows languages and dialects to be set side by side for comparison by both teacher and students.

10. They can help the teacher learn to be sensitive to areas of cross-cultural conflict, and provide classroom techniques for getting at those areas and dealing with them.

11. They can provide the teacher with some answers to the multitudinous "Why's?" that plague them in the language arts curriculum. For most of the "why" questions there are reasonable answers that students can understand and that are a considerable improvement over the ancient "because it says so in the book."

12. They can make the insights of generative transformational grammar available to the teacher in a format that is *not* like a mathematics problem, and can provide a model for the use of such materials in the classroom that need never require the drawing of intricate tree diagrams or sets of esoteric squiggles.

13. They can help the teacher dispel the common myths about language that are typical in the classroom: such as that some languages are inherently harder to learn than others; or that phonological differences in dialect are due to differences in the shape of the vocal organs in different peoples; or that there are such things as primitive languages; or that the English spelling system is a hopeless and utterly random mess.

14. They can provide the teacher with suggestions for new ways of teaching the basic reading and writing skills, both in the native language and in foreign languages, based upon recent research and new discoveries in these areas of learning.

15. They can provide the teacher with basic techniques for observing and interpreting the nonverbal communications of students, and for noting when there is a mismatch between these messages, and the oral or written ones—keeping in mind that in such cases it is frequently the nonverbal communication that should be trusted.

Now, I have just violated—fifteen times—one of the most venerable traditions of my profession about appropriate use of language. It is customary for scholars (linguists, for example) to adhere to a code of academic modesty, something like the code that forbids doctors to advertise. This is why, in scholarly journals, one is never supposed to say "I," and why everything said about the writer's own work is expected to appear in passive sentences. When asked what he or she can do, the applied linguist is expected to shuffle the feet, look mysterious, and refer the questioner to a list of publications that will clear the matter up. Most emphatically, we are *not* supposed to say that we can do *X, Y,* and *Z,* and *P* and *Q* to boot.

This attitude is one of the reasons behind the lag in the introduction of applied linguistics research into real classrooms, and it is a luxury we can no longer afford. It is not considered immodest for a surgeon to state that he or she can do an appendectomy, a hysterectomy, a tonsillectomy, etc.; and we would be reluctant to put our trust in one who refused to tell us what operations he considered himself competent to perform. Similarly, linguists cannot expect educators to accept their help, much less ask for it, until they are willing to set aside the mystification tradition and say, right up front, what it is they think that they are good for.

The list of suggested readings at the end of this chapter has been carefully chosen to direct you to sources presenting information about the items on my list, insofar as that can be done; a certain amount of overlap is obviously inevitable.

EXERCISES AND PROBLEMS

1. The following quotation is from Jeanne Herndon's text, *A Survey of Modern Grammars*: "The dictionary of Samuel Johnson and the school grammars of John Wallis, Robert Lowth, and Lindley Murray were not only aimed at establishing 'correct' usage but at pointing out 'errors.' Their criteria for such decisions were often based upon a familiarity with the requirements of Latin grammar, which was secure in its centuries of scholarly prestige. . . . The task of forcing English into the Latin grammar mold was doubly difficult because English is not derived from Latin but from old Germanic dialects."[5]

    Look up one of the three grammarians mentioned by Herndon in a reasonably adequate source such as the *Encyclopedia Britannica*; if possible, read a sample chapter from one of their grammars. Try to determine *why* these men felt obliged to write English grammar books based upon Latin syntax.

2. The phonological rules of Spanish do not allow any word to begin with /s/ followed by a voiceless stop. However, Spanish has many words which include this consonant sequence when it need not be pronounced as a consonant cluster, such as *estar, España,* and *escuela*. Can you

---

[5] Jeanne Herndon, *A Survey of Modern Grammars* (1976).

predict the effect these facts are likely to have upon Chicano pronunciation of English words beginning /sp/, /st/, or /sk/? List five hypothetical examples to illustrate your prediction.

3. Choose one of the three alternative approaches to the bidialectal-bilingual classroom situation described on pages 185–186 of this text. Write a paper of no more than three pages arguing for your choice, taking into consideration not only the philosophical and political issues, but the practical ones as well. That is, do not consider only whether something *should* be done; comment also on your opinion as to whether it *can* be done.

4. One of the most difficult matters of grammar for English teachers to explain to non-native speakers is the basis upon which an English native speaker decides whether to use *have/has* plus the past participle or *had* plus the past participle. The data below illustrate the problem.

   (a) She has always spoken French.
   (b) She had always spoken French.
   (c) Martha has already left the house.
   (d) Martha had already left the house.
   (e) José has been to Paris several times.
   (f) José had been to Paris several times.

   Consider the problem and see if you can write a brief explanation of your own basis for making this choice; remember that it should be an explanation that would be useful to a non-native speaker. (That is, only native speakers of English will be helped in any way by a statement such as "Use the one that sounds right in the sentence and makes sense.")

5. Many individuals who write articles and columns on "correct English usage" are involved in a sort of crusade to stamp out the use of the word *hopefully*. They do not seem to be making much headway; sentences such as "Hopefully, this will help the American economy" seem to be firmly entrenched in contemporary America. The interesting question is what it is about *hopefully* that is causing all this commotion. Unlike the word *ain't*, *hopefully* is not a marker of any nonstandard dialect. Look at the examples below and try to determine what factor in present usage of the word is responsible for the purists' concern.

   (a) Campers should handle matches carefully.
   (b) Campers should handle matches in a careful manner.
   (c) Quietly, Tomás attempted to explain the theorem.
   (d) In a quiet manner, Tomás attempted to explain the theorem.

(e)   Fortunately no students were hurt in the accident.
(f)   It is fortunate that no students were hurt in the accident.
(g)   Obviously the problem has a solution.
(h)   It is obvious that the problem has a solution.
(i)   *It is carefully that campers should handle matches.
(j)   *It is quietly that Tomás attempted to explain the theorem.
(k)   *In a fortunate manner no students were hurt in the accident.
(l)   *In an obvious manner the problem has a solution.
(m)   The nurse spoke hopefully of the patient's condition.

6. Taylor et al. (*Language and Speech*, April/June 1971) reported an experiment in which they tested the following hypothesis:

> ". . . the more sensitive an individual is to the feelings and behaviors of another person, the more likely he is to perceive and recognize the subtleties and unique aspects of the second language and incorporate them in speaking. In other words, the more empathic an individual is the more he will authentically pronounce a second language."

The focus of this experiment was on correctness of pronunciation in the foreign language being taught (usually called the *target* language), and the experimenters' hypothesis was borne out by the experimental results. Can you suggest reasons why it should be true that a student characterized by a high degree of empathy would also be characterized by skill in the pronunciation of a foreign language? Begin by determining clearly the meaning of the word *empathy*.

7. The phoneme inventories of three languages are given below. Assume that the phonetic realizations of these phonemes, except where otherwise noted, are approximately the same as their English equivalents, and choose one language for this exercise. Compare the phoneme inventory you have chosen with that of English and list some phonological problems that a teacher might expect to find in a first-grade class whose children were native speakers of that language and only secondarily speakers of English.

Language A: TAHITIAN
i, ii; e, ee; u, uu; o, oo; a, aa
p, m, f, v, t, n, r, h, ?

Language B: MEXICAN SPANISH
i, e, u, o, a
p, t, k, b, d, g, f, s, x, č, m, n, nʸ, r, r̃, l, w, y

Language C: JAPANESE
i, ii; e, ee; a; u, uu; o, oo
p, pp; t, tt; k, kk; b, d, g, h; s, ss; w, z, y, m, n, ṇ, r

NOTES: The Spanish /r̃/ is trilled; the Spanish /x/ is like a very breathy (fricative) /h/; the Japanese /u/ and /uu/ are not rounded; the Japanese /h/, /w/, and /y/ are all fricatives; the Japanese /ŋ/ is syllabic —that is, it can serve as a syllable without any vowel sound accompanying it; in Tahitian and Japanese the phonemes spelled as double letters are actually *long* sounds, and there are minimal pairs in these languages which are differentiated only by vowel length or consonant length.

8. This writer once supervised an independent study in the writing of formal English by a student whose native language was Chinese. The student was extremely fluent in English, both spoken and written, but was having difficulties with formal papers. After several discussions, we learned that he thought the following was a rule of English grammar and was attempting to use it:

   In formal and scholarly English, if a sentence contains a direct object it *must* be written as a passive sentence.

   The elimination of this non-rule was very helpful to the student, and put an end to most of the problems that had been plaguing him in academic writing. To find out why, choose a brief selection from a scholarly article and rewrite it, following the non-rule about obligatory passivization. What kinds of difficulties does this create for you as you write?

9. The student mentioned in Exercise 8 had never seen the "rule" written down nor been told that it existed; he had figured it out for himself. Can you suggest how such a misunderstanding could have occurred?

10. In courses the purpose of which is to help students become skilled in English conversation, one method of providing them with speaking practice is to ask questions and elicit their responses. Look at the following questions, which are typical of such sessions:

   (a) What is your name?
   Do you speak English?
   Where do you live?
   Have you finished your homework?
   Is this a pencil?
   Did you enjoy the story about the lady and the tiger?

   (b) What did you do this weekend?
   Where do you go in the summer?
   What are you going to do after you graduate?
   How do you feel about history classes?

(c) When did you stop speaking Albanian?
    How old were you when you learned Cherokee?
    When the dragon comes, what will you do?
    Why don't you like movies?

Questions such as those in group (c) produce more conversation, and are a more effective way of offering students opportunities to speak than those in either group (a) or (b). Can you explain why? (An effective way to tackle this exercise is to consider the possible answers one might give to questions in each group.)

11. I have repeatedly heard and read statements claiming that a particular student (or group of students) "doesn't know any of the grammar rules of English." However, examination of thousands of examples of written work from such students over the course of five years' research has failed to reveal even one example of a sentence such as those listed below.

(a) I behaved yourself.   (d) We behaved herself.
(b) He behaved yourself.   (e) Himself behaved them.
(c) You behaved myself.   (f) Yourself behaved you.

The rule for these constructions can be written as follows: In a sentence where the subject and the direct object of the verb are identical in reference, it is necessary to supply as the form of the direct object a member of the set of English reflexive pronouns which agrees with its antecedent in the features of number, gender, and person. This is a rather complex rule, to say the least, and it is not violated even by those speakers who use *hisself* for *himself* and *theirselves* for *themselves*. Can you explain how, if the students do not know the reflexive rule, they are able to avoid violations of that rule?

12. Linguists have been able to identify accurately certain features of non-standard English dialects that can be counted upon to provoke strong negative reactions in the classroom. (Two of the most reliable are the word *ain't* and the use of the double negative as in *I don't have no pencil.*) They have also been able to rank many of these features in terms of the relative strength of the negative reaction they will cause. Other features, such as the use of *like* for *such as*, provoke little or no reaction except in the most prescriptive teachers. Could you reverse this identification process? That is, could you make a list of ten or more features of Standard English that you feel are reliable as a means of provoking *positive* reactions in the classroom? (In order to keep this exercise within reasonable limits, restrict it to written language at the college level.)

13. Compare the list you wrote for Exercise 12 with those prepared by the other students in your class. Do you find that you and your classmates are in agreement on this matter?

14. Carol Chomsky has suggested that in teaching English spelling, teachers always present pairs of the following kind: *sign/signature; bomb/bombard; preside/president; photo/photography; electric/electricity.* This would involve teaching some very long words in the early grades of elementary school. Can you see any good reasons why this technique should be used in spite of the problem of word length?

SUGGESTED READINGS

ARTICLES AND EXCERPTS[1]

BARON, D. 1975. "Non-Standard English Composition and the Academic Establishment." *College English* 37:176–83.

BROWN, C. 1974. "Literacy in 30 Hours: Paulo Freire's Process in Northeast Brazil." *Social Policy*, July 8, 1974.

CHAIKA, E. 1978. "Grammars and Teaching." *College English* 39:770–83.

CHOMSKY, C. 1970. "Reading, Writing, and Phonology." *Harvard Educational Review* 40:287–309.

CHOMSKY, N. 1967. "The Current Scene in Linguistics." *College English* 28:587–95.

CONKLIN, P. 1967. "Good Day at Rough Rock." *American Education* 2:4–10.

CORDASCO, F. 1967. "Knocking Down the Language Walls." *Commonweal*, October 6, 1967.

COTTLE, T. 1972. "The Edge of the IQ Storm." *Saturday Review*, April 15, 1972.

COWLEY, D. 1977. "French First, then Mother Tongue English." *Christian Science Monitor*, March 7, 1977.

ELGIN, S. 1977. "Why *Newsweek* Can't Tell You Why Johnny Can't Write." *English Journal* 65:29–35.

———. 1978. "Don't No Revolutions Hardly *Ever* Come By Here." *College English* 39:784–89.

ERVIN-TRIPP, S. 1974. "Is Second Language Learning Like the First?" *TESOL Quarterly* 8:111–21.

EVANS, B. 1962. "But What's A Dictionary For?" *Atlantic Monthly*, May 1962.

FUNKHOUSER, J. 1973. "A Various Standard." *College English* 34:806–27.

---

[1] None of the articles listed here is technical enough to cause comprehension difficulties. Also highly recommended are the readings for the Psycholinguistics chapter, many of which are more difficult.

HOFFMAN, M. 1971. "Bi-dialectalism Is Not the Linguistics of White Supremacy: Sense Versus Sensibilities." *The English Record* 21:95–102.

JAKOBOVITS, L. 1968. "Implications of Recent Psycholinguistic Developments for the Teaching of a Second Language." *Language Learning* 18:89–109.

KEYSER, S. 1970. "The Role of Linguistics in the Elementary School Curriculum." *Elementary English* 47:39–45.

KOBRICK, S. 1972. "The Compelling Case for Bilingual Education." *Saturday Review*, April 29, 1972.

LAKOFF, R. 1969. "Transformational Grammar and Language Teaching." *Language Learning* 19:117–40.

———. 1975. "Linguistic Theory and the Real World." *Language Learning* 25:309–38.

LILES, B. 1972. "English Spelling." *Linguistics and the English Language*, pp. 256–83. Goodyear Publishing, Pacific Palisades, Calif.

LINK, T. 1970. "22,000 'Retarded' Children Face Second Chance." *National Catholic Reporter*, February 4, 1970.

LOGUE, C. 1974. "Teaching Black Rhetoric." *The Speech Teacher* 23:115–20.

NEWMARK, L. 1966. "How Not to Interfere With Language Learning." *International Journal of American Linguistics* 32:77–83.

ORTEGO, P. 1971. "Schools for Mexican-Americans: Between Two Cultures." *Saturday Review*, April 17, 1971.

ROSENTHAL, R., and L. JACOBSON. 1968. "Teacher Expectations for the Disadvantaged." *Scientific American* 218:19–23.

SHEILS, M. et al. 1977. "Teaching in English Plus." *Newsweek*, February 7, 1977.

SLEDD, J. 1969. "Bi-dialectalism: The Linguistics of White Supremacy." *English Journal* 58:1307–15.

SMITHERMAN, G. 1973. "God Don't Never Change." *College English* 34:828–33.

STAFF. 1975. "Can't Anyone Here Speak English?" *Time*, August 25, 1975.

TOVEY, D. 1976. "Language Acquisition: A Key to Effective Language Instruction." *Language Arts* 53:868–73.

WARDHAUGH, R. 1968. "Linguistic Insights Into the Reading Process." *Language Learning* 18:235–52.

WAX, R., and R. THOMAS. 1961. "American Indians and White People." *Phylon*, Winter 1961.

WOLFRAM, W. 1970. "Sociolinguistic Alternatives in Teaching Reading to Nonstandard Speakers." *Reading Research Quarterly* 6:9–33.

BOOKS AND MONOGRAPHS

ABRAHAMS, R., and R. TROIKE (eds.). 1972. *Language and Cultural Diversity in American Education*. Prentice-Hall, Englewood Cliffs, N.J.

ALATIS, J. (ed.). 1968. *Contrastive Linguistics and Its Pedagogical Implications.* Georgetown University Press, Washington, D.C.[2]

———. 1969. *Linguistics and the Teaching of Standard English to Speakers of Other Languages or Dialects.* Georgetown University Press, Washington, D.C.

———. 1970. *Bilingualism and Language Contact: Anthropological, Linguistic, Psychological, and Sociological Aspects.* Georgetown University Press, Washington, D.C.

ALLEN, H. (ed.). 1958. *Readings in Applied English Linguistics.* Appleton-Century-Crofts, New York.

BURLING, R. 1973. *English in Black and White.* Holt, Rinehart and Winston, New York.

CAZDEN, C. 1972. *Child Language and Education.* Holt, Rinehart and Winston, New York. .

DiPIETRO, R. 1971. *Language Structures in Contrast.* Newbury House, Rowley, Mass.

FASOLD, R., and R. SHUY. 1970. *Teaching Standard English in the Inner City.* Center for Applied Linguistics, Arlington, Va.

GREER, C. 1972. *The Great School Legend.* Viking Press, New York.

HERNDON, J. 1976. *A Survey of Modern Grammars,* 2nd ed. Holt, Rinehart and Winston, New York.

HUNT, K. 1965. *Grammatical Structures Written at Three Grade Levels.* National Council of Teachers of English, Champaign, Ill.

LAMBERT, W., and G. TUCKER. 1972. *Bilingual Education of Children: The St. Lambert Experiment.* Newbury House, Rowley, Mass.

LESTER, M. (ed.). 1973. *Readings in Applied Transformational Grammar,* 2nd ed. Holt, Rinehart and Winston, New York.

O'HARE, F. 1973. *Sentence Combining.* National Council of Teachers of English, Urbana, Ill.

OLSON, P. 1976. *A View of Power: Four Essays on the National Assessment of Educational Progress.* Center for Teaching and Learning, University of North Dakota, Grand Forks, N.D.

POLITZER, R. 1965. *Teaching French: An Introduction to Applied Linguistics.* Blaisdell Publishing Company, Waltham, Mass.

———. 1965a. *Foreign Language Learning: A Linguistic Introduction.* Prentice-Hall, Englewood Cliffs, N.J.

RUSH, S., and S. ELGIN. 1977. *An Experimental and Evaluative Approach to Teaching Basic Writing Skills.* California State University and Colleges, Long Beach, Calif. (Monograph Series).

WARDHAUGH, R. 1974. *Topics in Applied Linguistics.* Newbury House, Rowley, Mass.

---

[2] This and the next two entries are from the annual Georgetown University Roundtable Series; all volumes in the series are highly recommended.

NINE

Historical Linguistics

When we think of history we are accustomed to thinking of successions of kings, of sequences of wars, of conquests and discoveries, of one political system giving way to another. We think of facts that we can locate exactly in time, in a neat linear sequence. Even if we go back in time beyond the period when we can set down precise names and dates—for example, to ancient Egypt or Mesopotamia—we are still able to assign approximate dates for many events, and we know which event followed another.

When we come to the history of human language, however, the situation is markedly different. We cannot point to any particular date when language began, nor do we know what the first language of mankind may have been. Our written records of languages date back only a little more than a few thousand years. We do not know how many years before that time writing may have begun. We do know that all languages, so long as they have living speakers, change, and that such change is normal and has been going on since there *was* human language; but we are very short indeed on hard "historical facts." We can look at the English language today and see how difficult it would be for a linguist from the future to determine what it really sounded like from written records alone. For many languages, not even written records exist.

In view of this situation, certain questions become obvious. What does a historical linguist hope to do? How does he work, and on what sort of foundation does he make his claims?

To answer these questions we must first make clear a few basic matters about which there is often confusion. The most important may well be a clarification of the much-abused word *primitive*. We are continually tripping over this word in historical studies, in all fields. We read of *primitive man* and *primitive society*, of *primitive architecture* and *primitive tools*. We find groups of people living today described as having a *primitive* life.

In a very general way we can say that the use of *primitive* in these contexts is equivalent to *prehistoric*—that is, to a stage previous to any written records upon which to base conclusions. When contemporary peoples are described as primitive, the word is not given the same meaning except by analogical extension; usually what is meant is that the group described lives in a manner more consistent with what we assume to be true of prehistoric man's life than with our own. Along with this there has accumulated a heavy freight of negative connotations that is a kind of semantic contamination. The exclamation "How primitive!" is rarely intended as a compliment.

It may be that primitive humans, in the strictest sense of the word, spoke primitive languages. But we know nothing at all about any such language. Theories that picture man in the dawn of time communicating with a system of crude noises or calls are *only* theories. We cannot point to any language and say, "This is what a primitive language is (or was) like."

No group of human beings today, no matter what their lifestyle, speaks anything that could be called a primitive language. No records have ever been found of anything that could be called a primitive language. The most ancient languages for which we have written texts—Sanskrit, for instance—are just as intricate and complicated and comprehensive as any contemporary language.

For the linguist, then, the term *primitive language* can have only one useful meaning: a language which would be inadequate for ordinary human communication. Such a language might have no mechanism for adding a new word when a new object was introduced into the culture of the people speaking it, for example. No such language exists.

The second general issue is that of a "first" human language from which all other languages have developed. If at some remote period in prehistory there was a single language that was the ancestor of all languages spoken today, we do not know what language it was or when it began or where it was spoken. Some curious projects have been undertaken in the attempt to shed light on this mystery, including an "experiment" by the Egyptian Pharaoh Psammetichus in which two children were brought up in total isolation in the care of a servant sworn to silence. Psammetichus hypothesized that under these circumstances the children would begin to speak, free of any influence from the environment, and that their language would therefore reveal to us what the very first language had been. We are told that the first word spoken by the children was identified by scholars as a word meaning *bread* in Phrygian (now a dead language), and that this was assumed to have answered the "first language" question definitively. No one has yet learned anything more than Psammetichus did, although presumably our conception of what constitutes scientific investigation has become more sophisticated.

The historical linguist, then, finds himself or herself in much the same situation as the paleontologist. The paleontologist takes scraps of evidence—a bone here, a fossil there—and by combining these scraps and the principles of the scientific method by which he works, he proceeds to tell us about the appearance and habits of prehistoric animals. This process is called *reconstruction*. When you go to a museum and see exhibits of dinosaurs rampant with smaller animals in their mouths, you are not looking at an exhibit prepared from written records and pictures, but at a reconstruction.

The historical linguist is the paleontologist of language. From a few surviving clues, and the extrapolation of the principles of historical linguistics, he attempts to reconstruct languages that have now disappeared. He must take up the history of language in midstream, after written records already exist, even though he knows that the appearance of writing must be a very late stage in the development of language. That he can do this at all is due to what we know about the process of language change over time. For this study, which is also called *diachronic* linguistics, he has available two primary methods of research: the *comparative method*, and *internal reconstruction*.

In the comparative method, the linguist examines data from languages for which it has been possible to establish a historical relationship; in internal reconstruction he relies on diachronic data from within the single language being investigated. Only in those rare instances when a language appears to have no "relations" will he be forced to rely on internal reconstruction alone; ordinarily, both methods are used in combination, as each proves appropriate and useful.

Now, what does it mean, precisely, to say that languages are "related" or "of the same family?" This sort of thing sounds more like genetics than linguistics and is frequently misunderstood. It would therefore be a good idea to discuss it in some detail.

LANGUAGE FAMILIES

There are at least four thousand languages spoken in the world today. The number varies according to how strictly one defines the terms *language* and *dialect*. Linguists divide these languages into families of related languages, and typically display the postulated relationships by means of tree diagrams, as in (1).

(1)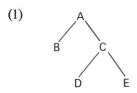

The family tree in (1) proposes that some language, Language A, has split into two languages, B and C, and that Language C has subsequently split into languages D and E. Languages B, C, D, and E are all said to be related because they had Language A as their common ancestor. Languages B and C are said to be *daughter* languages with respect to Language A (as are D and E, with respect to Language C itself), and *sister* languages with respect to one another. If written records exist for Languages B, C, D, and E, but all information about Language A is based upon reconstruction alone, Language A is called a *proto-language*. Thomas Pyles (1971) discusses this system as follows:

> . . . genealogical expressions when applied to languages must be regarded as no more than metaphors. Languages are developments of older languages rather than descendants in the sense in which people are descendants of their forefathers. Thus, Italian and Spanish are different developments of an earlier, more unified language, Latin. Latin in turn is one of a number of developments, which include Oscan and Umbrian, of a still earlier language called Italic. Italic in its turn is a development of Indo-European. Whether or not Indo-European has affinities with other languages spoken in prehistoric times and is hence a development of an even earlier language, no one is prepared to say with certainty; for, as we have seen, we are quite in the dark about how it all began. (*The Origins and Development of the English Language*, p. 80.)

English is a member of the Indo-European family of languages Pyles refers to. A chart showing the development of a representative sampling of the Indo-European languages is given in Table I.

Table I THE INDO-EUROPEAN LANGUAGE FAMILIES

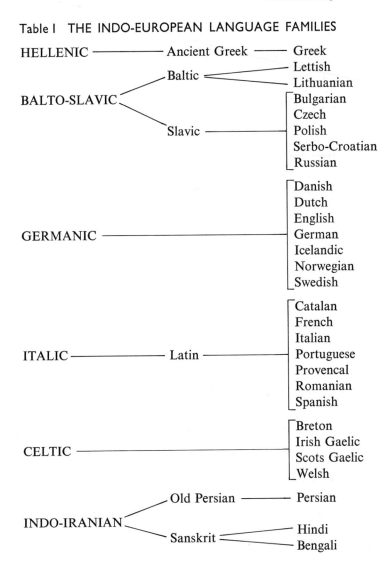

Note: Proto-Indo-European is the common ancestor of the languages in capital letters.

All linguists agree that the family tree concept, although useful as a way of presenting information, cannot be an accurate statement of actual language development. People do not go to bed one night using one language and get up the next morning using another, and the tidy splits shown in the diagrams have no counterpart in reality. At the present time there is much disagreement in historical linguistics about the proper description of historical change in language, particularly in light of recent research in language acquisition and sociolinguistics. We will not pursue this tangled question here.

It sometimes surprises the speaker of English to learn that English is a member of the same family—in the metaphorical sense—as Lithuanian or Bengali. The shared history of these three languages is so distant in time that a great deal of specialized training is necessary before the relationship can be seen and understood. It is much easier to see the relationship between English and German, because the surface resemblances between the two languages are still striking. Look at Table II, which shows a few examples of parallel forms from English, German, and two other contemporary Germanic languages.

Table II

ENGLISH	SWEDISH	DUTCH	GERMAN
blood	blod	bloed	Blut
hand	hand	hand	Hand
father	fader	vader	Vater
sister	syster	zuster	Schwester
hail	hagel	hagel	Hagel
hut	hydda	hut	Hütte
death	död	dood	Tod
birch	björk	berk	Birke
wind	vind	wind	Wind
door	dörr	deur	Tür

Even if the necessary allowances are made for the differences which always exist between the orthographies of languages and their actual pronunciations, the resemblances among the forms are too close and too numerous to be ignored.

If you examine Table II, you will see not just shared letters but shared *patterns* of letters, and this is what is important to the linguist. The simple fact that two languages have some of the same sounds means very little. What matters is the systematic shared patterning of sounds, and meanings, far beyond the possibility of coincidence.

All four languages in Table II have a similar two-syllable form meaning *sister*. Each form begins with *s* or *z*, has a *t* at the beginning of the second syllable, and ends with *r*. The odds against four languages showing a phonological pattern like this, and all four forms having the same meaning, are extremely high indeed unless we assume that they are developments from a shared earlier form. The four words for *blood* all begin with *b*, have a similar vowel, and end with *d* or *t*. This is the sort of systematic correspondence that the linguist looks for, and such word groups are called *cognate sets*. When many sets showing the same patterns can be found, as is true for the Germanic sub-family of Indo-European, we can assert with confidence that a historical relationship exists among the languages.

The historical linguist attempting to set up an inventory of the phonemes of the Germanic ancestor of English, Swedish, Dutch, and German, would almost at once propose a phoneme /b/, since all four languages show total agreement about this. The phoneme would then appear in his work as */b/, since reconstructed phonemes are by convention marked with an asterisk.

It takes many sets of related forms to establish and support a historical relationship. This is because it is not difficult to find a pseudocognate or two from almost any pair of languages. For example, Modern Greek has a word *mati* and Malay has a word *mata*; both words mean *eye*. We see here a possible pattern of correspondences: a two-syllable word beginning with *m*, having a *t* in the middle, ending with a vowel, and sharing the same meanings. In order to establish some relationship between Malay and Modern Greek, however, we would have to find many such sets, all showing a correspondence between Greek *m* and Malay *m*, Greek *t* and Malay *t*, and having Malay *a* where Greek has *i*. This cannot be done, and we are safe in attributing the pair of words for *eye* to chance alone.

Correspondences like this between unrelated languages are usually due to one of two factors. They may be the result of coincidence, as in the example just given. They may also be the result of both languages having borrowed a single word from another language, or one language having borrowed a word from the other. Navajo has a word *gidi* which means *cat* and is pronounced almost exactly like "kitty." From this we do not postulate a relationship between English and Navajo, but rather recognize *gidi* as a loanword. French has *le weekend* and *le whiskey*, both borrowed unchanged from English even though they radically violate the rules of French orthography. English has borrowed from French the expression *chaise longue*—literally "long chair"—and retained the French spelling, but pronounces the words as if they were written "chase lounge."

When a language borrows a word from a related language *after* the split between them has occurred, as in the French/English examples above, that word is not the result of their common linguistic heritage at all. It is as truly a loanword as if it had come from some totally unrelated language.

The linguist who attempts to demonstrate a historical relationship for languages must be very careful about such things as word-borrowing, since he must not confuse loanwords and cognates, and it is easy to do so.

The technique we have been discussing is the comparative method. The reconstruction of Indo-European has been its proving ground, because we are fortunate enough to have access to many ancient written texts for these languages. It had its "official" beginnings in 1786, with a famous address by Sir William Jones (scholar and founder of the Bengal Asiatic Society) demonstrating the historical relationship of Sanskrit to Latin, Greek, and the Germanic languages; this meant that we had Indo-European texts dating back to at least as long ago as the fourth century B.C.

The fact that the working principles of the comparative method have been borne out and reinforced by the available written records for Indo-European languages has made it possible for linguists to apply the same methodology, with reasonable confidence, to language families for which no written records exist, or for which writing is a very recent development.

HISTORICAL CHANGE IN ENGLISH

The history of English is traditionally divided into three periods, dated approximately as follows:

Old English	A.D. 450 to 1100
Middle English	1150 to 1500
Modern English	1500 to the present

As with the family trees, these divisions must be considered only as convenient notations. There were no abrupt breaks between one period of English and another, and each flows into the next with long transitional stages.

Old English is so different from contemporary English that reading it is like reading a foreign language. By the time one is well into the Middle English period the language looks more familiar, and although there are difficulties it can usually be read by anyone who reads English today. The English of the 1600's gives no modern reader any real problems of comprehension that cannot be settled by a good dictionary. A comparison of the following three biblical selections will make this progression clear. The first is written in Old English, the second is Middle English of the 1300's, and the third is from the 1611 version of the King James Bible; the lines quoted are from Genesis 8:6–12.

Old English Heptateuch

1. Ðā æfter fēowertigum dagum undyde Noe his ēahðyrl, ðe hē on ðam arce gemacode.
2. and āsende ūt ǣnne hremn: sē hrem flēah ða ūt, and nolde eft ongēan cyrran, ǣr ðan ðe ðā wæteru ādrūwodon ofer eorðan.

3. Hē āsende ða eft ūt āne culfran, ðæt hēo scēawode gyf ðā wætera ðagȳt geswicon ofer ðære eorðan brādnysse.

4. Hēo ða flēah ūt and ne mihte findan hwær hēo hire fōt āsette, for ðan ðe ðā wætera wæron ofer ealle eorðan; and hēo gecyrde ongēan tō Noe, and hē genam hī in tō ðam arce.

5. Hē ābād ða gȳt ōðre seofan dagas and āsende ūt eft culfran.

6. Hēo cōm ða on æfnunge eft tō Noe and brōhte ān twig of ānum elebēame mid grēnum lēafum on hyre mūðe. Ða undergeat Noe ðæt ðā wætera wæron ādrūwode ofer eorðan.

7. and ābād swā ðēah seofan dagas and āsende ūt culfran; swā hēo ne gecyrde ongēan tō him.

Middle English (Wycliffite Bible)

1. And whanne fourti daies weren passid, Noe openyde the wyndow of the schip which he hadde maad,

2. and sente out a crowe, which ȝede out, and turnede not aȝen til the watris weren dried on erthe.

3. Also Noe sente out a culuer aftir hym, to se if the watris hadden ceessid thanne on the face of erthe;

4. and whanne the culuer foond not where hir foot schulde reste, sche turnede aȝen to hym in to the schip, for the watris weren on al erthe; and Noe helde forth his hoond, and brouȝte the culuer takun in to the schip.

5. Sotheli whanne othere seuene daies weren abedun aftirward, eft he leet out a culuer fro the schip;

6. and she cam to hym at euentid, and bare in hir mouth a braunche of olyue tre with greene leeuys. Therfor Noe vndirstood that the watris hadden ceessid on erthe;

7. and neuerthelesse he abood seuene othere daies, and sente out a culuer, which turnede no more aȝen to hym.

Early Modern English (King James Bible)

1. And it came to passe at the end of forty dayes, that Noah opened the window of the Arke which he had made.

2. And he sent forth a Rauen, which went foorth to and fro, vntill the waters were dried vp from off the earth.

3. Also hee sent foorth a doue from him, to see if the waters were abated from off the face of the ground.

4. But the doue found no rest for the sole of her foote, and she returned vnto him into the Arke: for the waters were on the face of the whole earth. Then he put foorth his hand, and tooke her, and pulled her in vnto him, into the Arke.

5. And hee stayed yet other seuen dayes; and againe hee sent foorth the
doue out of the Arke.

6. And the doue came in to him in the euening, and loe, in her mouth
was an Oliue leafe pluckt off: So Noah knew that the waters were
abated from off the earth.

7. And hee stayed yet other seuen dayes, and sent forth the doue, which
returned not againe vnto him any more.

If one summary statement were to be made about the change in English
over the course of these three periods, it would be that the language began as
one with many inflections and has gradually developed into one with very
few. Inflections are morphemes added to other morphemes to carry information that in an uninflected language would be conveyed by independent
words; our verb suffixes *-s*, *-ed*, and *-ing* are examples of inflections.

As pointed out in Chapter One, languages vary in the sort of information that they find it essential to convey. In some languages sentences must
obligatorily be marked to indicate the source of the speaker's information;
in other languages the physical shape of a noun must always be indicated in
the noun phrase. Some languages are most particular about the gender of
nouns and whether they are singular or plural; other languages, although
they have resources for adding such information to the sentence, do not
consider it required for grammaticality. In all this variety there are, however,
three types of information which appear to be essential to communication
and turn up universally: *tense, aspect,* and *case.* Old English marked these
primarily by inflection, while Modern English relies heavily for all three on
independent words. The history of this major change is particularly interesting, since it resulted from the interaction of a number of different factors.

Tense

Tense can be looked upon in two ways. In semantic terms, it refers to
the time of the predicate in a sentence, while in morphology it refers to the
manner in which a verb is marked to indicate that time. Ideally there would
be a perfect match between the two, so that the attachment of a morpheme
meaning *present tense* would always and without exception mean that the
predicate involved was one in present time. In English, we do not have this
sort of ideal correspondence, and the so-called present tense forms of our
verbs in isolation cannot be relied upon to refer to present time at all. (We
will come back to this in more detail later.)

A full set of grammatical forms for a verb is called a *conjugation,* and
all sets of such forms, whatever their part of speech, are known as *paradigms.*
The paradigm in (2) is a present tense verb conjugation for the Old English
verb *keep*, the infinitive for which was *cēpan.*

(2) ic cēpe   I keep   first person singular
     ðū cēpest   you keep   second person singular
     hē ⎫   he ⎫
     hēo ⎬ cēpeð   she ⎬ keeps third person singular
     hit ⎭   it ⎭
     wē cēpað   we keep   first person plural
     gē cēpað   you keep   second person plural
     hī cēpað   they keep   third person plural

Almost all of the Old English present tense verbs had this set of four suffixes: *-e*, *-est*, *-eð*, in the singular, and *-að* for all persons of the plural. In Early Modern English the first person singular ending had disappeared completely, the second person singular had become *-(e)st* or *-(e)s*, and the third person was sometimes *-(e)s*, sometimes *-(e)th*. Plural endings in *-eth* were still found as late as the sixteenth century, depending upon the dialect. Nothing remains of this conjugation today except the *-s* of the third person singular, and even that does not appear in all dialects. The infinitive ending has also disappeared.

Notice that three kinds of information were conveyed by the Old English conjugation in (2). Inflectional endings marked a verb as present tense; they indicated whether its subject was singular or plural; and in the singular forms they also provided the information as to whether the verb was first, second, or third person. Today we know that an English verb is present tense because it has no *past* tense ending and because it is not preceded by the auxiliary verb *will*. The third person singular is still marked for us by an ending, but for all other forms we know the person and number only by the subject that accompanies the verb. Since there must always be a subject except in imperatives, and imperatives are restricted to the second person, the loss of the OE endings does not mean any loss of information. In fact, the third person singular marker is a superfluous marking (usually called *redundant* in linguistics), because no third person verb can appear without a subject and the number of all subjects is marked on third person noun phrases. (That is, plural nouns will always have a plural ending, and the pronouns have a separate plural form, *they*.)

The fact that the Modern English "present" tense cannot be relied upon to indicate present time is essentially a problem of terminology. It should properly be called the *non-past tense*, since it conveys that information unambiguously and without exception. (This situation is not confined to English grammars, by the way.)

To specify the time of the predicate precisely, we rely in Modern English on independent words and phrases. For example:

(3) a. Jeffrey arrives tomorrow morning at dawn.   (future)
     b. Jeffrey arrives every afternoon at three.   (habitual)

Even the addition of the words *right this minute*, as in "Jeffrey leaves right this minute," will not convey exact present time, since it is clear that Jeffrey is *not* leaving at the precise instant when those words are being spoken; this is a kind of immediate future.

Perhaps the only situation in which "present" tense is truly equivalent to present time is in such peripheral contexts as sports announcing or other live news reporting, where we may hear sequences like the following:

(4)   Jones sees an opening . . . He clutches the ball tightly. Now he runs down the field . . . will he make it, ladies and gentlemen? He *makes* it! The stands are going wild . . . .

Few English speakers are likely to have any opportunity to make use of this very specialized register. In any case, even this rare usage is accurately conveyed by the term *non-past*.

Aspect

Aspect in English has become inextricably mingled with tense. As a grammatical category, it has to do with the duration or degree of completion of a predicate, and in some languages will be divided into even more specific subcategories such as repetitive, intermittent, customary, and the like. A highly inflected language may have full sets of verb affixes to indicate all of these aspectual nuances.

Modern English has only two aspectual inflections, the *-ing* of the progressive which indicates lack of completion, and the completed (perfect) aspect marker *-ed* (sometimes *-en*). To indicate habitual aspect we use the "present" tense, plus a word like *always* or a phrase such as *every day, each morning*, etc. Paradoxically, the most likely meaning for any "present" tense verb in isolation, as in "Harriet dances" or "Leeanne runs" is habitual aspect.

In order to convey the fact that an action or state is still in progress we use what is called the *present progressive tense*, as in (5).

(5)   a. Ellen is eating (right now).
       b. The children are swimming (this very minute).

All the progressive forms require not only the *-ing* inflection of the main verb, but also a form of *be*. Similarly, the indication of completed aspect requires both a form of *have* before the main verb and the *-ed/-en* inflection attached to it. Nor does it end there, since multiple constructions like (6), while not common, are perfectly possible.

(6)　　We would have been being eaten alive by mosquitoes by this time if you had forgotten to bring the bug spray.

The progressive and perfect aspect system described above was part of Old English; and the possibilities for ambiguity appear to have been as great then as they are today, except that multiple auxiliaries such as those in (6) were not found and did not come into use until Middle English. There were more inflections for the verbs involved than Modern English has—for one thing there were several *be* verbs, each with its own conjugation—but no attempt will be made here to describe their development.

It was characteristic of OE that the past perfect was frequently marked only by the past tense of the verb, and this is beginning to be true of Modern English, especially in speech. Thus, instead of the technically correct forms in (7), it is common to hear the sequences of (8).

(7)　　a.　She had left before I got up.
　　　　b.　They had broken the toys by the time he arrived.

(8)　　a.　She left before I got up.
　　　　b.　They broke the toys by the time he arrived.

Case

In order for any sentence to be useful for communication, it is necessary for it to specify the case category of each noun phrase present—that is, its relationship to the verb. In Old English this information was provided primarily by a set of noun suffixes, which formed paradigms called *declensions*. Declensions are to nouns what conjugations are to verbs, and OE had a number of them. The most common paradigm was the one shown in (9), for the noun *hund* ('dog').

(9)　　*Singular*

hund	subject or direct object
hundes	possessive
hunde	indirect object and instrumental[1]

Plural

hundas	subject or direct object
hunda	possessive
hundum	indirect object and instrumental

---

[1] The instrumental case is the noun phrase category that indicates with what a particular action was accomplished, and is marked in Modern English by the preposition *with*, as in "We chopped the wood *with an axe*."

By no means does this convey the inflectional possibilities in the noun phrase of OE, however, since adjectives and demonstrative determiners were *also* declined. An example, with the demonstrative which served the function of Modern English *the*, is given in (10).

(10)   *Singular*
       se dola cyning   the foolish king (subject)
       ðone dolan cyning   the foolish king (direct object)
       ðæs dolan cyninges   of the foolish king (possessive)
       ðæm dolan cyninges   to the foolish king (indirect object)
       ðȳ dolan cyninge   with the foolish king (instrumental)

      Plural
       ðā dolan cyningas   the foolish kings (subject or direct object)

       ðāra dolra cyninga   of the foolish kings (possessive)
       ðæm dolum cyningum   to/with the foolish kings (indirect object and instrumental)

The list of case inflections in (10) is complete for that declension. The case categories as listed, however, are misleading, since some had additional functions. The category called *instrumental* would have been required for an NP like *in a gentle manner* and for *with the king* as in "The soldiers rode out with the king"; the *direct object* endings were needed for NP's such as *from the king*. Since there was not a separate case ending for every possible function of a noun phrase, ambiguities were frequently resolved by the use of prepositions, as in the Modern English examples.

By the Middle English period all these noun case inflections had been reduced to the single one we have today, the /s/ that marks the possessive. The many forms of the determiner had become simply *the*, and the only trace of the adjective declension was a single suffix, *-e*. We do still have remnants of case inflections in the pronouns of Modern English, where we find three forms—subject, possessive, and a form usually called the *object*, which is in fact used for an all-purpose non-subject/non-possessive category. Thus, we say *he* for subject, *his* for possessive, but *to him, from him, for him, by him, with him*, etc., as well as the simple direct object *him* without preposition.

It is tempting to summarize the course of case marking in English as follows: During the first stage case was indicated by inflections on the noun; during the second stage case was marked both by prepositions before the noun and by inflections, and the inflections began to disappear; in the final stage the inflections are almost entirely gone, and case is marked by word order and by prepositions. An analysis of this kind is appealing because it looks so logical. If case were marked both by independent words and by inflection, it would be redundantly marked, and one or the other of these mechanisms could be dispensed with. This is a great over-simplification, however, since there were always prepositions in English and some case inflections remain today. Certainly there were not three absolutely clear-cut time periods corresponding to the stages described.

Now that we have looked at examples of the move in English from a vast array of inflections to only a handful, the interesting question is: how can this change be accounted for? There is no complete and flawless answer, but we do have a considerable amount of information on the subject.

SIMPLIFICATION OF THE INFLECTION SYSTEM

One of the major factors responsible for the loss of inflections as the English language evolved was phonological change. Although we do not know why the phonological changes themselves took place, we can clearly see that one of their effects was simplification of the inflections. In order to describe these changes, we need to look briefly at the vowel phonemes of the three major periods of English.

Old English had seven long vowels and seven short ones. (The terms "long" vowel or "short" vowel refer here to actual duration of the vowel and not the traditional system used in dictionaries.) Linguists are not in complete agreement about the exact nature of some of these vowels; the list below represents one proposal. Note that it is customary, in discussions of the history of English, to indicate vowel length by a colon.

(11) *Long Vowels*
    iː, eː, æː, aː, oː, uː, üː

Short Vowels
    ı, ɛ, æ, a, ɔ, ʊ, ü

The vowels written *üː* and *ü* have disappeared from English completely; they are rounded front vowels, and similar to the one found in the French words *une* and *rue*. In literature on Old English you will often find these two phonemes symbolized by /y/ for the long vowel and /Y/ for the short; they are usually spelled with a macron or overbar (*ȳ*), to indicate length for the modern reader. Thus we find *fȳr* ('fire') and *fyllan* ('to fill'). Because the phonemic notation elsewhere in this text uses /y/ for the sound of *y* in Modern English *yard*, we have substituted /üː/ and /ü/ here. An example for each Old English vowel is given in Table III.

Table III   OLD ENGLISH VOWELS

iː	rīdan	to ride
eː	hē	he
æː	ǣrne	early
aː	þā	then
oː	blōd	blood
uː	hūs	house
üː	swӯn	swine
ɪ	him	him
ɛ	helpan	to help
æ	wæs	was
a	yldra	elder, older
ɔ	oxa	ox
ʊ	ful	full
ü	sylle	shall

In the Middle English period, /üː/ and /ü/ disappeared by merging with /iː/ and /ɪ/, respectively. In addition, the short vowels /a/, /ɔ/, /ʊ/, and /ɛ/ (represented in the inflections by the letters *a, o, u, e*) all fell together in unstressed syllables to become phonetic /ə/. This change immediately reduced the number of different suffixes drastically, since the suffixes were almost without exception unstressed. The final /n/ or /m/ which followed in numerous inflections also dropped, leaving only the schwa behind. The result for Middle English was the reduction to a single unstressed vowel of almost all inflections except the possessive case marker, the plural marker, and the marker of the third person singular present tense verb.

This was a phonological change, and a morphological one, with a radical effect upon the syntax of the language. The loss of inflections meant the loss of much syntactic information. It must be remembered, however, that this could not have happened had there not been other mechanisms available to provide the information that had formerly been conveyed by the inflections.

Word order had been very free in Old English, although it was never completely without restrictions. If it had remained that free as English evolved, the subject and object endings could not have been spared. Similarly, if English had not had ample resources in the form of independent words and phrases to convey tense and aspect, the verb inflections would have been indispensable. Without the prepositions to differentiate the majority of the cases, inflections would have been needed for the noun phrases. And without the English rule that every sentence must have a surface structure subject— and forms for that subject to indicate number, gender, and person where needed—some or all of the inflections from the verbs, adjectives, and demonstratives would have had to be retained.

It is impossible to say precisely how this intricate balance of functions is determined within a language. You cannot say that the word order became more rigid *because* the inflections were lost, or that the reverse is true. You cannot blame the phonological changes on the syntax, or safely claim the contrary. What *is* possible is to note the unmistakable counterpoint, a kind of trading-off among the various features of the language, to maintain the equilibrium necessary for effective communication.

EXERCISES AND PROBLEMS

1. The most common method for indicating negation in Old English was to place the word *ne* immediately before the verb. Somewhat later English developed a two-part negative, with *ne* still appearing but *noht* (or *nat*) being used later in the sentence for emphasis of the negation. By the time of Chaucer the *ne . . . nat* pattern was no longer emphatic, but an ordinary negative. Finally, the *ne* disappeared from the language. Suggest a reason for this developmental sequence, and support your hypothesis with evidence from another area (or areas) of the history of English.

2. Sometime during the fifteenth century the long vowels of English underwent a major phonological change known as the Great Vowel Shift. The vowels affected by this change are shown below.

	FRONT	CENTRAL	BACK
High	iː		uː
Mid	eː		oː
	ɛː		
Low		aː	ɔː

The changes that took place were as follows: /aː/ became /ɛː/ and then /eː/; /ɛː/ became /eː/; /eː/ became /iː/; /ɔː/ became /oː/; /oː/ became /uː/. The vowel /iː/ became first /aː/ and then /ay/; the vowel /uː/ became first /aː/ and then /aw/. Use the chart in this exercise and write a careful description of this change. (*Hint:* You will need three statements to complete this exercise.)

3. Although the Great Vowel Shift altered the pronunciation of many English words, the spelling system did not change to reflect that alteration. Thus, *hē*, which had been pronounced [he:], did not change its spelling to *hi*. For the Modern English words below, state what the most likely vowel would have been prior to the Great Vowel Shift.

sweet, house, root, home, teach, great, boot, moon, blind, brown, keen, field, break

4. In this chapter the statement was made that English personal pronouns are of three types: subject, possessive, and an all-purpose third form usually referred to as the "object" pronoun. (For example, *we, our, us*.) The one exception to this system is the pronoun used in traditional predicate nominative position, where the subject form is required, as in "It is I" and "The winners were she and I." Although this is the textbook rule, contemporary American speakers much prefer "It's me" and "The winners were her and me," and it is clear that there is a move in the language toward elimination of the exception. State at least two reasons why this should be so.

5. Compare the three versions given in this chapter of the excerpt from the story of Noah. Make as many statements as you can about the differences in word order in the three versions.

6. In Old English *f* and *v* were allophones of a single phoneme, not two separate phonemes as they are today. Look at the words below (written in phonetic transcription) and state the rule. Under what circumstances was the letter *f* pronounced [f]? Under what circumstances was it pronounced [v]?

fi:f	(five)
fi:fta	(fifth)
fi:vɛl	(sea-monster)
fædɛr	(father)
hɛovəna	(heaven)
hla:f	(loaf)
fa:	(foe)
wi:f	(wife)
wi:vɛs	(wife's)

7. All of the words below were borrowed from other languages and added to the English vocabulary. Go to a good dictionary (if possible, the

Oxford English Dictionary), and determine from what language each word came.

veranda, orange, ditto, spade, pylon, blouse, spinach, yogurt, zero, monk, mountain, castle, succotash, tobacco

8. The only case ending for nouns remaining in Modern English is the possessive /s/. Consider the information that is provided by this inflection, and the other mechanisms English has for providing that same information. Do you think that it would be possible for Modern English to drop this last case ending? Explain your answer.

9. In this chapter there was a brief mention of the English construction usually called the "present progressive" or "present progressive tense." Look over the examples and arguments in the text used to demonstrate that the present tense is not in fact an indicator of present time. Then construct examples and arguments of your own to show that the present progressive does or does not indicate present time as well as uncompleted action or state.

10. In the south of France near the Spanish border, many people speak Béarnais. Look at the pairs of words below and state the *systematic patterns* that prove the relationship between Béarnais and French. (An example is given at the end of this exercise to get you started.)

	Béarnais	*French*[2]	*Shared Meaning*
1.	abè [abɛ]	avait [avɛ]	had
2.	mountagne [muntañə]	montagne [mǫtañ]	mountain
3.	renar [rənar]	renard [rənar]	fox
4.	coum [kum]	comme [kɔm]	like, as
5.	yaméy [yame]	jamais [žamɛ]	never
6.	pèr [pɛr]	par [par]	by, on
7.	disè [dizɛ]	disait [dizɛ]	said
8.	nou [nu]	non [nǫ]	no
9.	gran [gran]	grand [grą]	large, great
10.	noublésse [nublesə]	noblesse [noblɛs]	nobility
11.	yudye [yudyə]	juge [žüž]	judge
12.	bloun [blun]	blond [blǫ]	blond

[2] In the simplified phonetic transcriptions used here, the small hook beneath a vowel indicates that it is a *nasal* vowel.

13. soubén [suben]   souvent [suvạ̃]   often
14. trouba [truba]   trouva [truva]   found
15. moumén [mumen]   moment [mɔmạ̃]   moment
16. Yan [yan]   Jean [žạ̃]   John
17. richésse [rišesə]   richesse [rišɛs]   richness
18. sabè [sabɛ]   savait [savɛ]   knew
19. pribilèdye [pribilɛdyə] privilège [privilɛž]   privilege
20. Yuransou [yuransu]   Jurançon [žurạ̃sọ]   (place name)
21. testemén [tɛstəmen]   testament [tɛstamạ̃]   testament

Example: Wherever French has a *v* between two vowels, Béarnais has a *b*, as in 1, 13, 14, 18, and 19.

11. In Old English the letter *c* represented two sounds—/c/ and /k/. Look at the word lists below and write the rule or rules that determined the proper pronunciation of *c* in these words.

[č]		[k]	
cild	child	boc	book
ceorl	peasant	cwæð	said
ic	I	cōm	came
celf	calf	clāð	cloth
ūsic	us	cūð	well-known
hēalic	exalted	folc	people
dīc	ditch	hōc	hook
sārlīc	painful	camp	battle
swālic	such	castel	castle
styric	steer (noun)	ēac	also

12. Many words change their meaning drastically over the course of time. Look up the following in a good English dictionary (preferably the *Oxford English Dictionary*) and make a list of the meaning changes for each.

(a) deer   (f) apple
(b) business   (g) girl
(c) lewd   (h) quit
(d) silly   (i) nice
(e) spill

SUGGESTED READINGS

ARTICLES AND EXCERPTS

BLOOMFIELD, L. 1933. *Language*, Chaps. 20 and 21. Holt, Rinehart and Winston, New York.

BRUNNER, K. 1953. "The Old English Vowel Phonemes." *English Studies* 34:247–51.

DOBBIE, E. 1958. "On Early Modern English Pronunciation." *American Speech* 33:111–15.

FRIES, C. 1940. "On the Development of the Structural Use of Word-Order in Modern English." *Language* 16:199–208.

FRISHBERG, N. 1975. "Arbitrariness and Iconicity: Historical Change in American Sign Language." *Language* 51:696–719.

HALL, R. 1950. "The Reconstruction of Proto-Romance." *Language* 26:6–27.

*HOCKETT, C. 1960. "The Origins of Speech." *Scientific American* 203:89–96.

———. 1965. "Sound Change." *Language* 41:185–204.

HOWREN, R. 1967. "The Generation of Old English Weak Verbs." *Language* 43:674–85.

JONES, C. 1967. "The Grammatical Category of Gender in Early Middle English." *English Studies* 48:289–305.

KING, R. 1967. "Functional Load and Sound Change." *Language* 43:831–52.

KIPARSKY, P. 1968. "Tense and Mood in Indo-European Syntax." *Foundations of Language* 4:30–57.

KLIMA, E. 1964. "Relatedness Between Grammatical Systems." *Language* 40:1–20.

LEVIN, S. 1964. "A Reclassification of the Old English Strong Verbs." *Language* 40:156–61.

MARTINET, A. 1952. "Function, Structure, and Sound Change." *Word* 8:1–32.

MENNER, R. 1945. "Multiple Meaning and Change of Meaning in English." *Language* 21:59–76.

PARKER, F. 1976. "Language Change and the Passive Voice." *Language* 52:449–60.

SAPORTA, S. 1965. "Ordered Rules, Dialect Differences, and Historical Processes." *Language* 41:218–24.

STOCKWELL, R. 1961. "The ME 'long close' and 'long open' Vowels." *Texas Studies in Literature and Language* 4:530–38.

*THIEME, P. 1958. "The Indo-European Language." *Scientific American* 201:63–74.

TRAUGOTT, E. 1969. "Toward a Theory of Syntactic Change." *Lingua* 23:1–27.

WEINREICH, U. 1958. "On the Compatibility of Genetic Relationship and Convergent Development." *Word* 14:374–79.

BOOKS AND MONOGRAPHS

*ALEXANDER, H. 1962. *The Story of Our Language*. Doubleday, New York.

BAUGH, A., and T. CABLE. 1978. *A History of the English Language*, 3rd ed. Prentice-Hall, Englewood Cliffs, N.J.

BLOOMFIELD, M., and L. NEWMARK. 1963. *A Linguistic Introduction to the History of English*. Alfred A. Knopf, New York.

FINNIE, W. 1972. *The Stages of English: Texts, Transcriptions, Exercises*. Houghton Mifflin, New York.

JESPERSEN, O. 1955. *Growth and Structure of the English Language*, 9th ed. Doubleday, New York.

KEILER, A. (ed.). 1972. *A Reader in Historical and Comparative Linguistics*. Holt, Rinehart and Winston, New York.

KING, R. 1969. *Historical Linguistics and Generative Grammar*. Prentice-Hall, Englewood Cliffs, N.J.

LEHMANN, W. 1962. *Historical Linguistics: An Introduction*. Holt, Rinehart and Winston, New York.

McLAUGHLIN, J. 1970. *Aspects of the History of English*. Holt, Rinehart and Winston, New York.

PYLES, T. 1971. *The Origins and Development of the English Language*, 2nd. ed. Harcourt Brace Jovanovich, New York.

QUIRK, R., and C. WRENN. *An Old English Grammar*. Holt, Rinehart and Winston, New York.

RIGG, A. (ed.). 1968. *The English Language: A Historical Reader*. Appleton-Century-Crofts, New York.

TRAUGOTT, E. 1972. *The History of English Syntax*. Holt, Rinehart and Winston, New York.

Index

Note: Pages in italics refer to exercises.